WENDELL
AND
ANN
PHILLIPS

WENDELL
AND
ANN
PHILLIPS

The Community of Reform, 1840-1880

IRVING H. BARTLETT

W • W • NORTON & COMPANY

NEW YORK • LONDON

Published simultaneously in Canada by George J. McLeod Limited, Toronto. Printed in the United States of America.

Library of Congress Cataloging in Publication Data
Bartlett, Irving H
    Wendell and Ann Phillips.
    1. Phillips, Wendell, 1811–1884. 2. Slavery in
the United States—Anti-slavery movements. 3. Aboli-
tionists—United States—Biography. 4. Phillips,
Ann Terry Greene, 1813–1886. I. Title.
E449.P56B36   1981   326'.092'4 [B]   80–27029

            ISBN 0-393-01426-6
            ISBN 0-393-00061-3 pbk

W. W. Norton & Company, Inc. 500 Fifth Avenue, New York, N.Y. 10110
W. W. Norton & Company Ltd. 25 New Street Square, London EC4A 3NT

            1 2 3 4 5 6 7 8 9 0

CONTENTS

WENDELL
AND
ANN
PHILLIPS

Photograph of Wendell Phillips c. 1859 by an unknown photographer. Reprinted from *Wendell Phillips Centenary 1811–1911* (New York, 1911).

Silhouette of Ann Phillips, believed to have been made in London in June 1841. It is the only known likeness of her. Reprinted from Francis Jackson Garrison, *Ann Phillips, Wife of Wendell Phillips: A Memorial Sketch* (Boston, 1886).

I. NEW PERSPECTIVES ON WENDELL PHILLIPS

1. The Making of an Abolitionist

MARK VAN DOREN once wrote that Benjamin Franklin would have been a great man at any time, anywhere.* Although one would perhaps not want to make the same claim for Wendell Phillips, the fact is that given his prominent family background, education, high intelligence, and remarkable platform talents in an age fascinated by oratory, Phillips was almost predestined to play a prominent role in American public life. What is less clear is why he chose the path he did—as a disciple of William Lloyd Garrison rather than a popular hero like Daniel Webster.

In attempting to answer this question some years ago I argued that Phillips made a conscious decision to choose reform as a vocation when he was about thirty years old. The decision was triggered by his marriage to Ann Terry Greene, an early follower of Garrison, by his apprenticeship years as an abolitionist after 1836, and

*In addition to the transcription by Patricia Denault and Sally Sweet of almost all of the letters published here, I have benefited to an unusual extent from the generosity, cooperation, and assistance of others. Crawford Blagden, sensitive from the beginning to the scholarly importance of the newly discovered manuscripts in his possession, generously allowed me to take the collection to Pittsburgh for a preliminary inventory. My wife, Virginia, assisted me in the early stages of that process. Once the papers were deposited at Harvard I was extended every courtesy by William Bond, Librarian of the Houghton Library, and Rodney Dennis, Curator of Manuscripts, who allowed me access to the papers while they were being catalogued. Suzanne Currier has been of enormous help in deciphering difficult hands, pointing out connections between manuscripts, and adjusting the pace of cataloguing to my own work.

None of the photographs and letters included here from the Blagden Collection may be reproduced without the written permission of the Houghton Library, Harvard University.

by his search for a calling consistent with religious duty and the tradition of leadership associated with the Phillips name.[1] This interpretation was generally in accord with earlier biographies and with available sources. The sources, however, were scanty. Phillips left no family correspondence, no autobiography, and few letters written to him. According to the conventional scholarly wisdom, the main body of his papers had been lost by fire or destroyed by his wife after his death. The biographer was forced, therefore, to re-create the story of his childhood, youth, and early manhood on the basis of reminiscences by friends, a few school and college records, and Phillips's own scattered letters, written mostly after 1840.

The conventional wisdom was proved wrong early in 1977 when Crawford Blagden, a great-great-nephew of Phillips, opened a long-forgotten crate of family papers in the basement of his Tuxedo Park home. These papers, now available to scholars in the Houghton Library, include thousands of letters to Phillips covering his entire career, hundreds of letters between him and his wife, and a smaller but significant correspondence with other members of his family. The new sources enable us to reconstruct the development of Phillips's career in more convincing detail, as the unfolding of an organic process in which family tradition, religious concern, death, vocational uncertainty, romance, and birth all play an essential part.

When the Blagden Papers were brought to the Houghton Library they came in seven substantial boxes, one of which was devoted to the papers of Wendell's father, John Phillips, and to other early members of his family. Included in the box is a large notebook which Wendell began to keep at least as early as 1832, when he was twenty-one years old. On the first page he wrote, "Grandma left keeping store about 1803." Wendell would have had clear memories of his grandmother, Margaret Wendell Phillips. Not only was he named after her family, but she lived until his eleventh year and was a well known Boston personality in her own right. Descended from the Wendells who had come to New Amsterdam in 1645 and the

---

1. Irving H. Bartlett, *Wendell Phillips: Brahmin Radical* (Boston, 1961).

daughter of a prominent Boston merchant, she had married another merchant, Wendell's paternal grandfather, been widowed at an early age, and carried on the family dry-goods business on Washington Street while bringing up her family. She left an estate of more than $30,000 including a substantial interest in Long Wharf and the elegant brick mansion house on the corner of Beacon and Walnut Street where her grandson was born in 1811.[2]

Wendell would probably have remembered his grandmother most vividly as a formidable defender of the family faith. Money had not eased her agonized conscience and the letters which Wendell preserved show her constantly examining the state of her own heart. She worried about the weather and then felt guilty that she was ignoring the goodness of God in everyday events. When a girl, "who I had learnt the price of goods and on whome my dependence was to tend shop" suddenly quit, she blamed herself for "fear I have not done my duty to her while she was with me." [3] Called out one evening to assist a poverty-stricken friend about to have her eighth child, she brooded over the ways of Providence, "dark and intricate to such short sighted creatures as we are." [4] Despite a life of labor devoted to the fulfillment of earthly responsibilities, Margaret Wendell never forgot the fundamental importance of treating life as a preparation for death. Everything else, including maternal tenderness, was of lesser importance. When a sister reported the birth of a new grandchild, Margaret wrote:

> Congratulate you my dear in the acquisition to your family, may the dear baba live not only to bear up the name but to inherit the virtues of its dear grandmama. Thay are carefull comforts from the cradle to the grave, but the parent's duty is plain, to enjoy with moderation. If thay live to years of discretion instill into them good principles and resign them to there Heavenly Father, whenever he is pleased to take them out of life.[5]

2. "Memoir of John Phillips," *Boston Monthly Magazine* (November, 1825), 281–292. Suffolk County Probate Records, 121.1: 205.

3. Margaret Phillips to Phoebe Foxcroft Phillips, undated. All manuscript references are to the Blagden Papers in the Houghton Library unless otherwise noted.

4. Margaret Phillips to Phoebe Foxcroft Phillips, undated.

5. Margaret Phillips to Phoebe Foxcroft Phillips, December 20, 1799.

Although Wendell's father, John Phillips, had apparently disappointed her by studying law rather than for the ministry, he remained emphatically within the sphere of his mother's influence until he died. When she was in Boston he customarily visited her two or three times a day, and he wrote her regularly when she stayed with other members of the family at Andover. The letters are distinguished for their religious earnestness and formality. On one occasion, for example, when he was in his thirties and presiding over a large family of his own, John, after wishing his mother a safe passage to Andover added, "P.S. I humbly hope to keep in mind my eternal welfare agreeably to your kind admonition although I am too anxious to sublunary interest." [6]

Inevitably the grandmother's admonitions were passed to Wendell and the rest of the Phillips children. When an older brother, away at school, complained that he was being asked to wear hand-me-down trousers, his father wrote, "You are mistaken in thinking them made from those which Thomas had. The cloth was purchased a few days since for you. I find you have written *whare* instead of were. Pray attend to your spelling. . . . I hope you are attending with great diligence to your studies. You might recollect the examination you are (to) pass if your life is prolonged." [7] The point was to remind the boy that he might be taken at any moment, in which case the state of his trousers would hardly be the decisive thing. A few years later when Margaret Wendell died at the age of eighty-four, John Phillips paused in his grief to point out the explicit lesson of her death:

Your Hon'd Grandmother was on Thursday about half past nine o'clock released from a world of trial and discipline and as we humbly trust through the merits of her Redeemer received to that happiness which God has graciously promised to the faithful followers of Jesus Christ our Lord. She, my dear son, had lived a long & very exemplary life, but the near approach of that period when she must appear in the presence of her Maker & her Judge filled her mind with awe and dread. She urged upon us all and frequently,

6. John Phillips to Margaret Phillips, September 18, 1804.
7. John Phillips to Samuel Phillips, October 11, 1815.

the indispensable importance of preparing for the great change of worlds. Now, my dear son, you have not received the benefit which I trust the actual view of your expiring grandparent would have produced. Yet you may recollect all the admonitions & advice she has given you. She daily carried you in the arms of faith to the throne of Grace. This she no more does in this world. Pray therefore daily to God for his blessing & direction. . . . Read your Bible also every day and frequently repeat those hymns which you have committed to memory. It gave her great comfort & support in the near view of death to repeat such hymns as she had probably learned seventy years since. You may be called in a short time. If prepared it cannot be too soon. In the meantime Providence has directed us while on earth to be active & diligent in the discharge of duty. Apply therefore to your studies closely that if you shall be prolonged you may occupy some station in which you may benefit society & promote your own welfare. The most important hours are passing both as respects the present & the future life. Be studious, be virtuous & God will bless you.[8]

John Phillips must have appeared to Wendell as an embodiment of his own principles. Eminent in character and achievement, he was the kind of father any Boston boy could recall with pride. A judge, member of the Corporation of Harvard College, for ten years presiding officer of the Massachusetts Senate, and the first Boston mayor, John Phillips according to the *Commercial Gazette* "appeared born to serve the public and advance their interests."[9] His personality is described in markedly different terms from those that were later applied to his famous son. John Phillips was known as a "safe" leader, a man of "conciliatory" temperament and "conservative" sentiment—the right kind of man to keep the Establishment firmly established.[10] Always a serious man, he became even graver after his mother died. On June 23, 1823, he presided over the Massachusetts Senate as usual, cordially introduced the new President, and administered the oath to the clerk "in his customary solemn and impressive manner." During an interval in official business he told a friend that he was suffering from chest pains and

8. John Phillips to John Charles Phillips, March 1, 1823.

9. *Boston Commercial Gazette*, June 2, 1823.

10. *New England Historical and Genealogical Register* (October, 1866), pp. 297–299. James S. Loring, *The Hundred Boston Orators* (Boston, 1852), pp. 248–252.

shortness of breath. Nevertheless he continued his duties, accompanied the procession of legislators to the Old South Meetinghouse for the customary services, walked home, and went to bed.[11] The next morning he was dead. The funeral was a public event attended by the members of the Legislature and the City Council, and every Massachusetts senator wore crepe on his arm for the duration of the session. Meanwhile Wendell's father was laid to rest in the Granary burial ground across from King's Chapel between the graves of two other Boston leaders, James Otis and Samuel Adams.

Wendell Phillips was eleven years old when his father died. Although there is not direct correspondence between father and son in the Blagden Papers or elsewhere, and Wendell apparently seldom mentioned him in later life, he carefully preserved his father's business records, political correspondence, and family papers. As he grew older, detailed memories of his father would become dimmer but he would remember him as an important, respected leader who always performed his duty. His sudden death at a relatively early age would almost certainly have been traumatic for the boy. Only a few months before, his father had invoked the death of his grandmother to remind his sons of the fateful decisions still ahead for them. The most important hours were passing, he had said, "both as respects the present and the future life." The words were written to Wendell's older brother John Charles, but the sentiment was even more applicable to Wendell, who would now have to pick his way through the snares of adolescence without a father's guidance.

Sarah Walley Phillips lived more than twenty years after her husband's death. As the next to youngest child in a family of eight brothers and sisters, most of whom could fend for themselves by the time their father died, Wendell naturally received a major share of his mother's attention. However, there has been hardly a scrap of evidence to indicate how she helped to shape his development. The yield from the Blagden papers is unfortunately thin in this connection, but there are two helpful letters. The first was to Wendell's

11. *Boston Commercial Gazette,* June 2, 1823.

mother when she was a ten-year-old girl visiting relatives in Salem. Her father, Thomas Walley, wrote as follows.

It gave me pleasure to hear you got safe to Salem & that you are so happy with your Uncle & Aunt Hall. I hope you will behave in such a manner as to make your stay agreable to them as well as to yourself & though you are at present from under the eye of your parents dont forget to read yr Bible morning & evening, to address your Maker & thank him for the Many mercies bestowed upon you. Tho you are young you do not want for capacity. Improve your talents, right Religion is amiable in youth, it is no enemy to mirth & good humour. They that fear God, especially in their youth have most reason to rejoice. . . . I do not write as to a Baby, but to one that I know is capable of discerning & knows what is right & how she ought to behave.[12]

Although we can hardly generalize about Sally Walley's behavior as a mother on the basis of a single letter written to her as a little girl, we should notice that while she came from the same kind of middle class Calvinist merchant family as her husband's, the quality of the religious tradition in which she was raised was significantly different. She was encouraged to combine her religion with amiability, mirth, and good humor, qualities conspicuously lacking in Wendell's grandmother and father. Like other children, Wendell would build his own moral resources from the offerings of both parents. From his father he would derive a commitment to public service and an unfaltering faith in Providence, from his mother a marked indifference to theology and the ability to blend wit and humor with high moral earnestness in his own popular sermonizing.

There is only one letter in the Blagden papers in the hand of Wendell's mother. It is written from the family cottage in Nahant to Wendell's younger brother Grenville probably in 1839–1840, after most of her children had married.

The bearer is a market man & comes to my door every day & I have asked him to call at the House every morning & get the papers of the last evening & any note you might want to send. I thank you for the chickens sent by brother Tom but do not wish any more in that way. I send my butter box &

12. Thomas Walley to Sally Walley, March 18, 1783.

wish Lucy to take four pound of Henderson's butter in stamp, it will come tomorrow morning, the butter I mean. I have been expecting some of you down, that & the wet weather has kept me at home but I think I shall be up tomorrow for the butter. My horse is getting on very well. We went to John on Tuesday. I think to bring him back next week. How is Thomas, I want to hear that he is better. . . . We have anything but Nahant weather. The Walleys sit by the fire & find it very cosy. With love to all I am your best Friend & aff.

Mother S. Phillips[13]

There is an appealing homeliness to this letter. John Phillips's letters are austere and admonitory; Sally writes as a friend offering warmth, shelter, nurture. Posed on the edge of adolescence when his father died, Wendell sought the love, support, and guidance that he needed from his mother. When she died in 1845, he was thirty-four years old. "It seemed to me as if something that overshadowed and protected me, as if I were still a child, had gone," he wrote, "and I were left all out, by myself, with nothing here to hold to." [14]

Most of Phillips's formal education took place after his father's death, during the ten years he spent at the Boston Latin School and Harvard. The dominant image which we have of him during this period, based on the recollections of schoolmates and school records, is of a bright, socially conscious, conservative-minded young Beacon Hill Brahmin, who was quickly welcomed into the top clubs and seemed more bent on enjoying life than figuring out what to do with it. His efforts to prevent the organization of a Harvard temperance society and his reputation as one of the leaders of the student "aristocracy" are pointed to as examples of his behavior and state of mind at this time. [15]

The evidence in the Blagden Papers relating to Phillips' student experience is indirect. Although there are no letters during this period from Wendell, himself, letters from his brothers encourage us to draw a somewhat different picture. In the first place the notion

13. Sarah Walley Phillips to Grenville Phillips, undated.
14. Wendell Phillips to Elizabeth Pease, April 30, 1846, Oswald Garrison Villard Papers (Houghton Library).
15. Bartlett, *Wendell Phillips*, pp. 17-25.

of the Boston Brahmin as a type should not be overdrawn. No doubt Boston was more culture and class conscious than most other American cities. No doubt Harrison Gray Otis and other close neighbors of the Phillips family lived on a grand social scale. No doubt Bostonians who clung to the spokes thought they were living in "the hub of the universe." Nevertheless Boston was not London, Rome, or Paris, not even New York or Philadelphia for that matter, and it does seem to be straining the language to describe John Phillips's son, the grandson of Margaret Wendell, as a kind of Boston prince. The provincial quality of life that remained even in the best Boston families in the early nineteenth century is suggested in the letters which Wendell's older brother Tom wrote to his parents during a trip to Washington in 1818. Although Tom was twenty-one years old, leaving home brought out feelings of dependence and vulnerability. From Providence he wrote, "My next letter will be written in a better hand. I shall expect to hear from you whilst I am in N. York. Shall go to the Post Office every day. Grandmama & Mama may not be alarmed for fear of accidents, for I find these gentlemen with whom we shall proceed are altogether opposed to riding in the night." [16] In New York Tom Phillips and his friends stayed at the City Hotel. "It is remarkably supplied with servants," he wrote, "so much so that one of our Yankee travelers some time since expressed his surprise that so many well dressed gentlemen should be seen standing bout the dining table & eating nothing, when he was told that they were servants." [17] When he finally reached the national capital, Tom was prepared to think the more of Boston. His interviews with President Monroe and John Quincy Adams, which he seems to have managed as a matter of course, were apparently not worth describing, and Washington itself was no more than "an ordinary city," Henry Clay a "raw country lawyer," and John Marshall "the last man I ever saw whom I should set down for a man of talent." [18] If Wendell had been old enough to

16. Thomas Walley Phillips to John Phillips, January 27, 1818.
17. Thomas Walley Phillips to John Phillips, February 1, 1818.
18. Thomas Walley Phillips to John Phillips, February 15, 1818.

accompany his brother, his perceptions would probably have been the same. The Phillips boys were brought up to measure achievement by Beacon Hill standards. More than twenty years later Wendell would write his mother from Rome that St. Peter's Square was only two thirds the size of Boston Common.[19]

If the leader of the Harvard student aristocracy was not as aristocratic as he has been described, neither was he as light hearted as he appeared. While still a student at the Latin School, Phillips had passed through the kind of religious reawakening championed by Jonathan Edwards a half century earlier. The experience was launched by the preaching of one of Edwards's less consistent followers, Lyman Beecher, but Wendell's grandmother and father had prepared the way. Having been called to the altar of faith, he had also shown at the Latin School that he understood another kind of calling. "Let us then remember," he had written in a school composition, "that a man has been blessed by the creator with the most noble grand and invaluable faculties. Let us all be careful that we neither benumb them by idleness and disuse or degrade them by applying them to improper or unworthy objects." [20]

To understand the importance of one's secular or vocational calling was one thing; to act on it quite another. As he approached the end of his college career, Wendell must have envied his older brothers. Tom Phillips had been contentedly practicing law for years, John Charles, four years older than Wendell, was finishing his theological studies at Andover, and George Walley, one year his senior, was beginning to study law at Litchfield. Although Wendell went on to Harvard Law School immediately after his graduation, there is no evidence that he felt called to the profession. Perhaps sensing his brother's indecisiveness in the matter and fearing that Wendell might turn into a pedant, his brother John warned: "The man who bows down to learning is as much in bondage and in a degraded condition—viewed as an immortal being—as the votary of

19. Wendell Phillips to Sarah Walley Phillips, February 9, 1840.
20. Bartlett, *Wendell Phillips*, p. 13.

pleasure." [21] A visit to Andover, John thought, might encourage Wendell to think better of the ministry as a career.

The best evidence in the Blagden Papers that Phillips was only partially engaged by his law studies is found in the genealogical notebook that he began the year he finished college. The notation which he made on the first page about his grandmother launched Phillips on an exhaustive search for family roots. Eventually the 1832 notebook would become part of a voluminous genealogical file, but in the beginning Phillips seems to have been most interested in establishing his roots in seventeenth century New England.[22] He drew elaborate family trees tracing his mother's family back to "the patient and holy Walley" who, according to Cotton Mather, had been providentially appointed to heal the divisions of the church in Barnstable. In succeeding generations the Walleys moved from the pulpit into the countinghouse, and after Wendell became an abolitionist he searched for evidence of their involvement in the slave trade. An "Uncle Tom Walley" told him about an earlier ancestor who "spoke in his last years with great pleasure of his never having engaged in any slave trading or privateering—never owned a stick in a privateer," but an eighteenth-century Boston newspaper disclosed a John Walley trying to sell "a likely negro girl aged about 16 yrs, can do household work."

Even before he discovered the Walley slaveholder, Wendell had been more interested in the Phillipses. After drawing a chart tracing them back to the Reverend George, who had sailed with Winthrop on the *Arbella*, Wendell made a list of early members of the family settled in Massachusetts and wrote out a plan of research.

Write or go to each town, to the present town clerk, stating the dates of birth & marriage of any individual you want & request an *official certified* copy on a *full* sheet of such record.

21. John Charles Phillips to Wendell Phillips, February 1, 1830 and December 18, 1830.

22. All quotations in the following two paragraphs are taken from the Wendell Phillips Genealogical Notebook in the Blagden Papers unless otherwise noted.

N.B. Why not while about it record all the sons or all the children of
Samuel of Rowley & Saml of Salem & the rest.

. . . I should refer also to *town* histories etc. confirming the genealogy,
as for instance History of Andover, Gage's History of Rowley.

A reading of Phillips's genealogical files shows that he spent a substantial part of his time from 1832 to 1836 reading the standard
chronicles of seventeenth-century New England, consulting manuscripts in private hands, like Samuel Sewall's diary, and visiting town
halls, state archives, probate records, and cemeteries to clarify the
Phillips story. He learned that John Winthrop had advanced the
funds to pay for George Phillips's passage, that this first American
Phillips was probably not the George Phillips listed in the Bodleian
Library catalogue, but that he had established the first church in
Watertown, and had signed a petition still lodged in the Massachu-
setts archives on behalf of "a man who had been fined for having an
Anabaptist Book." By 1836 Wendell had become enough of an
authority on the Phillips lineage to offer suggestions to the New
England genealogist John Farmer. "Anything in the power of a
young attorney not much employed professionally," he wrote to
Farmer, "I should be happy to do for your assistance." [23] Eventually
he would employ genealogists of his own in England and learn that
Winthrop's friend George Phillips had descended from Richard
Phillips of Norfolk, whose will was proved in 1416.[24]

Why should Wendell Phillips at twenty-one have begun a serious
investigation of family origins? Well born Bostonians have always
been sensitive about matters of pedigree, and no Bostonian of his
generation was better born in this sense than Phillips. Moreover he
was coming to maturity at a time when the ideological heritage
which had sustained his father's generation was disintegrating. Federalist leaders and Federalist ideas were still respected in Boston,
but they had long since lost national credibility, and the new leader-

23. Wendell Phillips to John Farmer, April 2, 1836 (New Hampshire Historical
Society).

24. H. G. Somesby to Wendell Phillips, August 10, 1852.

ship in Massachusetts was symbolized by a man like Daniel Webster who seemed to embody the principles of the past while accommodating himself to the alien ways of the new democracy.[25] Like other young Federalist sons at Harvard, Phillips felt drawn into Webster's orbit. "I love the Puritans, honor Cromwell, idolize Chatham & Hurrah for Webster," he wrote in his class book in 1831.[26] Having lost his own father at an early age, Phillips naturally looked for other models to follow. Unlike his father, George Phillips of Watertown had been a respected Puritan leader willing to defy the established authority structure whenever conscience and the rights of his constituents demanded.[27] Toward the end of his life, long after he had come to realize that he could not honor Cromwell and cheer for Webster at the same time, and when Wendell Phillips was trying to evaluate the significance of his own career as a radical, he would emphasize the fact that the first Phillips in New England had also been a great dissenter.

He asserted that the churches of Rome were true churches. Winthrop—a noted intermeddler, came with his friends, to Watertown to punish this heresy. Mr. Phillips refused to receive them as magistrates & only accepted their advice as that of members of a neighboring congregation. This was one of the first protests here against a State-Church & an ecclesiastical tyranny. That same year he led Watertown in resisting a tax levied without its consent; an agitation [to] which Savage attributes the rise of the Massachusetts House of Representatives in its present form.[28]

Phillips would not have called John Winthrop an "intermeddler" in 1832. He was still too much the Boston gentleman for that, and on the surface at least his career continued to develop along conventional lines. After leaving law school in 1834, he spent a few

25. James M. Banner, *To the Hartford Convention* (New York, 1970).

26. Bartlett, *Wendell Phillips*, p. 31. Irving H. Bartlett, *Daniel Webster* (New York, 1978), pp. 70–74.

27. Henry Wilder Foote, *Mr. George Phillips First Minister of Watertown* (Boston, 1830).

28. Wendell Phillips, "Notes for Autobiography" (Houghton Library). This brief manuscript is written in Phillips's hand in the third person as if it had been prepared as an introduction to a book of essays or perhaps even as an obituary.

months in Thomas Hopkinson's law office in Lowell. Hopkinson, a friend of Charles Sumner and a college acquaintance of Phillips, was an ambitious young Whig lawyer, and shared Phillips's admiration for Webster. How much else the two young lawyers shared is conjecturable because Hopkinson came from a much humbler social background and would soon become notorious in abolitionist circles for breaking up a Garrison meeting in Lowell.[29]

Sometime early in 1835 Phillips left Lowell to open his own law office in Boston, apparently committed to the paths of respectability that Phillipses had been treading for generations, paths designed to keep him safely away from fanatical abolitionists and their violent opponents. If he inclined to dabble in reform there was even an approved path for that, as his brother Tom pointed out when he wrote to suggest that Wendell might make a name for himself in temperance.

I should advise you to join a temperance society and make speeches, not only because it is a matter of duty with every man so to do, but because I think it is getting to be almost the only way in which a young man can recommend himself to the notice of the public. These movements seem to me to occupy the place of political parties and meetings in that respect as they were some years ago.[30]

Upper class young men could turn their duty to personal advantage by making themselves custodians of lower class behavior. Thomas Phillips's letter, an admirable document in support of recent interpretations of early nineteenth-century reform movements, suggests the gulf that separated the Boston elite from the Boston poor. The gulf was generally widest when the poor were black. Wendell's brother George revealed the condescension the Phillips boys had been taught to extend to black people when he gave what he thought was a humorous account of the success which a group of local Negroes had in rescuing two alleged fugitive slaves from the Court House in Boston.

29. Thomas Hopkinson, *Autobiography and Letters* (privately printed, 1922), p. 60.

30. Thomas Walley Phillips to Wendell Phillips [c. 1834–1835].

The idea that the niggers in open day carried off from the Supreme Ct. room two prisoners has something so laughable in it that one can hardly appreciate the insult. Huggerford who behaved well was seized by a large black woman and pinned to the wall. The runaways were tumbled in a carriage and lugged off. . . . So we go. Nig is uppermost now for sure.[31]

This letter was written sometime in the late summer of 1836. By then Phillips would have been pleased to learn of a successful fugitive slave escape, but he must have been offended by the sneering tone of his brother's letter. A year earlier he might have laughed— but that would have been before he saw Garrison mobbed and met Ann Terry Greene.

A member of the Boston Female Antislavery Society, Ann Terry Greene had been driven into the streets along with her black and white abolitionist sisters by the same mob that had seized Garrison on October 21, 1835. Phillips had been a spectator that day. Not yet sympathetic to the antislavery cause, he had nevertheless been amazed and disturbed at the apparent unwillingness of Boston authorities to control the mob.[32] A few weeks later he met Ann Terry Greene and heard the story from her perspective. A petite, vivacious young woman with a caustic tongue, Ann seems to have fascinated Wendell from the beginning, and in the winter of 1836, as he fell in love with her, he began to meet abolitionists socially. He was introduced to Garrison for the first time at Henry and Maria Weston Chapman's house, the social center of Boston abolitionists, where Ann lived. In January 1836, he visited Ann's cousin Deborah Weston while giving a Lyceum lecture in New Bedford. The lecture was on a neutral subject, but there was an informal discussion afterwards in the course of which Phillips attacked William Ellery Channing's recent book on slavery in good Garrisonian fashion.[33] Meanwhile he continued to see Ann Terry, and became engaged to her in the fall of 1836. From this point on his

31. George Phillips to Wendell Phillips, 1836.
32. Wendell Phillips, "The Boston Mob," *Speeches, Lectures and Letters,* First Series (Boston, 1894), p. 212.
33. Deborah Weston to Anne Weston, January 22, 1836 (Boston Public Library).

involvement with the antislavery movement escalated rapidly. He began to have long talks with Garrison, subscribed to the *Liberator*, and soon felt as comfortable with the other abolitionists at Maria Chapman's house as he did in any Beacon Street parlor.[34] By the summer of 1837 Phillips's leadership role within the movement was officially recognized and he was commissioned as an Agent of the American Antislavery Society. In October of the same year he married Ann Terry Greene and two months later after the killing of the abolitionist editor, Elijah Lovejoy, he gave the speech in Faneuil Hall that attracted enormous attention in Boston and is usually regarded as his first major oratorical triumph.

In less than a year Phillips had moved from a rank outsider to become a leading spokesman for the Garrisonians. He would later explain it by saying that he had been abolitionised by the women in the Boston Female Antislavery Society. "I thank them for all they have taught me," he said on the twentieth anniversary of the Garrison riots. "My eyes were sealed, so that, although I knew the Adamses and Otises of 1776 and the Mary Dyers and Ann Hutchinsons of older times, I could not recognize the Adamses and Otises, the Dyers and Hutchinsons, whom I met in the streets of '35. These women opened my eyes, and I thank them . . . for that anointing."[35] Most of the anointing had been done by Ann Terry Greene, and if he had been more precise Phillips might have said that the experience of falling in love became happily tumbled together in his mind with the discovery of a calling. The Blagden Papers supply us with one love letter written during his courtship days that will

34. The group around Garrison called the "Boston Clique" was not large and included people like Edmund Quincy, Maria Weston Chapman and her sisters, and Francis Jackson, who came from the same kind of social background as Phillips, as well as abolitionists of lower class background like Garrison and Henry C. Wright. The Clique, which remained cohesive despite the independence and strong-mindedness of its members largely because of Garrison's leadership, offered Phillips a viable alternative to the traditional Boston society in which he had been reared. For an interesting analysis of group dynamics in the Boston Clique, see Lawrence J. Friedman, "Garrisonian Abolitionism and the Boston Clique: A Psychosocial Inquiry," *The Psychohistory Review* (Fall, 1978), 6–19.

35. Wendell Phillips, "The Boston Mob," p. 226.

help to make this point more understandable; it was written by Ann Terry Greene probably a few days before they were married.

'*Give me* your hand,' my love, is not this warm weather charming? Where do you think I have been?—To East Newton, to the Theological seminary there—it stands on a high hill & commands a glorious prospect of hill & dale; from it I saw Boston, *dear* Boston. Not that I love Caesar *less*, but Rome more. Don't imagine that I am going to study for the ministry or that I even asked admission to the dwelling, for though you know I *approve* of a profession, yet I do not intend to follow one. I only *profess* to love you, but no—I make no *professions* or *confessions* touching *that*. Thank you for attending to Jamie's request. Your note was delightful and I with the *grasping* spirit of the age, *wished* to have Uncle give it to me, but maiden bashfulness kept me silent,—but they 'know not my heart, who believe there can be one stain of this earth in its feelings for thee'

I have *stole* into your chamber today & yesterday '*fools rush* in where angels fear to *tread*' . . . I looked in vain for a trace of my beloved. Why did you not leave the print of your footstep on the floor (so easy that) or your crême in the drawer for the slightest thing affection hallows. Tomorrow! how much that little word bears on its bosom for me, for *us*, since, we trust it brings us together. 'If heaven a draught of heavenly pleasure spare one cordial in this melancholy vale, tis when a youthful loving' etc. Your *memory must* supply the rest, for it is too *tender* to be *written*. Farewell.

thy Ann.

As an afterthought she added in pencil on a corner of the letter which would be folded under, "Oh that you were here. I am *all all* alone, 'alone upon a wide, wide sea.' What a grand time we should have." [36] The young couple exchanged other letters before they were married, but this is the one that has been preserved. It is an enchanting letter, and it was as an enchanted lover that Wendell Phillips was transformed into an abolitionist.

Just as it takes more than romance to sustain a long marriage, so it takes more than an initial fascination to sustain a lifelong career. Phillips discovered abolitionism at a time when the movement was successfully identifying itself with the cause of civil rights in the North.[37] His first successful speeches had been in defense of the

36. Ann Terry Greene to Wendell Phillips [c. 1836–1837].
37. James Brewer Stewart, *Holy Warriors: The Abolitionists and American Slavery* (New York, 1976), pp. 76ff.

right of petition and freedom of the press and one could hardly be branded a dangerous radical for defending such rights in Boston. In 1837 Phillips was still a lawyer and a part-time reformer defending the abolitionist's rights in much the same way that he would defend the rights of any other client.[38] Although it was unusual for a son of John Phillips to get involved in such controversies, Beacon Hill could tolerate his behavior as long as the villains he pilloried were ruffians in Illinois or slave drivers in the South.

For Garrisonians there was no neutral ground regarding slavery; a person was for immediate emancipation or for slavery. By this definition everyone Phillips had been brought up to love and respect was guilty and should be condemned. After the Lovejoy speech which gave him instant visibility in New England, he became increasingly willing to link himself with the most extreme advocates of abolitionism. Everyone outside the movement was repelled by the fanaticism of the *Liberator*, but Phillips, who disagreed with Garrison on some matters, like non-resistance, publicly endorsed Garrison's paper. "I regard the success of the *Liberator*," he said, "as identical with that of the abolition cause itself." The fundamental principle on which the paper was conducted was the conviction "that rights are more valuable than forms" and Phillips intended to "pour its spirit into the mind of every one I can reach." [39]

Phillips had been impressed with the importance of putting "rights" over "forms" ever since he became an antislavery agent. In the summer of 1837 he had begun to fulfill his duties by lecturing, organizing new branches of the association, dispensing literature, and raising funds. Sometimes he even solicited from door to door. For the first time in his life he found himself in the houses of poor people, many of them black—people who counted their wealth in pennies and contributed what they could to the cause.[40] He was

---

38. Phillips apparently kept his law office on Court Street until 1851. *The Boston Almanac* (Boston, 1850), p. 78.

39. *Liberator*, January 11, 1839.

40. *Liberator*, April 19, 1839. Anne Weston to Deborah Weston, April 8, 1839 (Boston Public Library).

moved by the experience and confessed that, "He hardly dare stand by the side of those, who, by drudgery and daily toil, and by the sweat of their brows gained a living" and still "poured their all into the treasury of the common cause while others were pampered with luxury and never felt for their brethren in bonds as bound with them." Phillips was discovering that his association with the abolitionists had become a holy fellowship. "There lived the religion of the present," he decided, "while the pulpit was busying itself with forms of sin that had lain buried in the graves of 1800 years." [41]

In March 1839, Phillips defended this fellowship with a practical demonstration of what it could mean to put rights above forms. Earlier that winter a group of Lynn women, many of them black, had petitioned the Massachusetts legislature to repeal the law prohibiting marriage between whites and negroes. Predictably, the legislators ridiculed the petition and the Representative from Braintree, Minot Thayer, was quoted as saying he did not believe "there is a virtuous woman among them." [42] On March 11 the abolitionists staged a massive meeting in Boston's Marlboro Chapel to consider resolutions condemning the legislature for refusing to heed antislavery petitions including the Lynn petition on intermarriage. The meeting was packed not just with abolitionists but with "many people of property & standing & many of the legislature," and when it was all over the words that they could not get out of their minds were those of Wendell Phillips. What he said was not reported directly, but he singled out individual legislators for their behavior on the intermarriage petition and abused them in a way that left Garrison awe-struck. "One of the severest castigations," was all he could write, "ever inflicted by mortal man." [43] Phillips's cousin by marriage, Anne Weston, was more explicit. She claimed that he had torn the legislature to bits, "then ground them to atoms, then strewed them on the waters." The result, according to another abolitionist friend, was that Boston was "convulsed with rage" and

41. *Liberator*, June 21, 1839.
42. *Liberator*, February 15, 1839.
43. *Liberator*, March 15, 1839.

"ready to lynch Wendell." [44] Representative Thayer, who had not been at the meeting but had been one of Phillips's principal victims, immediately demanded an explanation.

I have just been informed by a number of gentlemen that you made use of my name, (in too plain a manner to be misunderstood) in a very unkind and disrespectful manner in the lecture you gave the last evening; that I was held up to public scorn and ridicule; and, that you pronounced the most severe and unjust sarcasms against my character, that I was only worthy of representing a *community of brutes;* that I polluted the carpet on which I spit upon and that unless my constituents *ousted* me from my situation they ought not to enjoy the privileges of citizens; and many other equally severe and ungentlemanly remarks. You can hardly conceive what my feelings must be when told that a son of an affectionate friend, with whom I had long been acquainted from early life, and above all others that I most respected, loved and esteem'd, one whose confidence I had always enjoyed almost to any extent, and whose family and children I have uniformly endeavoured to respect and treat with the most tender affection; and further by one whose amiable wife, was the daughter of an old and sincere friend— could have thus unjustly abused me without the least provocation—as it respects myself it is of little consequence; but you have inflicted a wound upon the feelings of my friends and family that can never be heal'd.

Thayer went on to say that his opposition to the Lynn petition had nothing to do with abolitionism or with any attempts to improve the condition of "the poor and unfortunate slaves." He opposed the petition because he believed on the best authority that the names of respectable women were fraudulently placed on it to attract the signatures of others.[45]

Phillips's reply to Thayer is not available in the Blagden Papers, but there is a fragmentary, barely decipherable pencilled draft of a letter which shows that he tried to distinguish between his strong disapprobation of Thayer's behavior and the intent to abuse him personally.[46] In any event he failed to satisfy the legislator, who terminated the correspondence by saying, "If you think that you[r] late venerable Father would approve of the course you have lately

44. Anne Weston to Deborah Weston, March 11, 1839 (Boston Public Library).
45. Minot Thayer to Wendell Phillips, March 12, 1839.
46. Wendell Phillips to Minot Thayer, March 1839 [draft].

pursued, I suspect you are equally mistaken as I hope you have been in regard to me, and as proof of my suspicion I would refer you to your respected Brother Thomas or any others of your family." [47]

There is an eloquent silence in the Blagden Papers concerning the repercussions within the Phillips family of the attack on Thayer. Phillips must have been uneasy about it. On the one hand he could feel that he had done his duty by showing that laws against inter-marriage were no less than an extension of slavery and those who supported them as guilty as slaveholders. On the other hand he knew that Thayer had been correct about the use of names on the petition; some of them had been used without authorization.[48] Eventually Phillips would be proud to be known as a master of the "elo-quence of abuse," but in his first venture at the art he had landed squarely on an old friend of the family. Was this the way he wanted to spend the rest of his life? Two months after the Minot Thayer affair, Wendell and Ann Phillips embarked for Europe. They would be gone for two years.

A few days before sailing on June 10, 1839, Phillips received a farewell letter from the Massachusetts Antislavery Society written by Garrison which explains in characteristically overstated rhetoric exactly why the abolitionists placed such a high value on the sup-port of their new colleague.

We feel that, in a worldly sense, few in the extended ranks of American abolitionists have made larger sacrifices upon the altar of Humanity than yourself. Descended from a highly respectable lineage—the son of a father who had "done the State some service," and whose memory is endeared to the people of this Commonwealth—connected with an elevated class in society—possessed of rare abilities, which qualified you to reach and to fill high and responsible offices in the gift of the nation—in the spring-time of manhood, when the love of popular applause, rather than of doing good, generally inflames the youthful mind—you turned your back upon the bland-ishments of a seductive world, repudiated all hope of political preferment and legal eminence, made yourself of no reputation for the benefit of the perishing bondman, and became the associate of those, who, for seeking the

47. Minot Thayer to Wendell Phillips, March 15, 1839.
48. Anne Weston to Deborah Weston, March 11, 1839.

abolition of slavery by moral and religious instrumentalities, are up to this
hour subjected to popular odium, to violent treatment, to personal insult.[49]

There was every reason for Garrison to be rhapsodic. Phillips
brought wealth, social position, and great talent to the cause, and
Garrison was not likely to let him get away. On the other hand, he
had hardly become the social outcast pictured by Garrison. His
behavior over the past two and a half years had startled many people
and infuriated some, but he remained Wendell Phillips, the former
mayor's son, a Harvard-bred lawyer with an office on Court Street,
and despite the unpleasantness over Minot Thayer he was still
accepted by the rest of his family. In Europe he would find health
for his wife and represent the Massachusetts Society at the first
world antislavery convention in London. But there was also a
hidden agenda, one which Garrison would not even have wanted to
consider. Phillips wanted to be sure that his love affair with abolitionism was more than a youthful enthusiasm.

Although Garrisonians accused everyone who disagreed with
them of being pro-slavery, Wendell knew it was not that simple.
He knew that his brothers and sisters and his mother "disapproved"
of slavery. While not following Channing in matters of religion
they would have agreed with his moderate, "Christian," and gentle-
manly indictment of slavery.[50] Wendell's brother-in-law, the Reverend George Blagden, was the only other member of the family to
appear in print on the subject, and he argued that since slavery was
recognized in both the Old and New Testament there was no scriptural basis for reckless denunciation of the institution or of those
involved with it, although it could be attacked for the specific sins
it encouraged. The sins of slavery, Blagden said, "form a theme for
passionate declamation and oratorical display, which affords one of
the best opportunities that has ever been offered for public speakers

49. William Lloyd Garrison to Wendell Phillips, June 4, 1839.
50. The *Boston Courier* for April 9, 1839, probably spoke for the rest of Phillips's
family when it applauded Channing for rebuking abolitionist extremism while
condemning slavery in a way which gave slaveholders "no reason to complain of
the severity of language which is used."

of warm feelings and vivid imaginations to distinguish themselves
. . . without troubling themselves to go into that Patient study of
the whole subject which alone . . . can effect any permanent
remedy." [51] Wendell would have had no patience with Blagden's
first point. He had already decided that the spirit of Christianity was
against slavery no matter what was written in the Bible.[52] But the
second point gave him pause. He had practically been swept off his
feet. Garrison and the other leaders of the movement were obviously courting him, and he was discovering powers within himself
as an antislavery orator that he would scarcely have believed a few
years earlier. Phillips was still enough his father's son to realize that
the big decisions in life are best made deliberately. It was possible
that his new associations had weakened his "individual independence," that he was "being hurried recklessly forward by the enthusiasm of the moment and the excitement of heated meetings." [53]
Therefore, he welcomed the opportunity to get away and take a
sober second look at a career that threatened to thrust him perma-
nently outside the mainstream of American life.

Wendell and Ann landed in England in the early summer of 1839.
After spending a short time in London, they planned to cross the
continent to Italy, where they would spend the winter months
before returning to London for the great antislavery convention in
the following year. Although he would be gone twice as long as
originally anticipated, it became clear at the outset that Phillips was
never in danger of becoming an expatriate. From the beginning he
viewed the Old World through a New England lens and described
it in language that his mother was sure to understand. Lizard Point,
his first sight of the British shore, reminded him of Nahant. The
Isle of Wight made him think of "the pet ideas of your life realized
& more than realized—it is a perfect garden, Nahant & Brooklyn

51. Bartlett, *Wendell Phillips*, p. 97.
52. *Ibid.*, p. 41.
53. Phillips wrote these words to Garrison toward the end of his stay in Europe.
Wendell Phillips, *Speeches, Lectures and Letters*, Second Series (Boston, 1894), p.
223.

combined," with its foaming waves, towering cliffs, and ripe fields.[54]
In London, peering into the windows of a fashionable shop at round
bars of soap he recalled how his old nurse Polly had pampered him
in his bath by cutting off the corners of the soap. What he seemed
to be saying was that he had not forgotten the loving care he had
received as a child and would not be tempted in Europe to depart
from the sturdy Republican virtues he had learned on Beacon Street.
Thus he repeatedly told his mother of his success in preventing
unscrupulous boatmen, porters, and coachmen from overcharging
him.[55] After seeing Voltaire's house in France he pointed out the
presence of Washington's portrait in the study.[56] By January they
were in Rome. "Did you ever dream you should have a son wish
you a happy new year from the Eternal City," he wrote,

keeping house too, though awfully troubled when he wants mutton chops.
. . . We have seen his Holiness and if one of the blessings he distributes
among the crowd in St. Peter's Christmas Day can be supposed to light on
a heretic, I may have caught one, for he flung his fingers right out to where
I stood & all others kneeled it would have hit me first.[57]

Unlike other Americans who were overwhelmed by their first
exposure to great works of art and architecture, Phillips was not
moved by Europe as an aesthetic experience. After visiting the Pitti
Palace in Florence, he wrote his mother and dutifully carried her
through the twenty heavily decorated rooms past the great can-
vasses of Corregio, Raphael, and Titian.[58] But it was not the splen-
dors of Italy that impressed him so much as the opulence "existing
at the expense of so much ignorance & suffering on the part of a
suppressed & deluded people." [59] He was offended by the masked
and costumed throngs overflowing the streets of Rome in the

54. Wendell Phillips to Sarah Walley Phillips, July 26, 1859.
55. Wendell Phillips to Sarah Walley Phillips, June 24, 1839, January 2, 1840.
56. Wendell Phillips to Sarah Walley Phillips, October 18, 1839.
57. Wendell Phillips to Sarah Walley Phillips, January 2, 1840.
58. Wendell Phillips to Sarah Walley Phillips, December 7, 1839.
59. Wendell Phillips to Sarah Walley Phillips, February 9, 1840.

BRITISH AND FOREIGN ANTI-SLAVERY SOCIETY,

FOR THE ABOLITION OF

SLAVERY AND THE SLAVE TRADE THROUGHOUT THE WORLD.

PROPOSED SCHEME OF BUSINESS,

FOR

THE CONVENTION,

June 12th, 1840.

I. SLAVERY.

1. GENERAL VIEW OF SLAVERY.—*Define Slavery; various kinds.*

    (1.) Its essential sinfulness, and its opposition to the genius and precepts of the Gospel.
    (2.) Its impolicy with relation to commerce, population, &c.
    (3.) Its influence on legislation, and the security of society.
    (4.) Its moral influence on the character of the enslaver and the enslaved.
    (5.) Its opposition to the advance of civilisation, education, and christianity.

2. PRESENT OPERATION OF SLAVERY.—*Number of bondsmen; features of bondage in*

    (1.) British India and Ceylon.
    (2.) French West Indies.
    (3.) Spanish West Indies.
    (4.) Dutch colonial possessions.
    (5.) Danish West Indies.
    (6.) Swedish West Indies.
    (7.) United States.
    (8.) Texas.
    (9.) South America.
    (10.) Mohamedan countries.

II. SLAVE TRADE.

    (1.) Its nature—means of obtaining slaves—deportation and middle passage—its physical, commercial, political, and moral effect.

    (2.) Its progress and present extent—victims of professed Christian nations—State of the internal Slave-trade in the United States of America—victims of Mohamedans.

    (3.) Causes of its continuance and increase.

The original program of the London Anti-Slavery Convention on the back of which is Ann Phillips's pencilled note to her husband.

Wendell
Please to maintain the
floor — no matter what they
do dont give up yr right to —
Please deny for me who
never saw Mr Prescott
his assertion with regard to the
women saying they doubted
whether they shld be accepted &
Massachusetts was appointed
conditionally —
Ann

Ann Phillips's admonition to Wendell to "Please to maintain the floor." For a transcription of this note, see pages 29–30.

carnival before Lent ("Christian fools with varnished faces"),[60] and assured his mother that he would not live in Rome "if they gave me the Vatican to live in & Naples for a mantel piece ornament." [61]

The lesson which Phillips was learning in Europe had little to do with art, culture, or geography. The high point of his trip on the continent, significantly, was in Geneva where he visited Calvin's church. "Sat & stood in the pulpit, where, *as it was stone*, he may have stood. I attacked the officiating minister & in bad French" asked if Calvin had used the same pulpit, "but like a stupid user of liturgies . . . he couldn't tell. Think of standing in Calvin's pulpit & never having the curiosity to find out." [62]

Geneva must have reminded Phillips of the pulpit he had left behind in Boston. He would resume his abolitionist role only once in Europe, at the antislavery convention in Freemason's Hall, London, in the spring of 1840. The story of the convention has been told many times and does not need to be repeated here. Two groups of American abolitionists attended, the Garrisonians who counted a number of women in their delegation, and a more conservative group of politically oriented abolitionists led by James Birney, who were determined to keep the women from being seated. The conservatives carried the day and forced the American women into a segregated seating section behind a curtain at the end of the hall. At this point Ann Phillips left her most prominent mark on the historical record. Furious at being tucked away behind a curtain, she demanded that Wendell carry the fight to the convention floor. "No shilly-shallying," she is quoted as saying. "Be brave as a lion." [63] The Blagden Papers support this anecdote. On the back of a printed convention program is a pencilled note.

Wendell
   Please to maintain the floor—no matter what they do dont give up your right to—Please deny for me . . . [the] . . . assertion with regard to the women

60. Wendell Phillips to Sarah Walley Phillips, March 9, 1840.
61. Wendell Phillips to Sarah Walley Phillips, April 4, 1840.
62. Wendell Phillips to Sarah Walley Phillips, October 18, 1839.
63. Bartlett, *Wendell Phillips*, pp. 67ff.

saying they *doubted* whether they shld be accepted & Massachusetts was appointed conditionally.

Although Phillips was unable to get the American women accredited, he seems to have been decisively affected by his own active role in the debates and by the approval that he and his colleagues received from many people in Britain. As one of the leading American delegates he headed a deputation to meet Lord Brougham, was introduced to Carlyle and to famous reformers like Buxton and Clarkson, and was entertained by the Duchess of Sutherland and Lord Morpeth. "I tell you all this," Phillips wrote, "to show you how far from *vulgar* the *Liberator* would be, Ma, in London. Why the clergy whose names were familiar to me on title pages praise us so much in their speeches and the politicians followed in the strain that I got real sick of it." [64]

A year earlier, in his first letter home, Phillips had told his mother that in political discussions on board the boat, he kept up the family fame "by hitting the happy medium." [65] Now, reinforced by his heady experience in London, he began to lecture the other members of the family. Hearing that brother George was attending the church of Hubbard Winslow, who had condemned the abolitionist martyr Elijah Lovejoy, he dismissed Winslow as "a base minded, timeserving, truckling priest." Phillips asked his mother to remind his brother that he bore "the honored name of *George*" of Watertown and was "bound to think if he can conscientiously give such a man his support." Associating Winslow's name with his brother-in-law, the Reverend George Blagden, he also asked his mother to pass on what he had recently heard from a respected British churchman. "Why Sir, said he, the name of a New Englander stinks in the nostrils here. Nobody believes a New England Christian anything but a hypocrite unless he is an abolitionist."

After reprimanding the two Georges, Phillips attempted to close on a more domestic and tranquil note by writing "as for shirts Ma,

64. Wendell Phillips to Sarah Walley Phillips, July 24, 1840.
65. Wendell Phillips to Sarah Walley Phillips, June 24, 1839.

you do not seriously think that after using such ones as you make I would wear the horrid scant things that hang up in Paris shops?" [66] He would still wear the family shirts but he had outgrown the family ideas.

By the autumn of 1840 Wendell and Ann were back in Italy. Wendell's brother John, an orthodox Congregational minister, had asked if he had any plans for church affiliation when he returned. This occasioned another lecture to his mother.

Tell him I should be unwilling to join any church which admitted fellowship with a slaveholder not deeming such a Christian church, and even then perhaps I am too Quakerishly inclined to put my head even into that yoke. I don't like the church spirit as displayed in our days—as to frequenting the meeting house I shall hope to when other circumstances than those before on my return allow—but even there few ministers remember *religion*—But the parson & I will talk all this over when I get back. I hope before that time he will have awakened a little more thoroughly up to some stirring truths that I could name & which he who bears in this generation the mantle of the bold first George ought to be foremost in. I commend him to the study of his ancestor's spirit.[67]

Having admonished the two older brothers nearest to him in age on their moral responsibilities, Wendell turned to his oldest brother Tom, who as an enthusiastic Whig was singing the praises of William Henry Harrison's recent election. Tom had been more like a father to Wendell than anyone else in the family, and he treated him with more respect. He would not, however, celebrate the Whig victory.

There will have to be a more potent revolution than merely turning one selfish set of men out of office to put another equally selfish one in, before all we suffer from will be removed. A long argument this—the proper text of which would be the golden rule & the duty of each man's holding himself for a steward only of what God has given him & thinking he has sent us all here for a higher purpose than making money merely or spending it when it is made. Boston is full of good revolutions & I hope the family will take some share in them. They owe it to the name they bear.[68]

66. Wendell Phillips to Sarah Walley Phillips, July 24, 1840.
67. Wendell Phillips to Sarah Walley Phillips, November 19, 1840.
68. Wendell Phillips to Sarah Walley Phillips, January 22, 1841.

Having invited his brother to take part in one of the "good revolutions," Phillips extended the invitation to his mother. Garrison, he wrote, had named his recent son Wendell Phillips Garrison, and he hoped his mother would acknowledge the honor in a suitable manner.

Well I was thinking Ma had been at no expense for new years presents to me the last two years as I have been away. Now it would give me great pleasure if you should get some good *useful* thing & handsome too & send it to him in *your own* name—you do not know how much gratification such an attention would give to a noble hearted man. I ask it seriously & know you will be glad to please me in this. I know of nothing, hardly, which I should feel so much or so deeply as a kindness from you & *in your name* as I have asked. Do think of it my Dear Mother. . . . Do grant me this favor Dear Mother. I beg it as you love me—& remember Mrs. Edgeworth's favorite proverb—'Who gives quickly gives twice.' [69]

A few weeks later he wrote again to remind his mother of the request. "I know my little namesake will find by *rich* experience how kindly my mother remembers the name she gave me—for which I thank her always." [70]

There is no record in the Blagden Papers of Sarah Walley Phillips's response to this request or to any of his other letters, and there is no mention in Garrison's letters of having received a gift. The important thing, however, is to understand what Phillips was doing. He knew the importance Garrison would attach to being accepted by the Phillips family, thus the repeated emphasis on her sending the gift in her own name. And he must have known how difficult it would be for her to do it. His mother would have perceived Garrison through the eyes of people like Minot Thayer—a lower class rabble-rouser who represented everything the mayor had despised. How could she formally endorse linking her son's name with his?

Phillips had finally created a crisis that his mother could not avoid. Like most family dramas, this one proceeded on more than

69. *Ibid.*
70. Wendell Phillips to Sarah Walley Phillips, February 18, 1841.

one level. Phillips had made a conscious decision to spend his time in Europe pondering the extent to which he would commit himself to a career as a reformer. Having made this decision, he was announcing it to his mother. If she loved him, she would embrace the man whose example he had chosen to follow. On a deeper level he was demonstrating that he had discovered what it meant to be a Phillips. "I shall be home soon," he wrote his mother on April 28, "to try to bear *worthily* the *philanthropic* & ambitionless name we have inherited." [71] He had found the models he had been searching for ever since his father died. One was dead but bore the family name; Wendell had repeatedly urged the rest of the family to emulate their ancestral father, George Phillips of Watertown. The other was very much alive and bore the spirit of George Phillips in the form of William Lloyd Garrison. Phillips embraced the opportunity to be godfather to Garrison's son because the uniting of the family names symbolized the kinship he felt toward Garrison. Although they were close in age, he would over the course of a long and fruitful association lavish on his friend the affection and material support of a loving son. "I owe you Dear Garrison," Phillips would write five years after returning from Europe, "more than you would let me express—and my mother and wife except, more than to any other one. Since within the sphere of your influence I trust I have lived a better man." [72]

Phillips and his wife came back to Boston in July 1841 and he soon settled into his chosen career. It was a philanthropic career as he had promised his mother but hardly ambitionless. By finding a vocation consistent with his religion, his sense of family, his marriage, and his desire to lead, he was able to give his talents and harness his substantial ego to the great humanitarian causes of the

71. Wendell Phillips to Sarah Walley Phillips, April 28, 1841.

72. Wendell Phillips to William Lloyd Garrison, January 6, 1846 (Boston Public Library). Phillips paid for his namesake's education at Harvard and over the years he frequently gave Garrison and his family expensive gifts, including gifts of money, and on one occasion donated the services of a servant to the Garrison household for several months. William Lloyd Garrison to Ann Phillips, August 13, 1849.

nineteenth century. Eventually he would be rewarded with power and fame, but not without paying a price. After his mother died in 1845, Phillips wrote to a friend describing his overwhelming sense of loss. Then he sorrowfully confessed, "My own mother, the best, kindest and most devoted of mothers could never agree with me in any of my favorite views & looked sadly on my way of life as almost wasted." [73]

2. *Ann and Wendell Phillips*

AFTER ascending Mt. Vesuvius, Phillips proudly wrote to his mother: "Ann *walked* up the cone. Many men and most women are carried up, but she told the guide notwithstanding his arguments if she went at all she should go on her own feet." [1] The Vesuvius expedition and Ann's vigorous participation in the anti-slavery convention activities at London the following month suggested a reserve of physical vitality which she simply did not possess. Even before they returned to Boston she had fallen ill again, and after they moved into their house on Essex Street she was seldom seen in public. "A life long invalid, rarely leaving her room," Thomas Wentworth Higginson recalled, "she had yet such indomitable courage, such keenness of wit, such insight into character, that she really divided with him the labors of his career. It is impossible for those who knew them both to think of him without her; it is sad to think of her without him." [2]

Phillips would have agreed with his friend Higginson's description, and so would other friends who were close enough to know his wife. They all sympathized with Ann, but some of them sympathized with Phillips even more. After visiting the Phillipses in 1846, Edmund Quincy reported that Ann looked well,

---

73. Wendell Phillips to Elizabeth Pease, April 30, 1846, Oswald Garrison Villard Papers (Houghton Library).

1. Wendell Phillips to Sarah Walley Phillips, May 10, 1840.
2. Thomas Wentworth Higginson, *Wendell Phillips* (Boston, 1884), p. viii.

But they told me she was very ill. It is one of those mysterious complaints in which organic disease is mixed up with a good deal that is imaginary. But this is a dead secret, for neither of them would ever forgive such a suggestion. The end of it will be, I have no doubt, what a physician said of a connexion of my own in somewhat similar circumstances . . . Long Life.[3]

What Quincy and other abolitionists objected to was Phillips's unwillingness to leave his wife for extended lecturing jaunts. Such husbandly devotion was noble enough in lesser mortals, lamented Quincy, but it did seem "as if God had given [him] his great powers for something better."[4]

The fact that Ann Phillips with all her symptoms outlived her husband lends credibility to Quincy's diagnosis. The real problem in trying to understand what Phillips's marriage was like, and how it may have affected his career, has been the absence of direct evidence. Lacking letters between Phillips and his wife, biographers have been forced to rely on what other people said about them. Except for the candid remarks of Quincy, these observations have been very much in the Victorian style. Ann was a lifelong invalid. She and Wendell had a marriage practically without social life, with no children, and perhaps with no sex. Nevertheless, the older Phillips biographers assure us that the marriage was made in heaven and the couple were angelically content.[5] The temptation today is to reject this interpretation and look for a darker linkage between an unsatisfying marriage and Phillips's career as an angry, unrelenting, lifelong reformer. One of the exciting surprises in the Blagden Papers, therefore, is the discovery of a large number of letters between Wendell and Ann Phillips. Most of the letters were written between the early 1850's and mid-1870's. Intimate, informal, and graphic, they make it possible for us to establish Ann Phillips as a strong personality in her own right, a very modern if physically beleaguered

---

3. Irving H. Bartlett, *Wendell Phillips: Brahmin Radical* (Boston, 1961), p. 79.
4. *Ibid.*, p. 165.
5. George L. Austin, *The Life and Times of Wendell Phillips* (Boston, 1888), p. 87. Francis J. Garrison, *Ann Phillips, Wife of Wendell Phillips, A Memorial Sketch* (Boston, 1886).

woman, and to demonstrate that the Phillips marriage was very much as Higginson described.

Like Phillips, Ann Terry Greene claimed a distinctive lineage. Her first American ancestor had been an associate of Roger Williams in Rhode Island.[6] Unlike Phillips, Ann developed a taste for the unconventional early in life. Her mother died when she was very young and her retired merchant father, Benjamin Greene, died when she was ten. With an inheritance of more than $93,000 she and her three brothers were undoubtedly the richest orphans in Boston.[7] Ann was packed off with her share of the family fortune to live with her uncle Henry Chapman and his wife Maria Weston. Growing up as an adolescent and young woman in Maria Weston Chapman's house decisively shaped Ann's development. Harriet Martineau called Maria the handsomest woman in Boston and the most intimidating. John Jay Chapman remembered his grandmother less as a person than as an "embodiment"—a cameo-like creature who carried herself like royalty and fought like an Amazon for whatever cause she served. In 1834 that cause became Garrisonian abolition, and Ann Terry Greene, along with everyone else in the Chapman household, was swept into the ranks as Maria Weston began to raise money for Garrison, assist him in the office, and sometimes edit the *Liberator*.[8]

The few scraps of information we can glean about Ann's early life in the Blagden Papers reveal her fondness for unfashionable ideas. In a packet of letters written by her older brother Benjamin to their grandmother Mary Grew, there is an interesting description of Ann when she was eighteen. Benjamin was lamenting his religious condition, his inability to experience the "change of heart" that customarily accompanied conversion. "I was resolved to strive that I might be 'in Christ' if I was not," he wrote. "But alas! The more I

6. There are several genealogical charts apparently in Phillips's hand in the Blagden Papers tracing the origins of the Greene family.

7. Suffolk County Probate Records, 120:2:360. See the *Boston Commercial Gazette*, November 11, 1822, for an obituary of Benjamin Greene.

8. John Jay Chapman, *Memories and Milestones* (New York, 1915), pp. 209–225.

strove the more discouraging did my state appear, so that I have very little hopes of ever getting to Heaven." Then he told his grandmother in some exasperation: "I had a long conversation with my sister Ann lately on the subject of religion. She is very blind. She does not seem to believe the Atonement any more than if she was in a Heathen country." [9] Like all the early abolitionists, Ann Terry took religion seriously, but coming to adulthood as she did in the Chapman household in the early 1830's meant that she was touched more than Phillips by the "newness" capturing young New England intellectuals at this time. A gossipy letter from one of her youthful friends written a few years after her marriage suggests the intellectual climate in which Ann was raised.

I had a note from our friend Jeannie a few weeks since. Oh the child is so *transcendentalised* that I hardly know what to make of her. She regrets very much that she did not see you before you left us, but says that she quite forgot that while she was loving you at Chelsea you could not know it. . . . In my opinion the child's head is half burned. What with Waldo Emerson, Miss Margaret Fuller, Miss Peabody, Cary Sturgis. She is bewildered. This is her state as nearly as I can make it out. Miss Fuller has conversations at the Masonic Temple every Wednesday with a certain number of young ladies, her disciples. They are conversing now upon the Heathen Deities. I was asked to go, but thought *I could not stand it*. Does transcendentalism suit friend Wendell's taste? [10]

Ann Terry Greene was a tiny woman and her silhouette, the only likeness that we have, shows a pert profile accented by a firm chin and a slightly upturned nose. As a young woman she was considered pretty, but Wendell would have been as fascinated by the quality of her mind and personality as by anything else. He had been brought up in an orthodox family surrounded by conservative-minded brothers and sisters who had unquestioningly taken up the life style of their parents. Ann was a new kind of woman with ideas of her own about everything, especially about the place of women in the world. Phillips knew something about strong women through his

9. Benjamin Greene to Mary Grew, November 11, 1831.
10. Unidentified correspondent to Ann Phillips, December 8, 1839.

grandmother and mother, but their strength had been expended on family and business matters while Ann's was directed toward new ideas and unpopular causes. Although there is no reference in the Blagden Papers to the marriage ceremony, we can assume that Phillips's mother was not thrilled by it. One of Ann's cousins captured the mixed quality of her parental blessing when she noted that "the old lady Phillips . . . behaved like a perfect dragon at the wedding." [11]

Ann liked being different. In London she was visited by Mrs. Joshua Bates, wife of the wealthy American banker. "Abolitionist" was too strong a word for Mrs. Bates, and she asked if the Phillipses, like Mrs. Chapman, were "anxious for the slave." Ann had replied that they decidedly were. Mrs. Bates was politely incredulous. "I think she thought us rather odd folks," Ann reported happily to a friend, "everywhere we pass for queer folks." [12]

Before leaving for Europe Ann Phillips made out her will.

To my dear Wendell — My 'Testament', formerly my sister Mary's. All his letters to me to dispose of as he thinks best. The ring he gave me as a token of our pledged love to one another. Also 'Bryant' 'Coleridge'. The 'Cowper' his kind mother gave me. My watch since I had it round my neck the first day we met and it has pointed so often to our glad hour for meeting, and so kindly *warned* me that we must part. 'The boy's own book of poetry' given to me by him in New York. The little trunk with its key that has held his gems of letters. My two extract books. 'Schiller', 'My Early Days', 'The Skeptic'. My seal motto this 'Mon amour dure apres la mort.' My journals for him to burn as soon as he has read them. The little smelling bottle his mother gave me.[13]

This document makes us wish that Ann Phillips had kept the "gems of letters" written by her suitor before they were married, but they do not appear in the Blagden Papers. The only letter before their marriage was written by Ann and quoted earlier in connection with Wendell's conversion to abolition. That letter together with the

11. Anne Weston to Deborah Weston, October 17, 1837 (Boston Public Library).

12. Ann Phillips to Maria Weston Chapman, July 30, 1839 (Boston Public Library).

13. The undated manuscript will is in Ann Phillips's hand and appears in the Blagden Papers with other manuscripts from the 1830's.

will suggest the ardent and sentimental side of her nature which, combined with moral earnestness and an independent spirit, represented her essential personality.

It was not uncommon for a person in 1839 to make a will before undertaking a trans-Atlantic voyage, but Ann was probably thinking about more than the possibilities of disaster at sea. She knew that she had been close to death not long before she had become engaged. Her health improved remarkably after Wendell proposed, but her old symptoms had not disappeared, and the ostensible reason for going to Europe was to find a cure. In the absence of a medical diagnosis it has been difficult for biographers to do more than speculate on the nature of her illness. Early writers on Phillips talk vaguely about a possible "defect in nervous organization," an old-fashioned term for neurasthenia, a common nineteenth-century condition characterized by chronic debility and a variety of physical discomforts.[14] The Blagden Papers are helpful at this point because they contain a letter in French from the Boston physician Henry Bowditch describing her case.

This letter will be presented by one of my friends Mr. Phillips who intends to leave tomorrow to tour Europe. His wife accompanies him. She has been sick for three years past and makes the trip in the hope of finding a cure. The illness began with a light inflammation of the lungs and although all the symptoms relating to the lungs disappeared in a short time she has not been well since that time. As I am not her Doctor I cannot give you too many details but my colleague who treated her tells me that all her bodily functions seem in good condition but she suffers from extreme feebleness which prevents her from carrying out the most ordinary occupations without great fatigue. Her state of mind above all has a great influence on her strength. I hope it will not be necessary for her to seek the service of a doctor during her absence, but in case the malady returns while she is in Paris I have told her to consult you.[15]

14. Carlos Martyn, *Wendell Phillips: The Agitator* (New York), 1890), p. 86. Bartlett, *Wendell Phillips*, p. 80.

15. Henry Bowditch to Monsieur Louis, June 4, 1839. While there is no internal evidence to confirm the identification, this may well have been Pierre Charles Alexander Louis [1787–1872], the famous Parisian physician whose clinical approach to medicine was well known in Boston medical circles. See John Harley Warner, "'The Nature-Trusting Heresy': American Physicians and the Concept of the

After using this letter to consult with physicians in Paris and Germany, the Phillipses returned to Boston two years later with Ann no better than before. When they moved into their house on Essex Street, Ann's friends wondered if she would be able to stand the strain of housekeeping even though there would be servants and the place was tiny. Ten years later Garrison commiserated with her for the "long unchanging confinement to your little bedroom." [16] By this time everyone except Wendell seemed to accept the fact that Ann was a confirmed invalid. Not one to accept lost causes of any kind, he took his wife off to an isolated hotel in western Massachusetts to try the water cure in the summer of 1851. At this time she was so weak he had to carry her downstairs and have a bed installed in a private railroad car in order to make the journey. Like all the other cures they tried, this one also failed. Whatever her problem, it was crippling and debilitating rather than killing. She was not always bedridden, was frequently cheerful, always mentally alert, and occasionally even able to venture out of the house alone. Periodically she would be struck down by headaches, fever, pains in her back, arms, and legs, and swelling joints. Edmund Quincy thought she was developing a crooked spine, and one doctor told Wendell that her condition was hereditary.[17]

This evidence, together with Bowditch's description, would be consistent with a diagnosis of rheumatic fever or acute rheumatism, a disease that usually appears first at a relatively early age and periodically recurs with prostrating symptoms. It is also a disease in which the mental and physical condition of the patient are closely linked—"Any depressing cause acting upon the general health such as over work or anxiety, may precipitate an attack in persons predisposed to them." [18] Assuming the plausibility of this kind of retro-

Healing Power of Nature in the 1850's and 1860's," *Perspectives in American History*, 11 (1977–1978), 296–297.

16. William Lloyd Garrison to Ann Phillips, January 1, 1851.

17. Bartlett, *Wendell Phillips*, pp. 163–165. Wendell Phillips to Maria Weston Chapman, September 29, 1874.

18. William A. R. Thompson, *Black's Medical Dictionary* (New York, 1976), pp. 724–726.

spective diagnosis, we can say that Ann Phillips's health problems were organic, chronic, and serious enough to prevent her and her husband from enjoying a conventional life together. As we will see, however, despite her illness they were able to sustain a long, affectionate, and mutually supportive marriage in which she remained fully engaged in his career.

By the mid-1850's Phillips and his wife seem to have come to terms with her condition; at the same time improved rail and telegraphic facilities made it possible for him to make periodic lecture tours through the western states. Their correspondence begins at this point. "Your last sweet kiss dearest still lingers on my lips & though you have gone to fatiguing work still I feel glad you are away from home." [19] They had been married twenty years when Ann Phillips sent these words to her husband, and her letters to him over the next twenty years would always be touched with this kind of romantic intimacy. Sometimes she would write more playfully. "I have a note from Dear Edmund [Quincy] beginning *Dearest* Countess. I *may* let you see it. Think of that. *You* don't call me *Countess!* What do I care for you!" Sometimes her mood was more dependent. "When you get this you will have taken your first step towards home. Oh darling what would little char do without you." Her letters never lost the spontaneity and ardor of a young girl in love.[20]

Phillips was celebrated on the platform for his rhetorical assassination of the high and mighty. In perfect diction and without the slightest rancor, he would announce that Daniel Webster was "a great mass of dough," Edward Everett "a whining spaniel," Senator Robert Winthrop "a bastard who has stolen the name of Winthrop," and Abraham Lincoln "the slave hound from Illinois." [21] The same people who were fascinated and offended by this abusive eloquence would have been astounded to discover that he frequently used baby

19. Ann Phillips to Wendell Phillips, May 8, 1856.
20. Ann Phillips to Wendell Phillips, December 5, 1856.
21. Irving H. Bartlett, "Wendell Phillips and the Eloquence of Abuse," *American Quarterly* (Winter, 1959), 509–520.

talk to his wife. Like other lovers Wendell and Ann Phillips developed a vocabulary of endearment that was all their own. She referred to him as "Gra," a mysterious nickname that sometimes gave way to the more commonplace "little darling child." Wendell's basic nicknames for her were "little char" and "Andy Tandy," but he was as versatile in finding sweet names for his wife as he was in discovering epithets for the famous, and saluted her variously as "Little dud dud," "Dear *Bird*," "Puss Puss," "Little Twee" and "Wholly loveley Darling." "Baby Beauty," he wrote in 1867, "How I long to see you. I think as Gra grows older he hates all the more to leave her. Every hour his thoughts come home to little Essex. . . . Slept as usual. But had no little *feelums* in the morning—no baby to pet me—no little Char to sweeten my breakfast—poor Gra." [22] The following year he sent her a letter in an envelope which he had dipped into the Mississippi, "just to amuse my baby," and four years later when he was more than sixty years old he sent her a special gift.

I enclose a precious relic—a veritable bit of Gra's *toenail*. It will remind you of his cutting yours & is quite as good a vehicle of sentiment as a lock of hair. You need not tell of it as nobody will understand it but Char & Gra.[23]

Obviously such passages were not intended for the eyes of historians, but they are historically significant because they demonstrate that despite her invalidism, Phillips and his wife enjoyed an enduringly affectionate marriage built around a multitude of shared domestic pleasures and an open exchange of feeling. In old age as in youth they continued to enjoy each other and this dispels the suspicion that he may have persisted in his radical activities in order to get away from a sexless invalid.

Sometime after the war John T. Sargent heard someone say that Phillips did not mean what he said, that he wore "a false bosom." Sargent replied to this accusation in verse and sent it to Ann.

22. Wendell Phillips to Ann Phillips, November 1867.
23. Wendell Phillips to Ann Phillips, April 10, 1872.

> Go, ask *his wife* (if you can risk the assaults
> of *angel darts* from out her flashing eye!)
> ask *her* if *she* thinks Wendell's bosom's false!
> And then—*go make your will! Prepare to die!*[24]

Sargent knew that Ann Phillips could be a formidable woman when
the occasion demanded, and the Blagden Papers support his insight.
Like other dutiful husbands, Phillips never left home without a list
of instructions on how to behave. He would: comb his hair, check
his socks and night caps, avoid coughs, bathe, and exercise his chest.
He would not: "eat pastitles," read on the train or "speak on Sunday." [25] Enclosing a menu from a Dubuque hotel, Phillips wrote, "I
have drawn a pencil mark round all those things I *ate* for my health's
sake & put admiration marks to those I longed for but abstained
from for your blessed baby's sake." [26] On another occasion he
proudly wrote from Illinois that he had not lost anything with the
exception of a hair brush that "stopped in a minister's study in Ann
Arbor," but he trembled to think of his return, "when you call the
rolls of hdkfs." "Are you not ashamed to hear that your husband,
the HEAD—trembles a thousand miles off when he thinks of your
terrible ways?" [27]

Ann Phillips had committed herself to abolitionism and had con-
fronted hostile mobs before her husband had even begun to think
about the cause. Although she stopped going to meetings in the
1840's she continued to insist on the validity of her own ideas. One
of her recurrent anxieties was that Phillips might be taken in by
politicians. When the long-time political abolitionist Joshua Giddings wrote referring to "our cause" as if he and Wendell were
confidants, Ann sent the letter on to her husband, with a note saying,
"A very impertinent letter. He is not one of us & never was." [28]

24. John T. Sargent to Ann Phillips [c. 1866–1868].
25. Ann Phillips to Wendell Phillips, November 1854.
26. Wendell Phillips to Ann Phillips, 1868.
27. Wendell Phillips to Ann Phillips, April 10, 1872. There is a good deal of
bantering discussion in their correspondence about who was the real "HEAD"
of the family.
28. Joshua Giddings to Wendell Phillips, October 30, 1859.

Hearing that Phillips had been entertained by Salmon Chase in Ohio, she immediately sounded a warning note.

You can *sometimes* decline company & do more good to the cause. I wld. never have taken tea with Chase who *allowed* to say the least a woman & her family to be sent to slavery. Such a free soiler as he *does more harm to anti-slavery* than Pierce, Douglas & Co. There is no doubt of it in my mind. Do not, pray, forget *what men do*.[29]

Phillips's great popularity on the lecture platform came during and just after the Civil War. He became popular in part because of his ability to build an intellectual foundation for the radical position, partly because of his eloquence, and partly because he was sensational. In attacking the government he would fill the air with spectacular accusations against those in power. Some of his barbs would hit the mark, some would miss, and some would rebound. His wife did not like this kind of shotgun approach and told him so. In 1862 she wrote as follows:

Oh, my dear sweet child do let yr speeches be of a more serious character. Why cannot the slaveholders be told to free their slaves & *then* we pay what we choose? It is not right to bribe people to do right. Do think of these things. My heart is pained & I am very ill & the sacrifice of having you gone is great. Do try to satisfy me. It is so hard for me to have you differ from what I think is right. Do think of these things. *Please* do not thank God in your speeches. Poor Stone [Gen. Charles Pomeroy Stone, Union officer accused of negligence and perhaps collusion with the enemy] *do not mention him*. Do you remember he is soon to be on trial for his life & he is a prisoner & not in our service. Why throw at a man already down? . . . do let us abolitionists stick to anti-slavery. Leave worldly measures to worldly men.[30]

In March 1862 Phillips went to Washington, where he met the

29. Ann Phillips to Wendell Phillips, December 5, 1856. Margaret Garner, an escaped slave, was seized in Cincinnati and returned to Kentucky while Chase was Governor of Ohio. Albert Bushnell Hart, *Salmon Portland Chase* (Boston, 1899), p. 166.

30. Ann Phillips to Wendell Phillips, March 20, 1862. Phillips was supporting Lincoln's recommendation to compensate slaveholders in the border states for emancipating their slaves. *Liberator*, March 14, 1862.

President and was introduced on the floor of the Senate. His lecture at the Smithsonian, attended by many Representatives and Senators, was widely reported by the press and read by millions. It was a moment of personal triumph, but his wife was troubled because Phillips's popularity seemed to depend on his supporting an immoral war effort.

> I feel you are nearly popular *because* you have gone to the worldly men; they have not come to you. They of course like the Demon war, the Union & *compensation*. Think are you not going too much over to them unconsciously that is. What you *have got to look at*, do not be the least deceived by their coming over. They *always* went for compensation, Union & War & their own selfish interests carry them to Emancipation. I see no change in them & feel no encouragement *whatever* from it.[31]

Convinced that Phillips's role was to act as a moral critic without political obligation to anyone, Ann was disturbed when he allowed himself to be misquoted. "Emerson & other speakers would not allow themselves to be put before the public all wrong," she wrote, "you ought not to allow it." [32] Occasionally she thought Wendell was carried away by his own language ("Don't speak of our *revenging* on their prisoners. Vengeance is mine saith the Lord"), but her main concern was to hold him to a radical position based on moral principle.[33] During the impeachment proceedings against Andrew Johnson, Phillips was reluctant to approach his friend Sumner, who would sit in judgment on the case. "Yr delicacy about Sumner strikes me as ridiculous," Ann wrote. "He of course shld. with propriety be reticent to *you*, but not you to him. *You* are not a *judge*." A confirmed Johnson-hater, Ann urged her husband to keep the drums beating for his political execution.

> If they dont bring him in guilty it will be dreadful, though I think trying

31. Ann Phillips to Wendell Phillips, April 3, 1862. In the *Liberator* for March 14, 1862, Phillips was quoted as saying, "Every cannon fired by Halleck or McClellan (he never fired one) is a better lecturer than I." His wife disapproved of such glib acceptance of the war.

32. Ann Phillips to Wendell Phillips, March 23, 1862.

33. Ann Phillips to Wendell Phillips, December 23, 1864.

him only is better for the morals of the country than the imbecile state the country was in before, letting him go on in his cause. . . . Now do be rousing up the people with all the fire you can that they have got to *keep up* the Senate to impeachment—to let them constantly see that the country *demands* it & by our crying aloud to keep them in such a state they will be afraid not to impeach him.[34]

As an instinctive feminist, Ann supported her husband in his labors for women's rights but was decidedly cool to his efforts on behalf of the Irish and the labor movement. Despite vehement attacks on him by the Catholic press, Phillips correctly perceived that the Irish were an oppressed class in much the same condition as northern Negroes. His vehicle for combating prejudice against Negroes was a lecture on Toussaint L'Ouverture; for the Irish, a lecture on Daniel O'Connell. The O'Connell lecture, which always brought cheers from Irish audiences, worked no magic on his wife.

Wendell I cannot be left for you to lecture to Catholics and Copperheads. Cannot you get off? Is it not a mistake? I understood you to promise after lecturing for that wicked nation on D. O'Connell last winter that you would not any more. I cannot be left for Irish. Cannot you get off? You *promised* me you would not any more. How can you lecture for people who burnt blacks to death only four years ago [the draft riots in 1863] I dont see. It is incomprehensible to me. I am sorry to write so, but I cannot bear it.[35]

Two years later Phillips was still addressing Irish audiences and his wife again took him to task, making it clear this time that it was not the Irish attitude toward the war that distressed her, but their religion.

You ought never, even in the most [ ] way to help the Catholics. In the course of a hundred or less years, there has got to be a new Reformation & a new Luther. *Protestants* are doing the work which they have got to *give their lives* to undo. While you help yr age in one way, dont embarrass it in another.[36]

After the war Ann became increasingly reluctant to see Phillips

34. Ann Phillips to Wendell Phillips, March 1, 1868.
35. Ann Phillips to Wendell Phillips [c. 1866–1867].
36. Ann Phillips to Wendell Phillips, February 17, 1869.

go away on long lecture tours, especially when his speeches were not always directly concerned with the rights of the freedmen. In January 1872, for example, upset at discovering that she did not know his exact itinerary, she fired the following protest off in what she hoped was his general direction.

Write at once what you are going to do . . . for if I needed you this very day *I have no idea where you are* . . . dont make any promises for another year *whatever*. I dont want to hear next fall, 'now I just want to fill a few back engagements!' I have rec'd a dreadful blow. I find that Labor Convention that you told me of a̲s̲ a Labor one is a *political one*, no more or less than the making of a President! Why did you not tell me? I hate to see you have anything to do with the making of presidents. Politics in this country are awfully wicked. Do not meddle with them. Cannot Labor be a *moral* question? If it cannot be I would not have anything to do with it . . . Goodbye dear—would you please explain to me why you prefer lecturing to anything else in the world? Cannot you be happy doing something else?[37]

There is nothing neurotic about Ann Phillips's letters. She writes as an intelligent, articulate, assertive wife, informed about public issues and determined to participate in his career. Like his wife's correspondence, Phillips's letters to her convey the flavor of direct and intimate conversation. Some of them are valuable as detailed glimpses of life on the lyceum circuit, some for the insights they provide into his personality, and others for what they tell us about his goals and strategies as a reformer.

Lecturing was an arduous business in the middle of the nineteenth century. Phillips would sometimes meet as many as twenty-five engagements in a three-week period. Occasionally he would be put up by abolitionist friends, but most of the time when he was not on the platform he was in a train or stagecoach. In December 1856 he wrote Ann that he had been spending so much time on trains that he had averaged less than three hours of sleep and one meal a day over a two-week period.[38] Phillips's ability to sleep almost anywhere was a standing joke between him and his wife, but he encoun-

37. Ann Phillips to Wendell Phillips, January 11, 1872.
38. Wendell Phillips to Ann Phillips, December 7, 1856.

tered hazards in his western travels that were difficult to overcome. One was crying babies. "Lots of babies scream & cry in all notes," he wrote from Iowa, "awful babies—terror of western travellers— eight in these cars!! You ought to travel here & be satiated with babies. You have them in every variety of scream noise & nuisance— all ages, all sorts of dirt & always in the way—specially to folks who plan as I do, to sleep all day." [39]

Drunken passengers provided another distraction. The more Phillips travelled the more he found his temperance convictions confirmed. Approaching Pittsburgh ("dirty, cloudy, muddy, coal dusty & vile"), for example:

A drunken fellow has been shouting & crowing like a cockerel—pays no attention or little to the conductors . . . seeing a negro pass, he cries out 'all n – – – s ought to be slaves—I'm for freedom & Texas.'

This case is however an *exception*. Except for spitting, swearing, rough & dirty clothes & skins innocent of soap & lack of newspapers you'd fancy yourself in dear Yankee land.[40]

Less offensive but equally fatiguing were well-meaning admirers who refused to let him rest. Having just arrived in Hartford after a sleepless night, Phillips encountered "a man who sells shoes but was laudably in search of improvement [who] tired me nearly all the time with questions about spiritualism, slavery, history, man, politics." [41]

Although Phillips turned down his glass whenever the wine was poured, he liked to keep his plate full and was always complaining about hotel food. Happily surprised by a palatable pancake in Illinois, he immediately reported it to Ann. "Tell Polly" [their cook], he wrote, "that for the first time at any hotel I ate buck-wheats deserving to be on the same plate with hers. They were very nice, so good that I stated aloud that they were the first buckwheats

39. Wendell Phillips to Ann Phillips, March 15, 1868.
40. Wendell Phillips to Ann Phillips, January 1, 1858. The description of Pittsburgh is taken from an undated letter from Phillips to his wife, probably written in the mid-1850's.
41. Wendell Phillips to Ann Phillips, December 29, 1865.

deserving the name that I had eaten since leaving home." [42] A more characteristic response to western cuisine was his amazement at "the brisk, confident tone ('as if one were at Delmonico') when a waiter says 'Beefsteak sir?' & then brings you a tiny piece of his last year's shoe." [43]

Occasionally Phillips would sound a depressed note when he was away. "I am tired of going about," he wrote after leaving a train full of drunken Germans in Altoona, "the novelty is over. I fret at the bore of it." [44] But for the most part his complaints about the lecturer's life were made in entire good humor and designed to make his lonely wife laugh with him. As he shuttled from place to place there were more than enough compensations to make up for whatever hardships he suffered. The babies could be tolerated, for example, especially after 1860, when more and more of them were named after himself. Although Phillips prided himself on his willingness to court public hostility in the interests of truth, he enjoyed approval as much as anyone else and was especially gratified when travelling in distant states to learn that black people recognized and appreciated him.

Yesterday a colored man travelled 7 miles to hear me—insisted on paying my fare in the cars! & treating me with apples & such & by asking '*my name in writing to carry*.'

There, Baby is tearing I know. I treated him as tenderly as *you* could wish or command, gave him a ticket to my lecture—shook hands with him lots of times & made much of him.[45]

From a hotel in Keokuk, Iowa, in 1868 Phillips wrote,

I have had thousands ask for autographs. But this morning at breakfast a poor black fresh from New Orleans asked me for my name 'just to have all de time' & then he wished me 'good luck & a good time wherever I went.' These men always bring me the hottest cakes & the best piece of steak and sometimes speak, but this one is the first who asked for something to keep.[46]

42. Wendell Phillips to Ann Phillips, January 13, 1858.
43. Wendell Phillips to Ann Phillips [c. 1867].
44. Wendell Phillips to Ann Phillips, undated.
45. Wendell Phillips to Ann Phillips, March 28, 1867.
46. Wendell Phillips to Ann Phillips, March 15, 1868.

He was discovering that those who champion unpopular causes are frequently rewarded in surprising ways. When a Jesuit priest threw a drunken Irishman out of one of his audiences, Phillips decided, "That was O'Connell's work—bread cast on the waters." [47]

Once when he was behind schedule on a train to Chicago, some friends stopped a train passing in another direction so Phillips could board it and make his engagement.[48] Another time he was carried forty miles in Iowa on a railroad hand car. "Four nice Germans turned the crank," he wrote his wife, "alternately sputtering Dutch & rolling me along at the rate of twelve miles an hour. It was like a horseback ride, safe, easy, quick, in the open sun. . . . It saved me driving through 30 miles of mud which would have taken 11 hours." [49]

Although he enjoyed the special attention he received in the West, what kept drawing him back were the audiences and community leaders he met in connection with his lectures. "I am the only one who has uniformly made money for the Lyceums," he proudly reported to Ann in the spring of 1868. "All others have *often* not made their expenses." [50] He considered the lyceum to be a forum for the American elite and during the high tide of radicalism after the war he believed that his lectures and the informal meetings he held with local leaders were influencing the people who shaped public opinion at the grass roots.

I was never better—never had so many *leading* men come to me—lawyers, colonels, generals, ministers, judges—to talk & discuss. I never reached so many minds. And what is very very pleasant, I never met so many persons who told me that they *owed* their first thought on these subjects & their resolutions to a speech of mine.[51]

47. Wendell Phillips to Ann Phillips, February 24, 1867.
48. Wendell Phillips to Ann Phillips, January 18, 1856.
49. Wendell Phillips to Ann Phillips, April 7, 1867.
50. Wendell Phillips to Ann Phillips, April 6, 1868.
51. Wendell Phillips to Ann Phillips [winter, 1867]. Before the war Phillips's strategy was to give a literary lecture for a fee and follow it with a free anti-slavery talk. In December 1856 he did this in Iowa City before an audience which included two thirds of the Iowa legislature. Wendell Phillips to Ann Phillips, December 11, 1856.

In the winter of 1868, when the national attention was riveted on the impeachment proceedings, Phillips felt that the West could swing the balance. "Just now I am most enthusiastically listened to," he wrote. "These folks make the next *President* & they are in a *mouldable* state. . . . I get here audiences made up of the *leading* minds much, very much more than in the East." [52]

Phillips went to extraordinary rhetorical lengths to influence public opinion, but he always knew that symbols did more than rhetoric to move people. He responded to John Brown ecstatically because he knew that Brown's execution supplied the radical North with an extraordinarily powerful symbol. After Brown was hanged, Phillips went to New York to meet Mrs. Brown and collect the body, which Governor Wise of Virginia had allowed to be sent North. Many abolitionists expected Phillips to persuade Mrs. Brown to allow her husband's body to be exhibited in Boston, where it could be used to mobilize radical sentiment and raise funds for the cause. In terms of strategy the proposal made sense, but as a practical matter he found himself unable to push the idea and explained in a letter to Ann why he was taking the martyr's body and widow directly to the family homestead in upstate New York.

To separate her & the remains she has endured so much to secure . . . would be too cruel. I could not, tho I tried, propose it. She avoided all intimations in regard to it. She only says 'by & by I will not object to its going to Mass. My children want to see him once more. Sometime Mass shall have it.'

Then second—to take the body thro the great cities & Boston for a public funeral & demonstration seems to some not justified by the seeming *condition* of Gov Wise's letter (for decent interment among his kindred) . . . I did not feel like taking the responsibility of doing anything that seemed tricky or taking advantage to produce an effect & putting it with her *wishes* & *health* have concluded to leave the question to after & fuller debate . . . & to go with her to Elba.[53]

In 1862 Phillips discovered another symbol in John C. Frémont, the Union general who had lost his command for attempting to free

52. Wendell Phillips to Ann Phillips, February 22, 1868.
53. Wendell Phillips to Ann Phillips, December 5, 1859.

Missouri slaves with military power. He met Frémont and his celebrated wife Jessie for the first time at a Washington dinner party in
March 1862. His account of the affair is interesting because it shows
how seriously Phillips took himself and was taken by others as a
shaper of public opinion at this time.

> Fremont was all I fancied him, modest, able. Jessie was charming & very
> attentive to me, leaving Sumner who offered her his arms . . . to come across
> the room & take mine. . . She told me many good things, especially all
> about her & Fremont coming incog. to hear me in NYC. He disbelieved
> somewhat his friends assertion that the *masses* loved him & she advised his
> going, guessing I shld allude to him & then he'd *see* the effect. He was totally
> overcome & convinced by the first uproar made when I alluded to him even
> without mentioning his name & wished instantly to escape, but Jessie made
> him stay to the end.[54]

In Washington Phillips also met Lincoln for the first time. Heretofore what happened at their interview has been a matter of speculation based on scattered references in Phillips's speeches later that
year. His letter home gives a detailed report of their conversation in
the President's White House study.

> He came in. He shook hands—had a key in his hand & was trying to clean
> it, muttering, "I cannot make this key go into the lock." I said, "Mr. Pres.
> you've got a far worse lock than that to fit a key to." He smiled, said "yes
> I guess so," threw down the key & entered into conversation. His beard &
> full hair make [him] look better, less quaint than his pictures show him.
> He struck me as perfectly honest—trying to do what he thought his duty,
> but a man of very *slow mind*. He had been three months on this message—
> all by himself, no conference with his cabinet. I praised him for that &
> restoring Fremont—told him what I thought of these acts & something as I
> did in my speech. He did not think I valued the message quite enough &
> as usual told a story. "Did you ever hear of the Irishman who in Maine
> liquor days in Maine asked for a glass of soda & said, 'Could'nt ye put a drop
> of the crathur into it *unbeknown to myself*'—well I've put a good deal of
> Antislavery in it unbeknown to themselves." He said he told the border state
> Senators & Rep. not to talk to him about slavery. They loved it & meant it
> should last—he hated it & meant *it should die*. He said, "Mr. P. if only men
> over 50 voted we could abolish slavery. When men are soon to face their

God they are Antislavery—it is the *young* who support the system. Unfortunately *they* rule too much" etc. etc. . . . We talked an hour or so. I said
what I could, not all I wished, because he talked so fast & constantly it was
hard to get a word in edgewise. On the whole I felt rather *encouraged*. He
is better than his Congress fellows.[55]

It is difficult not to believe that the estimate of Lincoln as "a man
of very slow mind" was directly related to the President's refusal
to sit quietly in his study while Phillips told him what to do. Shortly
before their meeting Phillips had publicly deplored the fact that "a
Kentuckian" was in the White House, and a few months later he
would be quoted as saying that "Lincoln is doing twice as much
today to break this Union as [Jefferson] Davis is." [56] He employed
this rhetoric deliberately, to goad the government into an emancipation program, and there was nothing Lincoln could do to prevent
such criticism short of letting abolitionists dictate public policy. In
a personal confrontation at the White House, however, the President could make Phillips do the listening, and he did.

There was always an element of condescension in Phillips's attitude toward Lincoln. Recognizing the President's essential honesty
and sense of justice, he could not tolerate his willingness to put the
value of the Union above emancipation, and attributed to slowness
of mind what he was reluctant to blame on corruption of character.
But he was even harsher on Lincoln's successors. Ten years after his
first meeting with Lincoln, Phillips again visited Washington.
"Then to see Grant privately for an hour," was all he wrote to Ann.
"He is stupid." [57]

Considering his skill in provoking hostile audiences, it is remarkable that Phillips was never manhandled by a crowd. He was hooted
down a few times and during the winter of 1860–1861, when he
took over Theodore Parker's pulpit in the Boston Music Hall to
preach disunion, the abolitionists supplied him with a substantial
bodyguard. The closest he came to bodily harm, however, was in

55. *Ibid.*
56. Bartlett, *Wendell Phillips*, pp. 247, 252.
57. Wendell Phillips to Ann Phillips, February 23, 1872.

Cincinnati only a few days after his meeting with the President. Driven off the platform by a flurry of stones and rotten eggs, Phillips did his best to reassure Ann that the incident had only served to enhance his visibility and elicit a deluge of invitations from "the *mayors* of great towns."

It has done me great good as *all* the papers discuss me *pro* & con & gives me most crowded houses & all day my rooms are full of *first citizens,* so I lecture all day.

You . . . would laugh over the new coat covered with egg. I took two hours getting it off using only *water* as Bessie would have wished. There was some vitriol about but none thrown & some knives, but I saw none. Still it was only a trick slyly played on the audience. Had it been suspected an hour before the meeting, *my Germans* would have pitched all the drunken Irishmen out of doors.[58]

Alarmed by newspaper reports, Ann was not comforted by Phillips's explanation, and accused him of using the disruption to prolong his trip.

Cincinatti I should *never go to again* till they have done *their duty* & *turned* out their mayor & police. Dont *think* of going. When you left home you thought you should be home (the outside) by the 5 of April. That is this Sat. Now! you *cooly* state that on Sunday the 6 you are to be in Chicago, not having *started* for the way even of home. Well I will get along if I can, but I have been very ill ever since you went.[59]

The Blagden Papers show that Phillips generally accepted his wife's criticisms and advice in good humor and tried to accommodate her. At the same time he seems to have felt that he knew better than she how to be effective in public.

I am *serious* in my speeches, very much so. I think they even think me a little dull. I am so very solemn & give them such sad views of deep responsibility. As for paying for slaves, I present it in such a way as to avoid all I can Bessie's objections. Little darling must let her Gra do his work in the way his conscience dictates after weighing all she says.[60]

58. Wendell Phillips to Ann Phillips, March 27, 28, 1862.
59. Ann Phillips to Wendell Phillips, April 2, 1862.
60. Wendell Phillips to Ann Phillips, March 28, 1862.

One sign of a healthy marriage is when a man and wife find it possible to express not only the affection they feel for each other, but also the sense of frustration and hostility that occasionally creeps into even the most idyllic intimate relationship of any permanence. Ann Phillips was not backward in this respect, and on some occasions, at least, Phillips seems to have turned his cutting gifts upon her. In 1874, for example he apologised for seeming "pettish" and "for all his sharpness to her at parting." Phillips was then 62. "Dear Char," he wrote Ann, "I must love her more & more as the time grows shorter— & she'll never remember any of Gra's hastiness or petulance. He never means anything & is sorry instantly." [61]

As a reformer and orator, Wendell Phillips at the height of his career was one of the most visible men in the country, but as a married couple he and his wife became increasingly isolated as they grew older. During the war Phoebe Garnaut, the orphaned daughter of an abolitionist widow, who had lived with them for almost ten years, married and moved abroad.[62] Whatever fragmented social life the Phillipses had enjoyed was connected with the "Boston Clique," a name given to the small group of abolitionists clustered around Garrison who set the policy of the Massachusetts and American Antislavery Societies. Most of the socializing of this group was done at Maria Chapman's house, where Ann had grown up. After they moved into their Essex Street house, Ann rarely went anywhere, but she would still occasionally have old friends like Maria, the Weston sisters, or Edmund Quincy in for tea. Phillips was forced to attend the regular antislavery socials, fairs, and meetings alone. After the war, when Phillips and Garrison split over the issue of continuing formal antislavery organizations, this form of social interchange became even more limited.

61. These references are taken from undated letters written by Phillips to his wife from Philadelphia, Worcester, and Montreal in 1874.

62. Phoebe married George Smalley, a notable American journalist and one of the first American foreign correspondents. There are hundreds of letters in the Blagden Papers from Phoebe before her marriage and from Phoebe and George Smalley when they lived in London and Paris.

If we can believe the Blagden Papers, contact between Phillips and his family was minimal. Except for an older sister, Sarah, who had married a New York educator, and his younger brother, Grenville, who lived for several years in Paris, all of Phillips's brothers and sisters lived close at hand, but he rarely saw them after his mother died in 1845. It had been customary for the family to get together every summer and share quarters in the summer house at Nahant left by their mother. Wendell and Ann dropped out of this arrangement in 1846 and his two brothers and two sisters were startled in the spring of 1850 by a letter from Wendell demanding exclusive use of the house for himself and his wife for the coming season.

> I have given up the use of my share for your accomodation, seeing the four needed all the accomodation. Do the same by me. Don't, in fact, make that useless to me & shut me out of my mother's house by (unbrotherly) (unsisterly) selfishness.
>
> Consider this & then say what I ought to think of four (brothers & sisters), all well, all able to pay their own board, yet insisting on occupying the place year after year, well knowing it to be to the utter exclusion of one who cannot come with them & unless he has it alone cannot use it at all.

Phillips argued that since Ann's health did not permit them to share the house, they deserved to have it alone for a season, but it was not the argument which offended his brothers and sisters as much as his tone. "I want *your* answer," he informed each of them, "not one dependent on what someone else will do." If they refused his request, he said, he could "only lay the facts by as an item by which to estimate his [their] character." [63] None of the rest of the family thought he had made a case for changing the traditional arrangements at Nahant. His brothers tried to reason with him, but his older sisters, remembering, perhaps, how they had handled him as a little boy, dealt with the matter more directly. While sister Miriam charged him with selfishness, sister Margaret wrote, "I hope you

---

63. Wendell Phillips to Miriam Blagden, March 5, 1850. Identical letters were apparently sent to Margaret Reynolds and to George and John Phillips. Wendell's older brother Tom had not been a party to sharing the cottage and was not involved in the controversy.

are not aware of the spirit which your letter breathes. I would rather think you are so accustomed to this mode of expression that you forgot you was addressing a sister who never knowingly injured you in thought word or deed." [64]

Margaret's response points up the significance of what might otherwise be dismissed as an innocuous family argument. Accustomed to his outsider role in society and in his family, Phillips instinctively turned every difference of opinion into a moral confrontation. He might not get his way with his brothers and sisters any more than he did with politicians, but he would force his adversaries to reveal their true characters. The Blagden Papers do not tell us whether Phillips won the use of the Nahant house on his own terms or not, but the incident could hardly have served to reunite him with the family he had ideologically separated from ten years earlier.

The last dated correspondence between Wendell and Ann Phillips to appear in the Blagden Papers is in 1878, six years before he died. By then the popular radical sentiment which had sustained him in the immediate postwar years was waning and Phillips found his audiences less willing to listen to the problems of the freedmen and more interested in his literary and cultural lectures. He was gratified to find that he continued to draw large crowds, and when he was away from home he still sought out his aging abolitionist friends. Meanwhile the solitary routine on Essex Street continued. Alone with one or two servants, Ann coped with her symptoms, watched every move that Wendell made, and was always ready with new advice. Perceiving that the abolitionists had played their role in history, she urged him to expand his associations.

I was very sorry you did not accept the Lotus Club. I wanted you to go & it seems very rude to me when they give you *any* time & have invited you once before. I wanted you to see a *new* circle in New York. The Powells [Aaron Powell, editor of the *National Antislavery Standard*] are nothing to see & this wld be a literary set. Is it too late now? . . . I am infinitely

64. Miriam Blagden to Wendell Phillips, March 9, 1850. Margaret Blagden to Wendell Phillips, March 9, 1850.

more comfortable now that rasping Rosa has left & Margaret has not stated *this* week that she intends going—new girl (wan image) comes tonight. *Do* find some *new* society to be with . . . I think if you could go to some *new* Hotel. . . .[65]

In 1882 the Phillipses fell afoul of the nineteenth-century version of urban renewal when the city of Boston decided to extend Harrison Avenue and condemn the little house that had been their haven for more than forty years. Moving to another house on Common Street, they never really recovered from the shock. Phillips became increasingly absorbed with taking care of his wife, who was now bedridden most of the time. During the same year a grandnephew, Wendell Phillips Blagden, was born in New York City. Phillips had never thought much of the Rev. George Blagden who had joined his family through marriage many years before, but he was delighted now to learn that his own name would persist in one branch of the family. "You'll both have to be seventy years old," he wrote his niece and nephew, "before you'll know how grateful such an affectionate remembrance is." [66] He had just begun to sort out his books and papers and probably decided at this time to leave his papers to the Blagden family.

On February 2, 1884, the heart condition which had struck down his father more than sixty years before finally caught up with Wendell Phillips. When they told him he was dying, he said he was ready to go but worried about his wife. "Who will care for her," he asked, "as I have done?" At the end they brought Ann into the same room on a cot. Despite her anguish, she remembered later, "I held myself in strong control, and did not groan, or moan even, for that would have made it so much harder for poor Wendell to die." She would join him two years later.

A Victorian eulogist wrote that Wendell Phillips was "the ideal husband of his time" because he joyfully took upon himself the burdens of an invalid wife and willingly subordinated "his life to

65. Ann Phillips to Wendell Phillips, February 8, 1874. She is referring to her servant problems at the end of the quotation.

66. Bartlett, *Wendell Phillips*, p. 396.

hers when occasion demanded it. . . . He always wrought with his heart leaning toward his wife." [67] The judgment is not fair to Ann Phillips. The Blagden Papers tell us that despite the limitations life imposed upon her, she served her famous husband as well as he served her, and that they wrought together in the great arenas of nineteenth-century humanitarianism, their hearts leaning toward each other.

67. Mary Livermore, "Does the Ideal Husband Exist," *North American Review* (February, 1896), 213. Although Mary Livermore does not indicate whether this account of Phillips's deathbed scene is taken directly from his wife or from another source, the story is consistent with Ann Phillips's character and with what we know about the marriage.

II. A SAMPLER FROM THE BLAGDEN PAPERS

T HE manuscripts chosen for publication here are intended to provide a sample of what scholars can expect to find in the Blagden Papers. Unless otherwise noted all letters are to Wendell Phillips. Although they have been placed in categories that help to illuminate aspects of Phillips's career, the letters have also been chosen to illustrate the depth and variety of the materials that have suddenly become available. Since the purpose of this sampler is to alert a wide range of scholars to the existence of these sources as promptly as possible, the editing of the manuscripts has been minimal. The original spelling, punctuation, and spacing have been reproduced as accurately as possible in typographical form.

1. Black and White Abolitionists

ONE of the most dramatic aspects of Phillips's conversion to the antislavery movement was the suddenness with which he found himself involved with blacks as a benefactor and a colleague. When Phillips joined Garrison in the 1830's, the latter was heavily dependent on the Boston black community for the support of his paper and his organization. Although the direction of the Garrisonian movement always remained in the hands of a white elite, the *Liberator* served as a platform for and a mirror of the local black community, and Phillips and other Garrisonian abolitionists repeatedly campaigned for the rights of black people in the North long before slavery was abolished. The following letters reflect the ambiguities in the abolitionist mind concerning blacks, provide concrete examples of the services provided by Phillips to individuals, and suggest a possible explanation for his high opinion of the capacities of black people.

Historians have long since discovered that fellowship between white and black abolitionists was not the love feast that it was once made out to be. A person did not have to like black people to hate slavery, and it is easy enough to find examples of racist thinking and behavior among supporters of the antislavery movement. Indeed it is doubtful if the moral argument against slavery could ever have been successfully transformed into a political movement if Republicans had not been able to exploit the racial as well as the antislavery fears and prejudices of Americans. Moralists like Phillips and Garrison were very much aware of the linkage between racism and antislavery politics and this reinforced their conviction that abolitionists should stay out of politics.

Most of the abolitionists with whom Phillips worked closely were sincere egalitarians, but, as Frederick Douglass wrote, almost every American "approaches a colored man with an air of superiority and condescension." [1] Although they were hardly aware of it them-

1. Frederick Douglass, *Life and Times of Frederick Douglass* (New York, 1967 [1881]), p. 376. For a favorable view of Garrisonian egalitarianism see Donald

selves, one of the biggest problems abolitionists faced was that most of them were white while the people they were trying to help were black, and the whites were never quite sure how much they should make of the difference. The ambivalence on this score is vividly illustrated in the first set of letters in this section. There is a moving request from Lydia Maria Child to be buried in ground owned by Negroes "as the *last* testimony it is in her power to bear" against racial prejudice in America. On the other hand, Harriet Beecher Stowe, who commanded an audience never approached by any other antislavery writer, complains that black people are unable to stand on their own. A lady from New Hampshire wants to arm blacks for the war; another wants to help them because of their superior "Christliness." Clearly the black image in the white abolitionist mind was ambiguous, but we get more than an echo of what Douglass meant when we read of Edmund Quincy's distress at being criticized by a black abolitionist from Salem. Blacks were colleagues as well as victims, and they sometimes spoke their minds, as Phillips must have realized very pointedly himself when Agnes Grant chastised him for not inviting black leaders to a John Brown sympathy meeting.

It has been argued that abolitionists like Phillips were excessively moralistic and abstract in their thinking, that in attempting to purge white consciences of the guilt of slavery they tended to forget black people as individuals. To support this contention, Phillips is quoted as saying, "If we never free a slave, we have at least freed ourselves in the effort to emancipate our brother man." [2] The quotation is correct, but the inference is false, as the second set of letters in this section demonstrates.

Although he spent his time on the platform goading the national conscience and flaying public leaders, Phillips also devoted a considerable amount of time and money to helping obscure black

Jacobs, "William Lloyd Garrison's *Liberator* and Boston's Blacks, 1830–1865," *New England Quarterly*, 44 (June, 1971), 259–277.

2. Jane H. Pease and William H. Pease, *They Who Would Be Free: Blacks' Search for Freedom 1830–1861* (New York, 1974), p. 11.

people in trouble. When he heard it rumored that Providence authorities were ignoring the possible murder of a black man, he investigated the matter himself. When a former slaveholder asked for help in finding a vocation for an emancipated slave, he replied promptly and constructively. One could cite many similar examples but none more interesting or affecting than the cases of Susan Randall and Bernardo. Susan Randall was unknown to Phillips when she wrote to him from Hartford that she had been left stranded and pregnant by an entertainer then playing in Boston. Phillips ascertained the facts of the pregnancy, located the father of the child, and arranged for him to send money to the mother. The correspondence printed here follows an entire transaction through the birth of the child. Phillips probably never met Susan Randall or her child, but they were surely more than abstractions to him. So was Bernardo. An illegitimate child, perhaps fathered by a white man, Bernardo came under Phillips's charge sometime in 1849. Bernardo's life was short, but Phillips and his abolitionist friend saw to it that he received the same loving attention that they would have lavished upon their own consumptive sons.

The unmistakable message in these letters is that Wendell Phillips, the harsh unrelenting reformer who claimed the public ear for bitter barbs launched at famous men, was in private a man of compassionate generosity who did more than his share for the poor, degraded, and inarticulate.

In the spring of 1859, Theodore Parker, who had gone to the Caribbean in a futile attempt to reclaim his shattered health, sent Phillips a singularly unflattering description of Negro life on St. Thomas. Parker had seen a black woman with ten children and no husband and suspected that she "probably had 20 fathers for the ten babies." According to Parker, the blacks were "licentious, excessively libidinous," naturally polygamous, cruel to their children, and uncooperative with each other.[3] Although no record of Phillips's reply to this letter appears in the Blagden Papers, he must have had

3. Theodore Parker to Wendell Phillips, May 14, 1859.

it in mind at an antislavery meeting later that summer when he discussed the significance of Haiti, which had been born in a slave revolt more than a half century earlier. In that glorious history, Phillips insisted, there was

not a single fact nor incident which the lover of the negro would care to erase from the record. . . . They have put their feet on the untrodden and unredeemed soil of Hayti, and said to the world 'This is ours', and held their own for seventy years. If that does not prove capacity for self government, the highest test of the capacity of a race, then I do not know where it is to be found.

Santo Domingo, Phillips concluded, was the "very jewel of antislavery testimony and evidence," regardless of what white visitors might report "in regard to morals and education." [4]

Haiti was very much in Phillips's thoughts during the late 1850's because it was during this period that he began to lecture regularly on Toussaint L'Ouverture. Heretofore he had not tried to analyze racial differences or argue the case for the equality of the Negro except on moral grounds. Now he admitted that he was trying to provide both a dramatic biographical sketch of the great revolutionary slave leader and an argument "to convince you that the negro race instead of being that object of pity or contempt which we usually consider it, is entitled by the facts of history, to a place side by side with the Saxon." Phillips's argument was distinctive among abolitionists. Few of them shared Theodore Parker's low opinion of black people. Most of the abolitionists, to the extent that they thought seriously about the subject of race at all, took refuge in what has been described as "romantic racialism," by asserting that black people were naturally sensitive, loving, loyal, dependent, religious. Although creditable to Negroes, the qualities emphasized by romantic racialism could have put them at a disadvantage in the competition with aggressive white Americans after slavery was abolished.[5] Phillips emphasized a different side of the Negro. Argu-

---

4. *National Anti-Slavery Standard*, July 16, 1859.
5. George Fredrickson, *The Black Image in the White Mind: The Debate on Afro-American Character and Destiny* (New York, 1971).

ing that a race should be judged by its courage, its sense of purpose, and its endurance, Phillips said that by these tests Negroes are entitled "to a place as near ours as any other blood in history."

To prove his case, Phillips cited the case of Toussaint, "an unmixed negro—his father stolen from Africa," who created an army "out of what you call the despicable race of negroes, debased, demoralized by two hundred years of slavery," and put to rout the best blood in Europe. In Phillips's lecture, Toussaint became an untutored Cromwell, a hero to be likened to Lafayette, Washington, and John Brown, and the slaves he led to revolution and to nationhood became a race of freedom fighters. "Go to Haiti," Phillips challenged his audiences, "and stand on those fifty thousand graves of the best soldiers France ever had, and ask them what they think of the negro's sword." [6]

Although Phillips had apparently been collecting material on Haiti for years, and claimed that his account was taken from sources in French and Spanish as well as English, his lecture was not so much a piece of history as a rhetorical device for expressing his conviction that black people had the physical, intellectual, and moral resources to seize and maintain their freedom in a white world. His own romantic ideas about black people were far different from the "romantic racialism" that inhibited other abolitionists, and it is highly unlikely that these ideas derived solely from his reading of history. Since he does not seem to have been interested in the growing scientific literature concerning racial differences, his thinking on the subject must have been influenced by his own experience with black people, an experience limited, for the most part, to his associations with escaped slaves and black abolitionists. The third set of letters in this section are from Phillips's black friends and colleagues. The letters show how highly blacks valued his friendship and assistance, but they are most remarkable for what they suggest about the achievement of the blacks themselves. Most

6. Wendell Phillips, *Speeches, Lectures and Letters*, First Series (Boston, 1863), pp. 468-495.

of them had been slaves and Phillips had seen them transformed through freedom. In Lewis Hayden's dignified awareness of his own worth, in the resourcefulness of Harriet Tubman, and the triumphs of men like Anthony Burns, Frederick Douglass, and William Wells Brown, Phillips discovered at first hand the qualities of courage, purpose, and persistence that he ascribed to the legendary Toussaint.

i) *Ambivalent Images of Blackness*

1. From LYDIA MARIA CHILD

WAYLAND, JULY 2D. 1860

My dear Friend,

I take a sizeable sheet of paper, because I have several things to say, with regard to personal affairs, and Anti Slavery affairs. In the first place, I want to draw on you for $100. I am going to Boston tomorrow, but as you are out of the city, I propose to procure the money by giving an order on you to Mr. Walcutt, at the Anti-Slavery Office; and if they cannot do it conveniently, I will apply to S. E. Sewall, and give him an order on you.

Mr. Garrison wrote to me about making a sort of very concise Anti Slavery Register. I decidedly think it had better be defered till another year. There is not time now to do it *well;* especially as I should have to make various journeys to the city to examine newspapers, pamphlets, &c.

But there is a Tract which I have planned out, which seems to *my* mind calculated to do much good; and if the powers that be think so likewise, I should be gratified to have it published and circulated by the Hovey Fund. I want to act on the next Legislature, concerning the Fugitive Slave Bill. There are some thrilling *Stories* concerning Fugitives, showing how we at the North are made legal instruments of cruelty. There are eloquent *Speeches* before the N. York and Massachusetts Legislatures, from which very effective extracts might be taken. In a Chapter by itself the *Unconstitutionality of the Law,* might be concisely and very clearly stated. And finally perhaps I might sum up with some urgent appeal of my own. This Tract, I want to send to every member of our Legislature, *as soon as they are elected,* that they may have time to read it in the quiet of their homes, undisturbed by the distractions of the city. What think you of my plan? If you think well of it, please indicate what extracts I had better make from your own Speeches; and remind me also of any *story* peculiarly illustrating the cruelty of the Law. I remember one several years ago, called "The Famished Hand," which affected me deeply.

I have a small Tract now on hand, which the Society may publish or not, according to their pleasure. It is all taken from *Southern* sources, and is so arranged as to be very sarcastic. I planned it so that *some* might distribute it, as a Political Campaign Document, being desirous to make use of the political excitement of the present year, to spread Anti Slavery Ideas. I shall take the MS. into Boston with me, and leave it at the Anti Slavery Office, with Mr. Walcutt. If the Society publishes it, it ought to be done *soon*.

There is a request, that I have long wished to make of you, but it is so difficult to catch you, that I have not succeeded in doing it. If you survive me, please see to it, that I am not buried at Mt. Auburn, or in any such place, and that no monument of any kind whatever is erected to my memory, in any such place. Please see to it that I am buried in some ground belonging to the *colored people*. Let the stone placed over my remains be very inexpensive; and for epitaph inscribe on it the following: Buried in this place, at her own request, among her brethren and sisters of dark complexion, as the *last* testimony it is in her power to bear against the wicked, cruel, and absurd prejudice, which so grievously oppresses them in a country that boasts loudly of its free institutions.

My dear friend, I have this matter much at heart. Don't allow the vanity or pride of relatives or friends to cheat me out of this post mortem testimony.

With affectionate remembrance to Mrs. Phillips, I remain always your very grateful and truly attached friend

L. Maria Child.

P.S. Previous to my father's death, we were taxed only for the Northampton Farm, in addition to Poll and Highway tax. Since his death, I have told the assessors that *half* of what my father was formerly taxed for, now belonged to me; and they tax accordingly. The Farm and Wood lot of my brother James were for many years taxed to *him*, and not to my father. Therefore, by the half of my father's property, I mean that which *you* divided between me and my brother Convers. I mention this because I think it not unlikely the assessors will be trying to pump you on the subject.

The small sums from my earnings, which I placed in Mr. Loring's hands, from time to time, of course were not a part of my *father's* estate; and Mr. Loring so managed that they were never taxed.

Dont touch a hair of Charles Sumner's head, in your speeches. No politician has ever served our cause so honestly and faithfully as *he* has. It sticks a dagger in my heart to hear him found fault with.

Mr. Francis, my bookseller, has failed; and the *plates* of all my books, except The Girl's Book, will be sold at the Boston Trade Sale, early in August; subject to my small percentage on what may be *sold* of the books. I presume they will be sold very low; for the market is now glutted with plates sold by booksellers that have failed.

Now that the Anti Slavery Society have such nice rooms, I have thought that perhaps they might make a little profit by selling my books. Or would it be too many irons in the fire? I would buy them myself, if I could.[7]

7. Lydia Maria Child (1802–1880), a widely read abolitionist and author. Phillips was named executor of her estate and given $2,000 "in token of personal friendship, and of gratitude for the faithful and gratuitous care he has taken of my financial affairs, during many years." Helene G. Baer, *The Heart Is Like Heaven: The Life of Lydia Maria Child* (Philadelphia, 1964), p. 311. Mrs. Child was buried in Wayland, Massachusetts, near the graves of two slaves.

2. From HARRIET BEECHER STOWE

[1854]

Dear Mr. Phillips

Please accept my thanks for your kindness in forwarding the books & pamphlets—the books I herewith return—they I think will be what I want & I shall probably get the set—as well on my own account as for some students of art in our vicinity.

In regard to the pamphlets—I have not yet read them—My *head* is very poor at present & I find it difficult to attend to any thing requiring much thought—but I have a presentiment that your position is the true one—at least in some respects. This last clause you can make as much or as little of as you choose.

But I have been most excessively annoyed in reading the account of Parker Pillsburys late debut before the Anti Slavery Conference in London. I have always had an instinctive aversion to that man, founded on a deep impression of a want of honor & purity in his character—this confirms it in a most striking manner. What annoys *me* personally is that this Mr Parker Pillsbury is accepted by you all apparently as representing in England the American Anti Slavery society & then in the same breath I am cited in the English A. Slavery Advocate as having come openly forward in the late fair to give assistance to the Am Society on *account of my sympathy with the workers.*

Now for the same reason that I abhor slave holding I abhor injustice of every kind. The right of men to *character* is as sacred as the right to "life liberty &c" & the man who *for popular effect* so states & colors, that truth produces the impression of falsehood to the taking away of his neighbors good name, is in my view guilty of a sin the same in kind with the slave holder—I have no confidence in such a man's moral honesty—no confidence that were time & circumstances favorable he would not become a slave holder & a defender of slavery.

I have noted the course of such men before. There was not a more bitter unscrupulous, untruthful abolitionist in Lane Seminary than Henry B Stanton—& see where *he* has landed—& *this* man is as vile in my eyes as the most unscrupulous pro slavery politician because he shows an utter insensibility to the holiness & sanctity of truth.

To my mind, he who fabricates an untruth out of whole cloth, is less repulsive than he who so states true things by artful intermingling of false & effects of *stage lights* as to produce the impression of falsehood—the more particularly when it is done amid the cheerings of a popular audience.

I do not believe that the course of the American Board has been what it should be—& had Mr Pillsbury told the simple truth about them I had been well pleased—But these monstrous abominable charges I read with indignation greater than I have felt since the recapture of Burns & of the same sort for I think that white men ministers & churches *have rights* as well as black men. Lest you should not have read the account, I send herewith that number of the *Independent* in which I read it.

Meanwhile I see, by F. Douglas's paper that the poor foolish folk are murmuring & repining still about an industrial school—of all vague unbased fabrics of a vision this floating idea of a colored industrial school is the most illusive. If they want one why dont they have one—Many men among the colored people are richer than I am—& better able to help such an object—Will they *ever* learn to walk?

Sometimes I think I see that God does not design our efforts to turn the nation to repentence should be successful, since he suffers divisions to cripple the efforts of the A. Slavery party to such a degree—In principle I could agree very well with your detachment in the main—in fact they seem to be the only party that have any settled radical principles—but if such men as Pillsbury are to be its exponents I cannot go with it. In fact, I must remain by myself— This note is quite confidential. I was *obliged* to speak to someone—[8]

> Ever truly yrs
> H.B.S.

May I trouble you to redirect to me this number of the Independent after you have read it.

> HBS

8. Here Mrs. Stowe expresses her unwillingness to be associated with extremists in the Garrison camp like the New Hampshire abolitionist Parker Pillsbury (1809–1898) or with the more conservative Board of the American and Foreign Antislavery Society. Henry B. Stanton (1805–1887), a leader of the latter organization, had been an adversary of Lyman Beecher at Lane Seminary. The reference

to Douglass relates to his misapprehension that Mrs. Stowe was prepared to sub-
sidize an industrial college for Negroes. *The Life and Writings of Frederick
Douglass*, ed. Philip S. Foner (New York, 1950), II, 272–275.

3. From M. J. FLANDERS

Mr. Philips:

Sir.

The time for action has come, and the day you have predicted has
arrived—

But what measures are now being taken to arm the race so long
oppressed—?

We know of none here, but feel that it should be done, and some
few of us who have longed for their redemption are ready to solicit
funds for the purpose of arming the free blacks here and in Canada.

I offer myself either for that purpose or to travel among them and
rouse them to action.

If men are not working for this object women should and I apply
to you for advice in behalf other ladies who are anxious to devote
themselves to the cause of Freedom—

Very respt

Miss. M. J. Flanders

Concord, N.H.
April 22,/61

4. From MARIA K. A. BENCHLEY

My Dear Mr. Phillips

Can there not be a bill introduced into Congress for the setting
apart of a Territory to be given exclusively to the blacks? I have
lived at the South for years and *know* that the *worst* reports of
outrages against the colored people are true. The hatred of the
whites is so virulent, so limitless, and so utterly unscrupulous. It
makes me ashamed of my race. I am burning to do something for
the negroes. I have studied them faithfully while teaching them and

know them to be so superior in all that constitutes Christliness. But I am poor and all the property I have, except a little wee home, is in Texas, and I could never get the control of it if I should do all I would for this persecuted people. Already I am hated and socially ostracised for expressions of sympathy while living in Texas.

But in the name of Heaven *you* procure a bill introduced into Congress for such land as may be best to set apart for our afflicted ones. I thought to go about and lecture on the subject, but cannot do it now. I will give all but the necessities of life toward *buying* such a tract, if that can be done. We look to you, our hero, our leader. God in heaven bless & keep you.

Marie K. A. Benchley
widow of Ex Lt. Gov. Benchley
of Mass.

Jan 19. 75
Ithaca
    N.Y.

5. From EDMUND QUINCY

BOSTON, OCT. 30, 1850

Dear Wendell,

I called at your house just now in hopes of finding you as I wish to consult you on a point of some difficulty, or at least delicacy. I am engaged to lecture at Salem next Sunday as I suppose you know. Well, last night I rec'd a letter from Salem from a coloured man, very well written & spelt, telling me that I had never done myself justice there & wishing me to prepare a written lecture or at any rate so to arrange my thoughts "so as to command attention & help the cause." You see my correspondent is very plain-spoken. He says "You are not a good extemporaneous Speaker. In fact, you are a very poor Speaker!"

Now, of course, it is of no particular consequence what this nigger says (though evidently an intelligent one,—perhaps Babcock—

for I forgot to say the letter is anonymous); but I have a suspicion that he has been put up to it by some of the ladies. As you lectured there last Sunday, perhaps you may have gathered something of their feelings about it. If they really feel so (for I can't *write* a lecture at this notice) is it too late to give up my lecture? If you would go down in my place, they would be more than satisfied. I should like to know your views at once, as there is no time to be lost.

I was at first inclined to think the letter a hoax; but the internal evidence is conclusive as to its good faith. The writer is evidently a well-meaning, honest fellow, who thinks he is doing his duty–& perhaps he is. My wife says he speaks her exact opinion & that she could not express it better herself. He is very humble & fearful of offending me, which of course he does not. I am only diverted by it. But to satisfy him that I take it in good part I think it best to have the enclosed notice inserted in the Liberator of this week if possible. If it can be he will see it before Sunday & if you think best I author-ize you to have my lecture put off until I can write the lecture (for I cannot but think it is the wish of the ladies there expressed in this roundabout way) or omitted altogether.

If you approve of the Notice please put it into Garrison's hands early tomorrow morning. Love to the Countess. I trust she bore her journey from her Thames Villa to Arundel House without fatigue.

Truly yours,
EDMUND QUINCY[9]

For the Liberator if W.P. approve.
For the Liberator.
E.Q. returns his grateful acknowledgments to his coloured corre-spondent & assures him that his advice is taken in good part & will be followed as far as possible. He begs to know whether his (his coloured friend's) mother knows he is out? He would respectfully

---

9. Edmund Quincy (1808–1877), son of Josiah Quincy, came from a family background similar to Phillips's, and became a Garrisonian in 1837. His proposed note does not appear in the *Liberator*.

inquire of him "*How's yer marm?* Whether he can truthful exclaim "O! Crikey don't I love my mother? He would say that he thinks him (his col'd friend) some pumpkins he does. And that he thinks he is a nigger living in Lynn. That a nigger quite capable of getting this up lives there he (E.Q.) has the authority of ——— Pike, Esq. He also thinks that his col'd friend was assisted by a wench living about as far towards the South Shore. You didn't suck in this child, this time. No, *Sirrr*, No *Sirreee*—horsefly!

6. From AGNES MARY GRANT

WEDNESDAY DEC 9, 1859
OFFICE OF THE ANGLO AFRICAN PAPER
400 BEEKMAN STREET

To WENDELL PHILLIPS ESQ.

MY DEAR SIR

I have just heard of a *sympathy* meeting to be held at the Cooper Institute tomorrow evening plenty of good & true *white men speakers,* but where are the *Black men* for whom this "Just Man" gave his life? Who asks such men as that courteous Christian Gentleman Henry Highland Garnet, to speak a loving word for the man with whom he was in the most intimate communion from time to time during 15 years and who entertained towards him the love of a tender Parent? Where is that young Appollo whose glowing words of eloquence & power mark him as one destined to be an orator & a leader among his people. Why is no invitation extended to the intelligent young Editor of the newspaper of the Colored People of this City? *Why is it* that *White men* are for ever making speeches & self glorifying themselves & these men with their bursting hearts & grand utterances are kept in the background in this so falsely called Free North, as much socially and politically proscribed almost as their enslaved Brethern? Why is it Mr. Philips? Now do send an invitation to the Revd H. H. Garnet & to Mr. Hamilton the Editor of the Anglo African Paper & *do yourselves* the *honor* of sympathising *with them* for whom this dear old man died, & with whom the heart of God itself sympathises—All his wants looking to. I am unable from illness to go about much & have come down to this office today *having to be out* on business of importance but hearing of this *Sympathy meeting*, I have written a line to the effect. I write this to you, to my Pastor Dr Cheever— you are a great speaker Mr. Philips & my Pastor is a great Preacher, but in my Country we are used to such things in white men. I would rather hear Henry Highland Garnet when God gives him the word than either of you.

> I am Sir
> Respectfully your Friend
> AGNES MARY GRANT

Please excuse this almost unintelligible writing—you will perhaps make out enough to know there are some who would like to hear the Black men speak about what it is presumed they are well fitted to speak viz. their own wants & their own wrongs—

I mean Mr. Brown entertained the feelings of a Father towards Mr. Garnet—I have been *very ill*, & can scarcely *think* clearly, but you will make out what I mean. Perhaps you could find out who constitutes the Committee & get them to call upon Mr. Garnet 52. Laurens Street. Mr. Hamiltons office is as above—by the young "Orator" I mean the Revd. J. Sella Martin of Boston—so lately a slave, now so brilliant & impassioned a speaker—[10]

10. Henry Highland Garnet (1815–1882), minister of the Shiloh Presbyterian Church in New York City. He had escaped from slavery in 1824 and had long been recognized as a leading black activist and orator. J. Sella Martin was minister to the Joy Street Church in Boston.

ii) *A Benefactor to the Blacks*

7. From WILLIAM E. WALKER

NEW HAVEN CON   APRIL 10TH/60

Mr Wendell Philips

Dear Sir

Having known you by reputation for a long time as well as having had the privilege and pleasure of hearing you on several occasions, I have long since concluded that you are a true friend of the colored race. Your life & character evince this fact—words as well as deeds are the evidence.

The object of this is to inquire if you are not acquainted with some one in Boston or *Mass* who has independence and liberality eneough to take an honest, intelligent, smart, active boy and learn him some useful trade or give him a common school education. The circumstances attending the boy are very peculiar which I will state. The boy with his Mother were slaves in Va until 1859. My Father who owned them died— I became Administrator and as one of the legatees Succeeded by considerable outlay of money & time in having them emancipated. The boy is now 16 years old and very well grown. he is as likely as any boy you can find, his Father is a white man his mother a brown skin woman—he has every mark of intelligence and is a very sober, manly youth—now I wish to give him a trade, and brought him to the *free North* for that purpose. I tried in Pa. without success. I tried in New York without success. I now make my last appeal to you, the boy is no more a relation of mine than you, I am no more under obligation to him than any one who never saw him. I have already spent what little patrimony I had in securing his freedom, in purchasing my mother's interest, and in other expenses attendant upon his emancipation and travelling and board. I now desire something done for him. Can it not be done? Mr Wm C Nell of the office of the Liberator knows me. Inquire of him I was offered $1000.00 dolls for the boy and a $1000.00 for his mother—now let us do something for him. Freedom is worth but little unless we have those elements within us (which is to be had only by the proper development of our natural faculties) that we may be rightly able to appreciate and use our liberty to our own advantage as well as to the best interest of our fellow man.

Let me then in conclusion earnestly request that you will use your influence and efforts to obtain for that boy a good mechanical trade with a common school education. You would admire the lad much he is very likely indeed, he will *make a man* I need add no more Please write as soon as possible and believe me yours in the cause of freedom and humanity.

WM E. WALKER

8. From WILLIAM E. WALKER

NEW HAVEN CON.   APRIL 21ST/60

MR. WENDELL PHILIPS

DEAR SIR

Yours bearing date April 15th was duly received. I thank you much for the interest you manifest on behalf of the boy; this feeling, this principle which characterise your life I do not find existing among abolitionist and Anti-slavery men generally: They care much about the slave and nothing about him when free. But to the letter. I called on Mr. Sprague, he was not long a resident and could say nor do anything at present—he kindly tendered his service to do what he could and referred me to several *gents* besides introducing me to Mr Sheldon and his partner, but neither of them could do anything nor advise at present; so the matter remains just as it was when I last wrote. I shall leave here near the first of May, perhaps about 3d. I should like to hear again from you before. Hoping that you may have been able to do something in that direction

I remain Yours
WM. E. WALKER

9. From ALBERT MORTON

STEVENS LINEN WORKS
WEBSTER, MASS., AUG. 4TH 1868

WENDELL PHILLIPS, ESQ.

Dear Sir:—I write you in the hope that you may know of some person in Providence, R.I. who will be sufficiently interested in the cause of justice to investigate the matter herein stated.

You have doubtless seen or known of a colored pianist in Boston named Samuel Thompson, generally known as "Blind Sam." His wife informed me yesterday that they had resided in Providence for several months past where "Blind Sam" was employed as pianist in a saloon on Eddy Street kept by an Englishman named James Whittam (Mrs. T. did not seem very clear about that name). On Friday July 3d, Mrs. T. did not call for her husband, as was her usual course, and he left the saloon about 10.30 P.M. saying he could find his way home. He was not seen by any acquaintances after that time but the following Monday or Tuesday his body was found in the river with one side badly beaten and his head bruised almost beyond recognition. There seemed be no interest taken to procure evidence and the Coroners jury returned a verdict of "Accidental drowning." Mrs. Thompson says that while she was at the dock where the body was placed a young Irishmen,—who did not know she was particularly interested,—told her "that man was beaten and kicked in his side and head and then thrown into the dock." Mrs. T. thought from his manner that the man was one of the parties concerned in the murder but was too confused to take any steps towards his arrest. I feel bitterly opposed to the Irish persecutors of a race superior in good qualities to their own and hope something may be done to bring the actors in this outrage to justice. I will pay a reasonable proportion of any expenses which may be necessary to procure evidence and teach the class who think they can perpetrate any outrage on a "Nigger" with impunity, a severe lesson.

Yours truly
ALBERT MORTON

10. From A. FAIRBANKS

AUG. IOTH
[1868]

DEAR FRIEND

Yours was rec'd yesterday   I called upon the coroner with whom I am well acquainted and read to him the letter. He produced all the papers and read to me the testimony of the woman and others. The jury found no marks of violence on the body of the man and she at that time thought he was drowned by accident, and my neighbour Dunbar Harris saw the body and could discover no marks of violence. He was a very dissipated man had been taken to the lock up a number of times and fined for drunkeness. He has been here off and on several times for 3 or 4 years—The Irishman's remark to her I dont think amounts to much—especially at this time and I know personally three of the jury that sat on the inquest—upright, judicious men—had there been any marks of violence on the body they would not have passed it by in silence and why did his wife not tell of it until a month afterwards.

Truly
A FAIRBANKS

11. From S. C. HEWETT

BOSTON, APRIL 13TH 1857

WENDELL PHILLIPS ESQR.
SIR.

I make you a statement in regard to which I do not wish my name to become known, as I do not wish to come in contact with that class of men. Two years ago last February Ephraim Hayes, who keeps a public house and barroom in Change Avenue, went to the South and bought a negro lad about 15 years of age. He brought him home and put him to work in his house in Change Avenue. He got acquainted with a young mulatto girl, and Hayes tried to break up the intimacy. He finally sent for a Doctor at the South end who formerly lived at the South and is used to such operations whose name I have forgotten, and took this young negro boy down cellar, gave him chloroform, tied him and castrated him. After the boy got well he attempted to run for Canada. Hayes telegraphed, and offered a reward for his recovery and he was brought back. He then got into a vessel, unknown to the Captain, and went to Norfolk Virginia, and from there went back to his former master who had sold him to Hayes. His former master was so put out at Hayes' treatment of the boy that he would not let him Hayes know where he was. But Hayes accidentally found out where he was, and went out within 40 days, and sold him, and bought a mulatto girl about 13 years old, and a mulatto boy about 15 and has them now in his house in Change Avenue. It can by proved by many persons that Hayes did have this operation of castration performed on the boy, and the following persons know that it was done, and have seen his testicles now preserved in Hayes' house. They examined the boy after it was done. He was seared with a hot iron, which created a great deal of Soreness and inflammation for three or four weeks. The persons who know the fact are Jack. Granger. Mr. Baker, brother of John Baker, Court Street, Sadler & Harnesses, and many others who were and now are about the house. Hayes told the whole circumstance before me and some 20 others and the whole affair can be proved. I wish the boy could be bought and brought on, and then prosecute Hayes.

Yours respectfully
S. C. HEWETT[11]

39 Harrison Avenue

11. Simon C. Hewett was a well-known Boston doctor who specialized in setting bones and treating diseases of the joints. His work was publicly endorsed by Bronson Alcott, Thomas H. Perkins, Ralph Waldo Emerson, and other prominent people in the community. See H. C. Hewett, *Dr. S. C. Hewett, Bone Setter* (Boston, 1835). Ephraim Hayes, John Granger, and John B. Baker all appear in the Boston Directory for 1857. Although there is no mention of Hewett's accusation in the *Liberator* and no report of a criminal action against Hayes in available court records, Phillips would have treated this report seriously and taken what action he could. It is unlikely that Hayes could have been tried unless the youth he was accused of mutilating was brought back to Boston to testify against him.

12. From SUSAN P. RANDALL

HARTFORD DEC 15TH /58

To WENDELL PHILLIPS

Dear Sir my unfortunate condition compels me to acquaint some one of my imprudence I am in great trouble by Carl Formes that is at present singing at the Boston Theater I have acquainted him of it and receiving no reply and being destitute of funds I borrow 7 dollars and visited New York two weeks ago I wrote him two letters and the last one on the day of my leaving New York for this city I inform him that as he was soon to visit Boston that I should try what the laws of that State would do in my behalf in consequence of which I received a letter from a person that he employed to write me that I should return to New York and board he bearing my expenses with the $7 dollars that was sent in the letter I did so on the first of Dec the second day I received a visit from this person calling himself Dr. A. Schutte saying that Mr Formes would assist me but having some doubt whether he was the cause of my trouble he left me promising to call in a day or two I remained a week & being in debt for my board & receiving no word from either after writing several times to them the lady Mrs. Elizabeth Jinnings was obliged to advance me $3 dollars besides Board of $3 that I might return to Hartford where I am now at no. 52 Village Street I consider that I have been greatly wrong by one or both of them I am destitute of money and this great trouble on me I feel as if there ought something be done to assist me by him I would like you to go and see him & plead for me I do not wish to make it a Public affair on the account of my Mother who is a respectable Woman in Florence, Mass where I became acquainted with him pleas to do all that you can for me as privately as possible unless Mr. Formes is determin to doubt my word and then if the law can do anything for me I will come on and prove it for I shall suffer if I do not have assistance from him For I am now nearly six months in advance do pleas to use all the influence that you can for me for I must not go home to my Mother I cannot give you direc-

Hartford April 26 '59

Mr Phillips

Sir I am still at No 52 Village St and through your kindness are doing as well as can be expected

My little Boy was five weeks old last Saturday and is quite well I do not intend to remain here any longer than it is necessary for me to do so

It is A pleasure to me to inform you what A relief your kindly assistance gave me I shall soon be able to earn my living again I can never forget your kindness to me as A stranger for you can never know the relief your kindness gave to my mind at that time I wish it was in my power to give you something for your trouble or in any way to express my thanks as I could wish

Believe me truly grateful and accept the humble thanks of

Susan R Randall
52 Village Street

One in the series of letters between Wendell Phillips and Susan Randall, a black woman who was the object of Phillips's philanthropy. See letters 12 through 18.

tions where to find him only at the Boston Theater in company
with Madll. Picclomini & others   I am not aware how long the
company is there but hope this may reach you in time you will
assist me in getting what it is his duty to do for me   Pleas to pardon
the liberty I have taken to write you of my serious troubles & let
them apollogiz for so unfortunate person as Susan P. Randall No.
52 Village Street

Hartford, ct

P.S. If Mr. Formes will consent to assist me will you be so kind as to
keep it in your possession for me which I hope he will without a
Public affair   SPR

13. To DR. G. B. HAWLEY From WENDELL PHILLIPS

Dr. G. B. Hawley
      HARTFORD

DEC 22 '58

Sir

I received this morning a certificate purporting to be signed by
you & relating to a woman named Randall whom I never saw but
who applied to me to make the person who has wronged her con-
tribute to her support. He agrees to do so provided he can have
evidence that she really is in the state she represents & he intended
that I should select some physician known to me, of whom to ask
this certificate. She has chosen to attend to the matter herself and
I have only to ask if you really signed the certificate which I have
received. May I trouble you to reply to this as soon as possible since
the person concerned, a foreigner, will leave Boston in a few days &
I am desirous to settle the affair before he leaves.[12]

Yrs

Wendell Phillips

12. Draft copy in Phillips's hand.

14. From G. B. HAWLEY

DEAR SIR

Yours of the 22nd is received. In reply I would state that a colored woman called on me stating that she was in a family way & said her name was Randall.

After personal examination I was of opinion that she was pregnant, & gave her a certificate stating that to be my opinion.

Yours truly,
G. B. HAWLEY M.D.

Hartford
Dec 23d 1858

15. From SUSAN P. RANDALL

HARTFORD JAN 9TH 1859

MR. PHILLIPS
DEAR SIR

I received yours of the 4th with pleasure accept my humble thanks for the great kindness you have done me for I was in need of your friendly aid. Pleas to to take something for your trouble from the sum that remains with you for I cannot express the relief that your kindness has given to my mind as I was without money and sick in mind and body. Pleas to pardon the liberty I took to trouble with my affairs and accept the humble thanks of

SUSAN P. RANDALL
52 Village Street

16. From SUSAN P. RANDALL

HARTFORD   FEB 13" /59

MR PHILLIPS

Sir Will you make it convenient to send me that sum of Money this week as I am about to leave this City the last of the week.

Pleas write me when I am to expect the next and how much there remain to be sent me.

I am truly greatful for the interest you have allready taken to assist me and hope you will not go unrewarded for the Kindness you have done me and many others.

Pleas to excuse the liberty taken to trouble you again.

> In Haste
> SUSAN P. RANDALL
> 52 Village Street

17. From SUSAN P. RANDALL

HARTFORD MARCH 14" /59

MR. PHILLIPS

I am at present in this city   I was disappointed in going by the person who was to go with me at that time but expect to leave here as soon as I hear from you again   Will you oblidge me by sending the next sum I am to have as I shall not be able to attend to it myself unless it is sent soon for my time is now very short

> In Haste
> SUSAN P. RANDALL
> 52 Village Street

18. From SUSAN P. RANDALL

HARTFORD APRIL 26"/59

MR. PHILLIPS

Sir I am still at No 52 Village St and through your kindness am doing as well as can be expected.

My little Boy was five weeks old last Saturday and is quite well I do not intend to remain here any longer than it is necessary for me to do so.

It is a pleasure to me to inform you what a relief your timely assistance gave me   I shall soon be able to earn my living again   I can never forget your kindness to me as a stranger for you can never know the relief your kindness gave to my mind at that time   I wish it was in my power to give you something for your trouble or in any way to express my thanks as I could wish.

believe me truly greatful and accept the humble thanks of

SUSAN P. RANDALL

52 Village Street

19. From ISAAC E. MAYO

HARWICH PORT   NOV. 8: 1852

BROTHER PHILLOPS

DEAR SIR

My daughter noticed in the liberator an advirtsment of A bright cuban boy   you inquire if there is A friend of the colord people who will give A home and instruction to   I have a wife and six daughters   I have no boy   I have often thought of taking one   my family wants mee to wright yow for to send for him to mee if you will send him I will make my home his home.

for information enquire of Gilbard Smith, Joshua H. Robins, G. H. Small and others of harwich or S. S. Foster Parker Pilsbry, W. L. Garison they have they have ben to my house often

Yours respectful

ISAAC E. MAYO

Harwich port   wright mee soon

20. From   G[ibson?] H. SMALL

HARWICH   NOV 30, 1852

W. PHILLIPS ESQ.

DEAR SIR

Your note mailed 26th has been received and in reply to your Enquiries respecting Mr. I. E. Mayo would say that he is a neighbour of mine and has been for some 20 years and he has always

appeared to me to be a man of good morale principale and correct
in all the affairs of life and has a very pleasant family   he is in moderate circumstances engaged in house carpentry and the making
sashes blinds and c. & also cultivates a few acres of Lands   I should
think on the whole that it would be one of the best plans if not the
Best for a Coloured boy in this region. Mr. *Mayo is a thorough
reformer and would not be likely to treat him ill on account of his
Complexion*   the chance for schooling is I presume about the same
here as in other parts of the state   boys from 12 to 15 usually attend
school about the 3 winter months   that is them that go to the Public
school only

Yours truly
G[ibson?] H. SMALL

21. From MARY W. RAYMOND

BATH FEB. 22ND 1853

SIR.

   I rec'd your letter a short time since, and have omitted writing on
account of my health. You wrote that you wished me to send Bernardo up to you, but as he has a good place now, and a good master,
(for that is what he needed) he is a very good boy. I cannot get him
now, but I will send him to you as soon as I can. I rec'd your letter
in which the ten dollar bill was enclosed and was much obliged to
you. I have had a great deal of care and anxiety attending him. He
was constantly running away, but could give no sort of reason for
so doing excepting "Because I wanted to." One thing I can say
however, he never gave me a saucy word while he lived with me,
but I guess I am the only one. He has done a great many things that
he ought not to do. When I send him and (that will be as soon as I
find a good chance) I will write to you in season, so that you shall
know when to expect him. When we send him shall we have him
left at the same place which you directed us to in your first letter?

Yours,
MARY W. RAYMOND

22. From HANNAH E. STEVENSON

MR. PHILLIPS
DEAR SIR,

Bernardo is here, looking so thin & ill, with a hollow cough that it excites the compassion of the household who have known him before. He arrived from N York, after perhaps too hard work, & finds his master Capt. Mayo, also here, discharging the Sam Slick, which is at Lewis's Wharf. The Captain sought you, in vain, yesterday; and Bernardo came in here in this intense heat at noon so exhausted & thin that I am keeping him till towards evening. He is on board the vessel with Capt. Mayo, who is desirous to see you. He tells me of such coughings & symptoms as seem to indicate grave disease; & I should think he had found a rather hard time with the last Capt. Capt. Mayo tells him he shall go to Harwich, & he is pleased with that. He says he wrote you the 8th June; but has not found an opportunity since. He thinks he is in a consumption, & perhaps he is right, but he does not look fit for hard work; lifting weights &c. brings on head-ache & he coughs violently when he lies down & when he wakes.

I offered to forward him to Nahant, but he thought it might be better to send a letter. Capt. Mayo may remain in Boston some days longer.

What a shabby letter to send to an elegant gentleman! But the height of the thermometer dims my sight, & the din of the little ones obfuscates all the bits that are not melted out.

> Yrs
> HANNAH E. STEVENSON

23. From BERNARDO

My Dear Friend I now take my pen in hand to let you now

what I have to you. I commence my School on monday success one day. and am going to morrow. Capt. Isaac Mayo is going to Boston to morrow the vessel is going to London she will be rady to go in the middle of the week and I dont think you will have any chanch to see him. cough plage me so that my writing looks bad my hand quiver so it makes it bad. my studies is this smith Arithmetic and Geography and wen ar you coming down? I shall be very hapy to see you hear. and I study book keeping I dont think you will find this out. I havent any mor to write you please answer this.

BERNARDO

24. From F. H. DRAKE

LEOMINSTER   SEPT 8TH/56

DEAR MR PHILLIPS.

Bernardo arrived safely on tuesday eve. He seemed greatly fatigued after the journey. consequently I kept him with me till the next day—then went with him to his lodgings. We find him a very pleasant and interesting lad. I am pained to see him so feeble. As soon as I saw him, I came to the conclusion that he was really more feeble than you had apprehended. I have had much experience in nursing people who were suffering from pulmonary affections, & I felt that his case was one of great doubt. I resolved to give him a mother's care & kindness. He has been with me a part of every day & I have made it a point to devote my time for his comfort or enjoyment—we walk or read & converse, as he may feel inclined.

I have been to his lodgings nights to aid him in fitting on his compress, (as he understood it) but more in fact to give me an opportunity of observing him under all circumstances. I find he coughs most when lying on his left side & many other symptoms seem to indicate ulceration.

I am not wont to look on the dark side when one is ill, but in this case the evidence seems irresistable.

Last week the cough was very hard & dry. Yesterday it was looser. He feels relieved in that respect & attributes it to the change of air—of course I encourage the idea, to him & cheer him with all the hope I can.

As we took our walk yesterday, I asked him to step in with me, to see our family physician (pray excuse the liberty I took, without your consent, I did it to relieve my own mind), Dr. C. C. Field (a very judicious & experienced physician in re-form practice) who confirmed my worst fears—He says the only possible hope of his recovery is, *to live outdoors*, & have very nourishing diet, & create as healthy an action of the skin as possible. This will surely make him more comfortable, & it may restore him, though he thought there was very little hope—of course Bernardo knows nothing of this doubt.

I thought it not best to send him to school, but invited him to come to me & read once a day, & spell, define, & take a short lesson in mental arithmetic. He has devoted one hour each day thus. He acts just as he chooses about it. I think he is pleased with the arrangement & seems to enjoy it much. The lad cherishes a lively sense of gratitude for all your kindness, he says no boy could desire a kinder friend than you are to him. I sincerely hope he may be spared, to enjoy a long life—so well begun. Nothing on our part shall be wanting to accomplish so desirable results.

How very sad the bereavement of our friend Remond & family! A heavy loss to us all.

Sadder if possible is the lamentable condition of Fredrick Douglass —poor weak brother! Heaven save him.

I will apprise you from time to time of the condition of Bernardo.

I am, very truly, yrs,

F. H. DRAKE

25. From F. H. DRAKE

LEOMINSTER, OCT. 2ND
[1856]

DEAR MR PHILLIPS

Your note of this date, with enclosed check for twenty-five dollars, is just rec'd.

I regret to inform you that Bernardo is steadily and rapidly failing. He is not able to walk except from the door to the street. His physician thinks it is desirable that he should ride as often as the weather will permit.

He is not inclined to take his bed, rather chooses to sit up the first part of the day, & lie on the sofa in the afternoon. His appetite is very little, eats mostly fruits. I have spared no pains in procuring the best of fruit for him, he seems to enjoy it greatly. His rides are a great comfort to him, we ride about two miles at one time (pay 25 cts a trip). We call on Dr. Field occasionally, he says the best medicine for the patient is a good ride. Every thing is done that can be done for the comfort & happiness of the boy. He is delighted with his watch, we paid $7.00 for it (the first one being sold before we rec'd your note of approval). I have bought a dressing gown for him, material & making cost about two dollars fifty. I found it necessary to get him some gloves, & cotton flannel drawers. I do not think he will need any thing more for clothing even if he should live several months, which is not probable. I do not think he has thought of the danger he is in till this week. he seems very sad & at times is quite overcome in view of his weakness. I asked him today what I should tell you for him. he said "I should like to see him very much." The dear child was greatly grieved today, & for the first time since he has been here, cried. I cheered him all I could, still he seemed grieved because his limbs were so weak.

I shall not say any thing to him of his danger, untill he first speaks of it. Tis sad to break such truth to one so young & hopeful.

I think he would be gratified to have a line from you.

It will be five weeks next Wednesday since B. went to Mr. Bates, his bill will at that time be thirteen dollars, the watch, carriage hire, & what clothing I have bought comes to twelve dollars. This includes all that has been expended for him, except three calls on Dr Field.

Should anything unusual occur I will write you speedily—Saturday next I leave town for two or three days to attend a convention at Westminster. I shall not leave till after the morning mail comes in (9 ½ o'clock) Sat. morning, if you wish to communicate anything to me before that time.

Very truly yrs,
F. H. DRAKE

26. From F. H. DRAKE

LEOMINSTER OCT. 12TH/56

DEAR MR PHILLIPS:

The basket containing the grapes & c. for Bernardo was duly rec'd. He was greatly delighted with all the things, particularly the grapes—which he seems to enjoy more than any thing of the kind he has previously had.

I asked him what I should say to you today. he says, "Tell him I think the grapes are the nicest thing I have tasted for a long time."

We have got him nicely moved to Mrs Whitney's. I moved him on Thursday. He seems to like quite as well as I expected. Mrs. Whitney is very attentive to him, doing many little kindnesses, which every true nurse knows to be essential.

You may be assured he will have every thing done for his comfort. I go every day to assist in any way I can. Some things he rather prefers that I should do for him, which I am very happy to do. He will soon get accostomed to his new position, & I am sure will be very happy in his new home & friends.

We have just been out to ride. He still enjoys riding more than any thing else. He takes the cod liver oil like a hero, the dear patient creature! every thing I suggest to him, is law with him. It rather amuses those who have some times ventured to advise him, to have him always wait for my judgment before he accepts their opinion.

I think for a few days he has more fully realised his situation. He has grown weaker since you saw him, & is much more inclined to keep his bed a part of the day.

Stephen Foster sent him some nice pears, which he relishes very much & also his sweet potatoes. We can get them in our market now.

My friends are very kind to send him syrups, jellies, & other little delicacies, which are ever grateful to the sick. I feel truly rejoiced that our people have this opportunity offered them to call out their sympathies for a persecuted class. I think it will be a blessing to them, & I am sure it will aid them greatly in overcoming their most wicked prejudices.

I will keep you apprised of the dear child's condition from time to time.

Husband joins me in kind remembrances.

Truly yrs
F. H. Drake

P.S.

You will find Mrs Willey at her home on thursday next, at 13 Minot St. if you wish to learn anything more definite concerning Bernardo.

FHD

27. From F. H. DRAKE

WEDNESDAY MORNING 10 O'CLOCK
[1856]

DEAR FRIEND,

Bernardo had an ill turn yesterday which he has not rallied from. I have been by him for twelve hours, & find he fails very fast. He cannot live through another such turn. He strangles. He cannot probably live till noon, certainly not till morning.

If you have any directions to communicate to me, in the event of his death, please do so by express this afternoon.

He told me this morning he should like to see you. I think it is *not possible* for him to live till you get here.

He is not willing for me to leave him so I cannot say more.

Haste,

F. H. DRAKE

P.S.

The Dr. has just been in, & says I am right in what I have told you. Says if you wish to see him you may possibly if you come this P.M.

28. From F. H. DRAKE

LEOMINSTER NOV 17TH/56

DEAR FRIEND,

On my return from my journey saturday eve, I found a line from you saying you would give us Thursday eve, at Fitchburg.

Thank you for your promise to come on any eve, it makes no difference to us which—I presume Pillsbury can come either eve—as he does not lecture week days. I have written him of your decision.

I owe you an apology for not writing you before I went my journey. As I was not able to settle all accounts at that time, & feeling in some haste to go before it was very cold weather, I defered writing till I should return.

I have now settled all the demands against me on Bernardo's account, & have in my hands about ten dollars surplus. I intend to be at the Basaar & shall take my accounts & receipts with me, for your inspection at that time.

Our good friend Mr Davis refused to receive any compensation for his trouble & expressed great satisfaction for the opportunity thus given him to speak for humanity—He certainly improved the opportunity in a very fitting manner—Every one present seeming to feel the force of his remarks. Although some were of the straight orthodox faith, & not a word hinted by Mr Davis about the repentance or condemnation of the departed, but rather the most kind & christian recognition of the pure life & character of the more than ordinary lad, the twice orphaned and lone one— Our Antislavery friends generally were present, & followed in procession to the cemetary. Mr. Benj. Snow Jr accompanied Mr Davis.

I have been to Fitchburg to look at a tombstone. I found a very proper kind for ten or twelve dollars, white or rather grey marble. There were also slate for seven & eight dollars.

The manufacturer seemed to rather advise the grey marble, as the Slate deface so soon. The lettering is 1 ½ cts a letter.

My grateful acknowledgements are due yourself for the generous testimonial bestowed on me, in consideration of my attentions to our dear adopted one. I am certain it is to you alone, that I am under obligations. Much as I value it for your sake, I had no need of other memento than the loved one himself bestowed. His last warm kiss —from icy lips. God only knows how great a blessing it was to me, to pillow his dying head on my bosom. Death were indeed a heavenly boon to such as him. I cannot trust myself to utter what I feel so intensely as I do, the wrong, visited on this victim of a twofold oppression.

With new resolves for more earnest devotion to humanity.

I am, gratefully Yrs,

F. H. Drake

29. From E. J. JOHNSON

WENDELL PHILIPS ESQ
SIR

Being fully aware of the deep interest at all times exprest by you for the welfare of my race must be my excuse for entering your presence. I trust you will not consider me presuming. I need not say to you Sir that one of the first acts of the next Congress will be, the admission of such of the Rebelious States as profess Loyalty to the Union; Such as was seeking admission at the close of the last Session will have the influence of the President to assist in the hasty completion of the work. The friends of the Negro have heretofore asked for these States to grant them the right of suffrage, under their new constitutions so far well if they can possibly accomplish this. But Sir will not those States possess the right at any time to disfranchise the Negro when they can find a sufficient number of whites to overwhelm them at ballot on change of State constitution this has been done *North* why not South? is there not a possibility of getting Congress to pass a law to give the right of suffrage to all Americans white or Black. if so will you be so kind as to say to me, what is the best plan to pursue to secure such an act, once more allow me to say my cause must [be] my Plea

With Respect
E. J. JOHNSON

Mrs. E. R. Johnson
  New Bedford
    Mass

A letter written by Lewis Hayden when he was three years out of slavery. See letter 30 and compare it with letter 31, written twenty-two years later.

30. From LEWIS HAYDEN

FRIEND PHILLIPS

the letter you wrote to the Dr was read to me yesterday informing me of my agency being stop and after the first of March you will I have no doubt consider where I am how far I am from home the season of year and that you will remember it cost me more than two months wedges to get here I do not complain at all though it will place me in a poor situation for by the time I get home I hope to be as well of as I was when I left home do you not think I ot to be well I do not think I shall be and I have not spent no more than I could help now if I had known this I should have said to friend Hathaway when he call on me in Boston well sir will you send me home again he would have said yes for he did not know then what I was he did not know but what I was a second yourself but he and you all know it is not so you know it is me jest three years from Slavery well let me say to you if I am not Wendell Phillips now it dought not appear what I shall be for I shall not leve one stone onturnd to obtain light I shall do all I can to make myself a man that is if nature has done her part this you know has some to do with the matter withought her I can not be of any use to my Brothren in Bonds all though I am not able to say my bread is shore I therefore would like to be sent home to Detroit Mich will you make this known to commitee and do what you can for me If you will you may do something to aid me on my way upward and onward to manhood you will please write to me at west winfield. you me not like my composition it is as good as any of yours when you was but three years old which is my age: remember me if I live to get home I will [   ] you letter

yours truly   LEWIS HAUDEN[13]
[Hayden]

13. Lewis Hayden (1816–1889) had recently escaped with his wife Harriet from slavery in Kentucky. Upon leaving the employment of the American Antislavery

Society he moved to Detroit where he helped construct a church. Later he opened a clothing store in Boston, became a leader in the black community, and turned his house on Phillips Street into a rendezvous for fugitive slaves. The Lewis and Harriet Hayden Scholarship for black students was established at Harvard in 1893 with funds from their estate.

31. From LEWIS HAYDEN and CHARLES L. MILLER

COMMONWEALTH OF MASSACHUSETTS

SECRETARYS OFFICE

BOSTON, FEBRUARY 28TH, 1870

WENDELL PHILLIPS

DEAR SIR:

There is a smouldering enthusiasm in the bosom of the people which will burst forth into a flame when the President shall proclaim that the fifteenth amendment forms a part of the fundamental laws of the United States of America; and, knowing as we do that your heart beats in sympathy with that of the Loyal People; we therefore invite you to be present with us and address the people of Massachusetts in Faneuil Hall on a day which will be hereafter named at which time the Citizens of Massachusetts will celebrate this the crowning event of American Liberty; (the ratification of the fifteenth amendment.)

Respct Yours

LEWIS HAYDEN, Chairman

CHAS. L. MILLER Sec.

I have written Mr. Hayden that I have forwarded this letter. It seemed to me that you would be wise to accept an invitation by the blacks of yr own state.

There may [be] other speakers but still it is the blacks endorsing *in a measure yr course* the past 5 years. Take it into consideration & at any rate answer them. All well *Wednesday March* 2d yr own

CHAR [ANN PHILLIPS][14]

14. The note after the letter from Hayden and Miller is in Ann Phillips's hand. She refers to Phillips's efforts to keep the antislavery movement alive after Garrison's retirement in 1865.

An invitation from Lewis Hayden to Phillips to celebrate the promulgation of the 15th Amendment. See Letter 31.

Ann Phillips's comment pencilled on the back of Hayden's invitation, urging Wendell to attend the celebration. See letter 31.

32. From HARRIET TUBMAN

WENDELL PHILLIPS ESQ

MY DEAR FRIEND

I write to let you know that I am about to start on my mission. I shall leave on Tuesday. As you promised if I would let you know in case I did not make up my $100. I will state I lack after paying my board $19 or $20 of that amount. I shall not take my money with me but leave it with Mr. Walcott to forward to me at Philadelphia. Whatever you do will be gratefully appreciated by

HARRIET TUBMAN[15]

Saturday Aug 4/60

I am as well as is usual for me to be and in good spirits

15. Harriet Tubman (1820?–1913) of Underground Railroad fame had escaped from slavery in 1849 and was well known among Boston abolitionists. The letter presumably is in the hand of an amanuensis.

33. From JOHN OLIVER

OBERLIN OHIO   11" JAN 1857

DEAR FRIEND

MR. PHILLIPS.

I took the liberty a few days ago to write you a few lines. I was very Sick when I wrote in bade my head was very much affected. So much so that I did not know that I should gete over it. though I am now very much better, I hope I may continue to emprove.

I was in Boston while you were West I left Oberlin that day you left Boston. I am now living in the most unhappy portion of my life, though I hope I am getting over it, my Wife is not the women she was before I went to California, her Brother knows it & so does her mother. Mr. Phillips you cannot tell how unhappy I feel when I think of it & how hard I have worked to make my wife comfortable and happy. all I can do now is to waight her movements, if she goes to Cort with that paper in the form in which it is now, I think it will be my duty to publish the hole affare in the Cambridge paper, I do not see how I can let any thing that is so much aganst me & so farren from the real trouth pass without letting those who know me know the real trouth in regard to the hole matter. I would now rather do any thing I could for her or suffer any thing I could than do anything to anger her in the least, but anything that is so completly brake me down I cant let it pass without letting those who have been my friends know the trouth. *I wish for nothing more*, & whatever there may be in it against me I am willing it should be known, however, I will dismiss this part of my letter and proceed to asked your advice in regard to my futuer corse & futuer Business.

I wish to stay at this School untill the close of the present term than I wish or that is this term will Close the last week in February, than I wish to go to Cleveland & Study in Mr. Folsom's Comercial Collage untell some time in may, the studys will be there Book keeping, Arithmetic & writing. After may I wish to undertake a new Business. I think I shall open a Book Store, with alkinds of Books paper pens papers that is newspapers, and Confiend my time & attention to the collection of anti-Slavery works of all kinds in Short keep a regular *anti-Slavery Book Store*. now if you please tell me where I shall find the best locality for such a business. I have thought of Two places Worcester mass is one & Syracuse new York is the other. now witch of the two do you think is best. I have though Worcester, because I could gete my goods from boston cheper to Worcester then I could to Syracuse from Boston. But what do you think of the places & which is the best for such a business, and the next thing is, is there *anti-Slavery feeling* enough *in either place* to patronize a colord man & such a store, what do you my Friend think of it, perhaps you might think of some place better still. I love the carpenter shop but I have been broken down in that business & will not undertake it any more if I can help it.

I am now Mr. Phillips without any mony & I have now four weeks board due it will cost me over 45 dollars here this term it

The letter from John Oliver in which was enclosed the photograph of a scalded black woman. See letter 34.

Mr Wendell Phillips

Dear Friend

I enclose to you a Photograph which is a very poor one but from to you will be able to be quite see the features of Maud as I now exist in Ring Witkin Co. Virginia in 1866 This girl with a twin sister and then (month) Mary Richardson was Slave to a Mr Henry Abrams his wife one of the Great-Great grand tear her in any instant the left eye by the clothes, and her constant habit has been to take the children and hear this Leave in the arm which the picture explains. This child is now 16 years old and was brought Ever at the [?] Creatures too want to write with [?]

[second page]

Dr to Dorothy (?)
I have her to [?] Ivey, he has had the care expense of and Mrs Anna Abrams bought into a [?] Fairwell's heart two years for her then I Loan Light of the Care and [?] of [?] this time the any [?] what has been I will be done with her then a ferm in Both. She was for a time anyhow [?].

Yours very respectfully

John Oliver

Richmond Va
July 6th 1866

I hope to be able to you you all the fact.

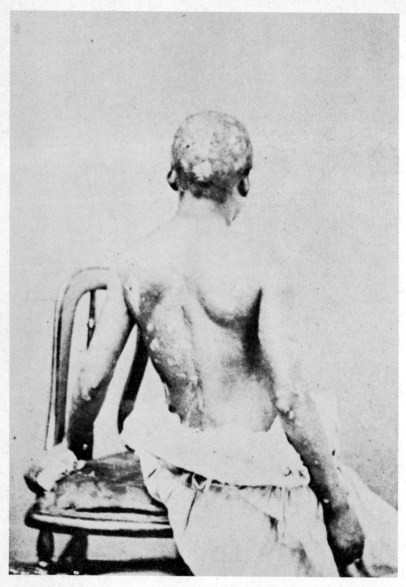

Photograph of a female slave who had been scalded by her mistress, as reported to Wendell Phillips by John Oliver. See letter 34.

being winter, and I want a pare of boots or shoes very much   I wish to gete you if you please to let me have 60 dollars if I hade not been sick I should not be behind in my board up to this time. please let me have a little money from time to time up to may, than I hope to go to work I wish to keep right oun untell then as I have begun to Study, I will used my little change as charful as I can   please do me the faver to let me have the 60 as soon as you can   I hope this may find you sir enjoying the best of health

Very respectfully
Yours   JOHN OLIVER[16]

16. It is not clear whether Oliver was an escaped slave or not, but at the time of this letter he was relying on Phillips for financial aid and personal advice. A decade later he had apparently become a Reconstruction official in Virginia.

P.S. 12" Jan PM. I have received your letter with the 40 dollars or the checke for 40, please except my thanks for your kindness. please let me know what you think of what I have asked when you have the time to attend to it.

OLIVER

34. From JOHN OLIVER

MR. WENDELL PHILLIPS
DEAR FRIEND,

I inclose to you a Photograph which is a very poor one but from it you will be able to see quite well the barbarism of Slavery as it now exists in King William Co, Virginia in 1866. This girl with a twin sister and their mother Lucy Richardson were Slaves to a Mr. Henry Abrams. his wife, one of the most cruel tyrant read of in any age put out the left eye of the mother, and her constent habit has been to take the Children and burn their backs in the mann[er] which this picture explains. this chil is now 16 years old and when brought to me at the freedman's Court was too weak to walk with me to square to gete something to eate. I took her to Gen. Terry. He has had the case worked up and Mrs Anne

Abrams, brought into a Judge Advocate's Court two weeks ago but then I lost sight of the Case and cannot up to this time tell any more what has been or will be done with her than a person in Boston. She was for a week under $5000 bonds.

> Yours very respectfully,
> JOHN OLIVER

Richmond Va
July 6th 1866
P.S.   I hope to be able to give you all the facts.

35. From JOHN OLIVER

RICHMOND AUGT. 22TH/67

MR. WENDELL PHILLIPS
DEAR FRIEND

Your Kind favor has been received. I am obliged to you for the cod and other information contained in your letter, and will make the best use of it I can.

With this letter I will mail to you a Photograph of the first grand Jury ever empanelled in Virginia composed of colored and white men. While seated in the Jury Room day after day, it oftened occured to me, that I was enjoying a privelege which you have been pleading for for me, more then thirty years, whenever I talk to the people I never fail to tell them of Mr Garrison, and yourself, and how many years you have labored for them. But while it is a matter of great intrest to them, yeat poor people they cannot appreciate it even as much as they seem to desire. How can they? Slavery left them without the knowledge of history, and their Children, and Childrens Children, only will know the sacrifices of the present age. I wish it might be possable some day not distent for you to come to Richmond, I know you would be richly paid, just to see the colored children of this city in school, and learn the progress they have made in Two years. some few of the youth, are already quite well advanced in their Latten Grammurs. How

Telegraphic Despatch.

Slavery Triumphant!!

FREEDOM KNEELS TO PIRACY!!!!

Boston, Friday Morning, 10 o'clock, A. M.

Commissioner LORING!! has ordered BURNS to be given up, and the Military are now out in full force to PROTECT the VILLIANY of SLAVE GOVERNMENT!! and sustain a band of INHUMAN KIDNAPPERS on soil consecrated to FREEDOM by the Blood of our Fathers !!!!!

"O Lord, God, to whom vengeance belongeth; O God, to whom vengeance belongeth, show thyself.

"Lord, how long shall the wicked, how long shall the wicked triumph?"

Southbridge, June 2, 11 o'clock, A. M.

Broadside decrying the fate of Anthony Burns, who was ordered returned to slavery from Boston in 1854. See letters 36–38.

Rocky Mount N C

My Dear Mr Daner I take the opperunity to Now write you A few Lines to inform you of My health I Am well at this time and hope that these few Lines will fine you and all of My freands in physician health peace and ~~happiness~~ hapiness have at tend you all the day Long I am Able to say that The god of your havinely father hath been with Me even un tell Now and he hath said that he would ever bee A god for me & pray on that god May strenpen you all in that you try to dow he was A god in delivering of Many City and he is the sam that he All ways was Mighty to dow this if we have the faith beleving in him that he will dow these things & dow Not hold your hand from trying for you know not when the Lord will deliver you all these Mighty foes for Let us be hold egypt how that the Lord did bring them out and he is Still Able to deliver More so pray on that your prayers May be heird through Much truble & Violence that you all hath hird grate Many lies but what I did say but I trust that you will Not begin to think So you Must expect to hear all this Now

But god All Mighty wise he knows the truth pray for Me that I Might once More Stept My foot on the Lands of that country once More I would tell you all of many things & gave My Love to Mr phillips And Mr parker Mr elis sys to all My friends and Brethern Brother Pills and to Brother Cole the preacher My best Love My Brother Grimes the preacher and tell them to write Me one of their Letters each of them in one and all of you write to A Letter and all the News what is don and what is dowing in the City all write Me soon As you can dow all you can for Me

I hope to see you all agin please god pray for me untill I com agin to you all with the healpe of god I will Not write Much More to you Now as the time is short & I am Living with A man who is A trader But he says that he will Not sell me I am tryinge to dow the best I can but if I can Get the chance I will com Agin all ways Look for Me and pray that the Lord will dow this But I say to you all My friends that their is But one way to deliver Me and Many others you Must do it with your sorte god will helpe you to do it

Letter written by Anthony Burns to Richard Henry Dana in 1854. See letter 36, and compare this with Burns's letter written from Oberlin, letter 37.

Oberlin Ohio August 2nd 1856

Mr Phillips Dear Sir

It is again that I avail my self of this opportunity to write you a few Lines which I truly hope will find you well and Enjoying gods blessings I have not had a Letter from you for a Long time but I hear from you and should have written you before now but having a Lame hand did not write untell now Sir I hope that you will not think me like the man who when Bound in Prison with Joseph who interpeded his Dreams and many other kind things did Joseph for him but when he was delivered did not remember his kindness any more I can Say thanks be to god I have not yet for gotten your kindness towards me for this is Enscribed on the tablet of heart there Long to be remembered and if I were not to write never again you may know that this act of kindness I will not for get I think of you most daly and Pray accoseldently that God may Bless you in all your ways I hope you are also praying for me that I may hold out faithful to the End I am going on with Studys dowing the Best I can & I hope to take up Lattain in the fall I am doing all I can to help my Self & I have Som times been put to it for means to go on but I hope that I Shall Obtein an Education

Please Excuse this hast
I will try and do better in
the next

I now Close my Letter Yours
truly Anthony Burns
write by return mail

I wish I too, had the opportunity now opening to them. We want now some of the best and tried friends of the Anti Slavery Cause to come, down here, and talk to the people at the most prominent places in the state. The Cities, Towns, and Court houses. Tell them of the passed, the present, and what the future demands in this hour of Reconstruction. the Jackson fund used in this work paid to the old friends of the negro, would have been used in its legitimate and rigtful channel. But I fear of using too much of your valuable time. Please except my thanks for your kindness

Yours very truly
JOHN OLIVER

36. From ANTHONY BURNS

ROCKY MT., N.C.
[1854]

MY DEAR MR DANER

I take the opportunity to Now write you A few Lines to inform you of my health   I am well at this time and hope that these few Lines will fine you and all of my freands in physician health peace and hapiness have at tend you all the day Long   I am Able to say that the god of your havenely father hath been with me even untell Now and he hath said that he wood ever bee A god for me & pray on that god may strinken you all in that you try to dow   he was A god in delivering of Many citys and he is the sam that he All ways was mighty to dow this if we have the faith beleving in him that he will dow these things & dow not hold your hand from trying for you know not when the Lord will deliver you all these mighty foars for Let us behold egupt how that the Lord did bring them out and he is still Able to deliver more so pray on that your prayers may be heird through much truble & I beleve that you all hath hird quote many lies Abute what I did say but I tust that you will Not begin to think so you must expect to her all this Now

But god AlMighty wise he knows the tuth   pray for me that I

might once more stept my foot on the Lands of that contry once
more I cuold tell you all of many things & give my Love to Mr
phillips and Mr parker Mr elissy to all my friends and Brethern
Brother Pitts and to Brother Cole the precher my best Love My
Brother Grimes the preacher and tell them to write me one of their
texes each of them one and all of you write to A letter and all the
News what is don and what is dowing in the city all write me sun
As you can dow all you can for me

I hope to see you all agin please god pray for me untill I com agin
to you all with the healpe of god I will Not write much more to you
Now as the time is shorte & I am Living with A man who is A
trader But he says that he will Not sell me I am trying to dow the
best I can but if I can get the chance I will com agin all ways   Look
for me and pray that the Lord will dow this But I say to you all my
friends that their is But one way to deliver me and many others you
must do it with you sorle god will helpe you to do it.

time is short   the Letter will close you and Brother Anthony
Burns write to me and call me James Black at Rocky Mount North
Callina for if you call my name I will Not get it
write Now to Me
pray for Me in all the chirches
one and all Anthony Burns[17]
              call me James Black
North Callina   I may get it

When I fine that I can get Letters from you then I Will write to
you all the News and what I wount you to Dow for me & if you
can cen A Letter to A friende of yours in Richmond and get them
to derect it Me in North Callina I can get it   think for your self how
to do it.

---

17. Anthony Burns (1834–1862) was returned to slavery after a celebrated trial
in Boston in 1854. Phillips, Theodore Parker, and R. H. Dana ("Mr. Daner") had
been actively involved in Burns's defense. "Brother Pitts" refers to Coffin Pitts, a
black businessman who had given Burns a job in Boston. Leonard Grimes, minister
of Boston's black Twelfth Baptist Church, eventually raised money to purchase
Burns's freedom.

37. From ANTHONY BURNS

OBERLIN   OHIO AUGUST 2D 1856

Mr Phillips   Dear Sir

It is again that I avail myself of this opportunity to write you a few Lines which I truly hope will fine you well and Enjoying gods blessings I have not had a Letter from you for a Long time but I hear from you and should have writen you before now but having a Lame hand did not write untill now Sir I hope that you will not think me like the man who when Bound in Prison with Joshef who interpeded his dreames and many other kind things did Joshef for him but when he was delivered did not remember his kindness any more I can say thanks be to god I have not yet for gotten your kindness towards me for this is enscribed on the table of heart there Long to be remembered and if I were not to write never again you may know that this act of kindness I will not forget I think of you most daly and Pray accorddently that god may Bless you in all your ways I hope you are also praying for me that I may hold out faithful to the end I am going on with Studys dowing the Best I can & I hope to take up Lattain in the fall I am doing all I can to healpe myself & I have sometimes been put to it for meanes to go on but I hope that I shall obtain an Education[18]

I now close my Letter   Yours
truly   Anthony Burns
write by return mail

Please excuse this last I will
try and do better in the next

18. Burns entered Oberlin College in 1855. In 1860 he was pastor of a black church in Indianapolis. He died two years later as minister of Zion Baptist Church in St. Catherines, Ontario.

38. From ANTHONY BURNS

OBERLIN   AUGUST 29/57

MOST HIGHLY ESTEEMED

  SIR

    I greatly fear that by my negligence in correspondence with you I have there by forfitted all claims to my Correspondence with you, but at the same time hope that you will forgive me in my negligence I again take my pen in hand in order to give you a few lines in the form of friendship and I truly wish that this will find you enjoying the Blessings of health I was some what expecting to fine you in Cleveland at that meeting held on the 26 and 27. I would have been glad to see you there and to heard you also There was not verry large number of Persons out at the meeting & sometimes it seems to me that I am almost ready to give up the hope of my Countrymen's ever being freed from there chains but yet I continue to hope for the day to come May God speed the right

  My great object in writing these hasty lines is to receive from you some Instructions in regard to a political life I feel as if I need some instruction and I new of no one able to instruct me in this point of view better then you therefore I write not that I might receive advice now only but at all times when you think proper to write and advise

  I think I need to be educated in these principals, as much as any thing else to which I may go into

  I hope you please excuse my hand write as my hand is burned & I thought I would not waite untill it would get well because I have waited two long all ready.

I am Yours
truly friend,
ANTHONY BURNS

39. From FREDERICK DOUGLASS

LYNN FEB. 10TH 1844

DEAR SIR,

In consequence of being absent from home during the past week, I did not get your letter of Feb. 4th requesting me to engage in the truly noble movement of holding one hundred Anti-Slavery conventions in this state, till late yesterday Evening.

There are two points in your letter, of which I wish to say a word, before I can answer your inquiry (will you go) in the affirmative. The first relates to the principle upon which compensation is to be rendered to agents, I think the sum to be paid should be deffinate, If I am to have 7 or 8 Dolls. per week I should have that and no more, If 7 dolls. is sufficient for an agent.—more is superfluous—and ought not to be given. For the Board to insure 7 Dolls. per week —and make a provission by which that sum may be increased to 12 Dolls. is (however unintentional) in my opinion to give the character of the movement a sort of mercinary coloring. Our A.S.S. Friends should be made acquainted with just what it will take to sustain us and should be made to feel that they are to give that and no more. The least element of speculation should be kept out of the dealings of abolitionists so far as their enterprise concerned. Your determination to strictly adhere to the principle of equality in compensating agents is good. I would not consent to work side by side with a Br. agent paying the same for the necessaries [of] life—laboring as hard as myself and yet for his labor getting less than myself. Nor could I on the other hand be satisfied with a reversed arrangement. by which I should have less than an equal fellow laborer. The principle you have here laid down and mean to carry out will secure harmony and good feeling amongst the agents, and prevent the jelousies, that might exist were a different policy pursued. The second point, of which I wish to say a word, relates to that part of your letter which says we expect due prominence to be given to the subject of liberty party. Now if by this it is meant that we are to make the liberty party as such a special object of attack, candor compels me to confess I am not a suitable person to be engaged in your service in carrying on the one hundred conventions. But if it means that I must as freely and faithfully expose the corruption of that party and it leaders—as I would expose the same in either of the great political parties,—I most heartily agree with yourself and the committee. I addopt the sentiment expressed so eloquently by yourself at the meeting of the american society. 'That we must carry our cause over the constitution of the United States, as well as over the heads of the political parties.'

With all else in your letter I most fully agree. And will gladly serve the cause under your direction, If it shall be your pleasure to employ me.

I have a few engagements to meet in Nov. which will take one week, after this I shall be at your service.

Yours Respectfully,
F. Douglass[19]

P.S.   Please write at Bradford N.H. at your earliest opportunity.
yours & c.
F. Douglas[s]

19. Douglass escaped from slavery in 1838.

40. From FREDERICK DOUGLASS

My Dear Mr. Phillips—I am glad to hear from you in any capacity whether it Be in the dignified character of a committee of *one* or in the affectionate character of a sincere friend. I have often thought of writing you a friendly letter since I came to this country and have only been deterred from assuming so much by my great inferiority to yourself. Do not scold me for this for I tell you the truth when I say that I have for you such grateful regard and admiration that I cannot bring myself to approach you familiarly. You have been to me a brother but so much more than a brother—in imparting to me information and good counsel that I feel more like a diciple to you, than a familiar friend. And this is by no means a painful feeling. I love to look up to you as such. Your advice to me on leaving the United States for this country I have strictly adhered to—I have not gone near the London Committee. I have acted in in every way independent of them and as if they did not exist. This course has made my path any thing but easy thus far—so far as the good opinion of that committee and those who sympathise with it is concerned. They look upon me with the same feelings with which they regarded yourself and Mr. Garrison in 1840. Still I have no reason to complain. I have got on thus far much better than I anticipated. I have sold some two thousand copies of my narrative—the proceeds of which together with what has been given me by friends who needed not to be solicited has put me quite at ease as to travelling expences, which by the way are very great in this country being about double to what they are in the U.S.

But to the business. You say C. L. Remond has presented a request to the Mass. Board to compensate him for losses in the cause the last four years or so.—And among those a horse which died in Pennsylvania—at the time of our one hundred conventions in the west. In regard to this last item you ask me the following questions (To wit) 1st Was the purchase of our horses an economical step &c. &c.

2d—Did it enable us to attend more meetings than we otherwise could have done.

3d—Were the localities such as friends would not have carried us from place to place.

4th—Was the travelling on horse back such a thing as a man with good judgement could have deemed for the best interest of the cause? Before answering these questions—Allow me to say that Mr. Remond did not travel with me. Nor was I with him when he bought the horse. He travelled with Mssrs. Gay & Monroe and I with Mr. Bradburn, and White. I cannot therefore undertake to

answer for him as to the need of his buying a horse. I can only
answer for myself. 1st I do not think it was an economical step—As
the travelling expences of my co-agents were I believe less than my
own. The second inquery and the third may be answered together
as follows—It is difficult to determine Whether in all cases we
could have got friends to carry us from place to place—for when
we got horses we had no need of asking them to do—or testing their
willingness to do so—the purchase of our horses might have enabled
us to attend more meetings—though I believe those who had no
horses attended as many meetings as I that had one. The fourth I
decline answering—Suffice it to tell you just why I bought a horse
at that time. I had nearly completed my western tour—having gone
through Indianna and the most of Ohio—and of course had been
carried by friends from place to place without any further expence
than that of occasionally stoping at Hotels. When about to leave
Ohio & finding that horse flesh was pretty cheap—I thought it would
not be a bad speculation to buy me a horse—with my own money—
bringing him on east. I supposed I could get a good price for him.
I bought one   I gave $40! for him, and deeming the labourer worthy
of his hire—When I had to put up at hotels I set his expences down
against the society—the faithful beast brought me from southern
Ohio to Philadelphia—a distance of 500 miles. There I sold him for
$50 to Mr. Purvis—Making just $10 on my speculation. There you
have in simple terms the history of my connection with horses
during that time. I had no idea when I bought the horse of making
the society a party to the losses or gains of my speculation—it was
purely an individual concern—and so I believe it was viewed by us
all at the time. Indeed, so far was I from supposing otherwise I hesi-
tated about charging the society with pay for my horse food. Feeling I had no right to charge a society with the keeping of a horse
which they did not othorise me to buy.

I am Dear Friend in great haste very truly[20]
Yours,
F. DOUGLASS
Glasgow 28th April 1846

20. Phillips and Douglass admired, but did not always agree with, one another. In 1853 Douglass claimed that Phillips treated him unfairly at a public meeting because he dared criticize Garrison. *Frederick Douglass' Paper* (Rochester), August 19, 1853. He referred to Phillips in his autobiography, however, as one "who has said more cheering words to me and in vindication of my race than any man now living." Douglass, *Life and Times of Frederick Douglass*, p. 376.

41. From WILLIAM CRAFT

1 2 CAMBRIDGE ROAD
HAMMERSMITH
LONDON
JAN[y] 26th 1858

DEAR MR PHILLIPS

A very dear friend of mine has just invented a very ingenious machine for blacking boots. & as there are several unprincipled persons in this country (among whom are Americans) that make a business of ketching up every new invention they can, & have it patented in foreign country & thereby unjustly deprive the inventor of the benefit of his own machine.

My friend has requested me to write to some respectable gentlemen in the U. States, whom I think may be so good as to have his invention patented in their own name, & hold it in abeyance for him till he has fully tested it in England, & can make it convenient to pay the large sum that the Patent Law of the States require of a Foreigner.

Therefore I take the liberty of enclosing you this note in the hope that you will be so kind as to have his machine protected for a short time.

My friend will be pleased to pay all expenses, & will forward you the specifications & the money as soon as he can learn the amount. Which by the way he has been informed is much less to an American than to an Englishman.

The gentleman has no desire to evade the laws of the U. States but simply wishes to prevent dishonest persons from robing him of the right to his invention before he is prepaired to have it brought out in America.

If it is not convenient for you to entertain the matter, will you be so kind as to try to get some suitable person who can?

If you will be so good as to state the sum of money required & also to give us a little information respecting the Patent Laws—I shall be extremely obliged.

My wife joins in grateful remembrances to yourself & to all the kind friends by whom you are surrounded.

Feeling that you are jenerous enough to pardon my intrusion

> I remain
> Your humble servant
> WM. CRAFT[21]

P.S. I enclose W. Wilson's note to me

21. The celebrated fugitive slave couple William and Ellen Craft had fled the South in 1848 disguised as master and servant. After living in Boston for two years they went to England, where they lectured successfully with William Wells Brown. Their experience in England is discussed in R. J. M. Blackett, "Fugitive Slaves in Britain: The Odyssey of William and Ellen Craft," *Journal of American Studies*, 12 (April, 1978), 41–62.

42. From WILLIAM WELLS BROWN

LONDON, SEPT. 28, 49

MY DEAR FRIEND

enclosed, is a check for ten pounds, which you will please get cashed and remit to Wm. C. Coffin, New Bedford, For my girls. Hereafter I shall remit through Baring Brothers and Co. I have made arrangements with them, but too late for this mail as they do not issue on Fridays. Geo. Thompson refered me to this house. I owe two small sums in Boston one to Bela Marsh the other to Geo. A. Curtis. I made an arrangement with them to wait until I sent the money. I will try to send the money for them by the next steamer, and Mr. Walcutt will pay the bills. My friends here, gave me an enthusiastic welcome last night at the Music Hall, I wish Father Mathew could have been there to have heard the applause that followed the words of condemnation heaped upon him, or in other words the applause with which that part of my speech was received that refered to his course upon the question of Slavery. He is condemned by all who speak of him here. He has lost his moral power. I took the skin off of them.

Please give my respects to all around the office   I shall send a letter to the Liberator by next mail.

Faithfully your friend
W. W. Brown[22]

W. Phillips

22. William Wells Brown (1813?–1884) escaped from slavery in 1834. After working for several years on steamboats on the Great Lakes, Brown became a lecturer and agent for the Western New York Antislavery Society. In 1847 his *Narrative of William Wells Brown, a Fugitive Slave* became an abolitionist best seller. He went to Europe in summer 1849 as a delegate to the Paris Peace Congress and for the purpose of lecturing on slavery in England. William Edward Farrison, *William Wells Brown, Author and Reformer* (Chicago, 1969). Father Theobald Mathew, famous for his temperance work in Ireland and England and a popular figure among the Boston Irish, had been condemned by Phillips for being soft on slavery. Irving H. Bartlett, *Wendell Phillips: Brahmin Radical* (Boston, 1961), p. 92.

43. From WILLIAM WELLS BROWN

DUNDEE, JAN 24TH
1851

DEAR FRIEND,

I have not heard from you for such a long time, that I begin to be of opinion that I am almost forgotten. You will see by the date of this that I am with the Scotch.

The Crafts and myself are paying a flying and short visit to the Highlanders, and the Patons and Smeals of Glasgow. Think we did the cause some good there.

Our Bazaar friends in Boston will be glad to hear that the new Ladies Society formed by Dr. Pennington in opposition to the Bazaar has received a death blow at our hands. Should I do no more in Scotland, the visit to Glasgow will repay me for comming to this part of the kingdom. Two of the Glasgow clergy spoke out well. The question of the writings of Mr. Garrison and H. C. Wright were the topics for discussion during the evening. The Revd. Mr. Scott said he would sooner work with H. C. Wright than with Pennington, who was never known to be a fugitive until he came to England where anti-slavery is popular. Dr. Pennington has done much to injure the Boston Bazaar, both in Glasgow and Edinburgh; he is the right hand man of Dr. Clandish or Candlish. As you have heard by the papers of the Glasgow meeting, I will let you judge of our reception there. I send you a paper to day, giving an account of our effort here.

I return to England with the Crafts, some time in Feb.

We defere a meeting in London until the arrival of our friend G. Thompson.

I delived a lecture on my painting on Thursday evening to 1600 persons. As a Yankee would say, the painting is a "*paying concern.*" The proffit of the Thursday evenings lecture being £ *12–6 shillings*. Enough on this point.

I send by this mail a draft for £ 28—and also, in a letter to Mr May another for £ 10—I sent the one to Mr May for fear that some dishonest post office clerk might do me as they did a short time since, steal my letter and contents. These drafts, though payable in London, can be sold at a *premium* in Boston, I suppose. If Mr Thompson returns soon, these might be of service to him instead of *U.S. Money*. And now my dear Mr Phillips, I have determined to see my daughters some time during the months of March or April, and as I cannot return to the United States with safety, I must get them to this country, and for this purpose I send the enclosed money. I shall write by this post to Mr Thompson and if he will see to them on the passage and you or Mr May will get them a passage on the same steamer with Mr Thompson, I think they can come very well without any other person with them. Clara is near 15 years, and Josephine near 12, and Mrs Fletcher would come with them to Boston. I dont think it possible to get a first class passage for them in any steamer, English or American. If you should get them a first class passage, they would most likely do them as they did H. H. Garnet put them on the steamers deck, in a state room alone. They would do the same if they should have only second class fare, Yet, after all I should rather they would have a first class passage, if they could be in the first class Ladies cabin. I have not sent money enough for a first class passage, and it is too late for to get another draft, but if I have time to send another before the sailing of Mr Thompson, I will send it. But I have an understanding with Mr T. and shall write him upon that point.

I dont know how my accounts in New Bedford stands, and therefore, I cannot tell whether I am in debt there, or not. But I wish all the demands against me to be paid up, and I will send by the next *mail* ten pounds more, which I am sure will be sufficient to pay all demands. If you should need this sum before the arrival of the next mail, if you will advance it, you may be sure of getting it by next post.

Mrs Fletcher will need a small sum to get the girls ready. Mr Coffin will let you know how my accounts are. And now my friend if you will oblige me in this matter, I shall be under many obligations to you.

If my girls do not come with Mr T—I must come home if for no other purpose than to get them and return. I do not expect to remain longer in England than when I can return with safety. But I can put my girls in a good school and that will be of great service to them. please drop me a line and let me your determination.

> In haste
> Yours with truth
> W.W. BROWN

W.P.—

My address is 13, Moseley street, Newcastle on Tyne, care of John
Manson[23]

23. White abolitionist sectarianism posed a problem for all black abolitionists. In
the first part of this letter Brown assures Phillips that he is supporting Garrison
while his black colleague, James W. C. Pennington, seems to be supporting the
anti-Garrisonian abolitionists. Andrew Paton and William Smeals were Brown's
patrons in Glasgow. George Thompson (1804–1878) was the most famous support-
er of Garrison in England and a member of Parliament from 1847 to 1852. Brown's
"painting" was a panorama depicting the evils of slavery.

44. From WILLIAM WELLS BROWN

PERTH
JAN. 31, 1851

MY DEAR FRIEND,

I wrote to you by the last steamer, and hope ere this, you have got
my letter.

I stated that I should send another draft by this post, for £10—for
the expenses and passage of my girls, provided my Mr Thompson
could see to them on the voyage, and my friends would see that they
were on the same steamer.

I send the enclosed draft for £12. This together with the £38
already sent will make £50. This I hope will be enough to pay up
what outstanding debts, that may be against me, on account of my
daughters, and to pay their passage. But should this not be sufficient,
if you will advance the required sum, I will forward the sum to
you by the return steamer. Should there be any after paying the
demands, you can send it to Mr Thompson. please write me a line.
My best regards to my friends in and about the anti slavery offices
and especially to our friend Mr Thompson. The Crafts are well, and
go with me to Aberdeen next week. They wish to be remembered
to all.

Your with truth
W. W. BROWN

W. phillips, Esq.

45. From WILLIAM WELLS BROWN

22 CECIL ST. STRAND

AUG. 8, 1851

MY DEAR FRIEND,

Your kind letter of the 17th inst. came duly to hand, and for which you have my best thanks.

I am more than obliged to you for the trouble you put yourself to, in making out the account of the receipt and expenditure of the different sums of money forwarded to you, and which I find to correspond with my own account   I have not yet heard from Mr Coffin.

My girls go to Calais, France, on Wednesday next. They go to an excelant boarding school. I met with your young friend Charles B. Sumner yesterday at Geo. Thompson's. He came over in 16 days. This was a quick passage. I saw the Chapmans and Westons the same day, also the Estlins.

You will see by the papers, that the "American Fugitive Slaves and their friends," had a grand turn out here, on the 1st of Aug. We gave Thompson a warm reception. The old Hero, made one of his best speeches, it was altogether one of the most enthusiastic meetings that has been held in London on the subject of slavery for years.

The Hall of Commerce where it was held is one of the most respectable Halls in the City, holding about fifteen or eighteen hundred persons.

It was jamed full, every part of it.

It was pleasant to see the faces of the Chapmans and Westons, in the room. Thompson seems to get on well in the Tower-Hamlets. He has avowed his intention to stand for a re-election in the event of a dissolution of parliament next year. How will this chime with his intended return to the "*Land of the Free*?" We shall try to get Charles B. Sumner into a good school.

The Crafts are well satisfied with their new home. Their vacation takes place next week, and they will come to town for a few days and then I shall see them. Spear is trotting about with a letter of introduction in one pocket from Webster and one in the other from Sir Geo. Grey. He makes little headway as yet. I fear he is not the man for the *mission*, if we can call it "a mission."

Father Hensen returns to day I understand that "snake in the grass," John Scoble, goes out with him.

You need to watch him, should he visit the states.

He is a great enemy of the American Society, and especially Mr Garrison. I dont often meet with him.

What mission of mischief he goes on, I cannot tell. But certainly nothing good.

Garnet is under the care of his mother Mrs Richardson of Newcastle and is but little [improved?].

"Burritt's Brotherhood Bazaar," which closed here last week, was a failure. Not more than 20 persons were in, at any one time. They did not sell goods enough, I understand, to pay the expenses of the affair.

Burritt is too much milk and water. He is neither a good Abolitionist, nor a pro slavery man in the general sense. He was in favour of admitting all persons to sit in the Peace Congress, but was out voted in the Committee. Since the failure of his Bazaar, his face looks considerably longer than it did before. But I must stop. The Queen prorogues her Parliament to day, at 2 o'clock, and my girls wants to see her.[24]

Yours very truly,
Wm Wells Brown

W.P. Esq.

24. Charles Spear (1801–1863) was a prominent American prison reformer. Josiah Henson (1789–1883), an escaped slave, was reputedly the original Uncle Tom of Harriet Beecher Stowe's novel. John Scoble was a clergyman and leading opponent of Garrison among British reformers. Henry Highland Garnet and his family were then living with Mr. and Mrs. Henry Richardson of Newcastle-upon-Tyne. Elihu Burritt (1807–1879) was a well-known American peace reformer.

46. From WILLIAM WELLS BROWN

22 CECIL STREET, STRAND
LONDON, SEPT. 1, 1852

MY DEAR MR PHILLIPS,

I feel confident that you will think me ungrateful in not writing for so long a time. However, the only alternative left me, is to confess my faults and claim a free pardon.

I am now in London resting and recruiting for the Lecturing season, which is just commencing. My daughters are in the "Home and Colonial School," in London. This is one of the best schools in the country, and where they train young women for teachers. My girls made but little progress in France, except in the Language. But are now doing well.

The Crafts are getting on finely at the Ockham School, where your young friend Charles Sumner is also a pupil. The Crafts bid fair to have an *increase* in their family. You have no doubt read the account of a suit brought by Box Brown against an editor for damages, in which he got a verdict for £100. The editor was certainly to blame, yet Brown is a very foolish fellow, to say the least. I saw him some time since, and he had a gold ring on nearly every finger on each hand, and more gold and brass around his neck than would take to hang the bigest Alderman in London. And as to ruffles about the shirts, he had enough to supply any old maid with cap stuff, for a half century. He had on a green dress coat and white hat, and his whole appearance was that of a well dressed monkey. Poor fellow, he is indeed to be pitied.

You have long since learned the news of the defeat of our friend of the Tower Hamlets. Few great men have lost position in every respect, more than Mr Thompson. I cannot account for it, yet it is the fact. No one regretted the result of the election as it regarded him, more than I. I gave him my tears, I could do no more.

A few of his friends are trying to get up an interest to present him with a Freehold house; but it like other attempts to aid him will fail. A paper to be called "The Metropolitan" of which he is to be the editor, is another scheme that will fall through. His case is a sad one, yet we must hope for the best.

If the publisher of my new book sends it to London in time, I will forward a copy to you by Miss Caroline. Although the work has been reviewed, it is not yet out. Should it be too late for Miss Weston, I will send it to you by the first opportunity. The work is published by subscription at ten and sixpence, or, about two dollars and a half. A high price, this, for a book from a fugitive. A cheap edition at five shillings is to be put out almost immediately. "Uncle Tom" is all the rage here. Seven different houses have published this wonderful book. The dearest edition is 7/6, or about one dollar seventy five cents per copy. The cheapest is 6^d—or eleven cents.

Miss Weston will tell you about "The Anti Slavery Advocate." We hope to make it take the place of the "A.S. Reporter." Mr. Estlin is the establisher of the "Advocate." I have seen much of the abolitionists of this country, and have a very high opinion of a great many. But above all, stands Mr Estlin. He has the most benevolent heart, of any one I have yet seen.

Elihu Burritt is doing little or nothing here. His movement appears to be asleep. You will no doubt see in the "Standard," a little account I give of a meeting with H. Clapp, in one of the Streets of the Metropolis. Where he is now, or what has become of him, I cannot tell! but believe he is in France. H. H. Garnet has accepted an appointment as missionary in Jamaica, where he is to go immediately. He can well be spared from this country, for he has done little more, since comming here, than to pander to the bad feeling of a few enemies of Mr Garrison.

I am thinking seriously of a return home, what do you think of the propriety of such a step? My old master Enoch Price was in London last year at the Exhibition. I did not see him, but he left his card with Mr Farmer. He looked for me, and I regret that I was out of town. Do you think I would be safe?

For some time I have turned my attention to Literature, and have got up some Lectures which I intend delivering before Mechanic Institutions through the country.

I have nine engagements already for the next month & October. How comes on my Gerrit Smith farm? I hope you will keep the tax paid up, and I will remit to you whatever you have to pay out. By the by I have never heard a word from W. C. Coffin, is it not singular? He is welcom to the one hundred and thirty dollars which he kept. I did not wish him to receive the money from you and hand it over to Mrs Fletcher, without paying him for his trouble. But I do think he should have written to me, and sent me his charges. However, he has "done the cause some service," and I forgive him. I must now close.

please remember me most kindly to my old friends, and believe me to be,[25]

> Yours very truly,
> W. WELLS BROWN

W.P.

25. Henry "Box" Brown had become famous as the slave who had himself shipped to freedom in a box. Brown's discussion of George Thompson relates to the latter's loss of his Parliamentary seat. John Bishop Estlin (1786–1855) was a noted surgeon and philanthropist in Bristol. The Charles Sumner referred to was probably a black namesake of the Senator.

47. From MRS. A. F. PILLSBURY

HILTON HEAD. S.C.
JUNE 29TH 1864

WENDELL PHILLIPS. *Esqr.*

SIR;

I take the liberty of sending you two pictures of an old man now residing on Hilton Head island, whose life has a strange historical interest. His name is Norice Wilkinson & he was a soldier in Toussaint L'Ouverture's army. I have gathered by questions & conversation some facts from his own mouth which I forward, as you will know their reliability.

Norice was born free at Porte Plate St. Domingo & is 78 years old. After Toussaint was taken & he had been three months in the mountains, with 18 others he was brought to Charleston. S.C. & sold into Slavery.

A Mr. Gaston came on board the ship & bought the lot. They were taken inland, & for many years, Norice was the "property" of the Stoney family, on this island—Was 18 years of age, when sold.—spoke French & Spanish & speaks it now, with charming accent.—Indeed, his English has the mellow coloring of those tongues.—Received four dollars per day for interpreting Spanish into French in application for "passes."

Says Toussaint's first general was Moyé—that he was told to take "Rigo" (or Arigo") Toussaint's enemy—Moyé tried two years & failed. "Sahlin" took him & Toussaint killed Moyé to give "Sahlin" his position. Says Bonaparte send 70,000 men, soldiers. "Know dey cant take Toussaint on shore"—"Fool him"—"Ask him on board to dinner, den take him!"

"Toussaint occupied a splendid *tree* story house"—"Sleep up dere" (third story) "Guard dere & dere & dere." (in each story) "Two big gun here & dere" (each side of door). "Toussaint rode a splendid bay horse" "dress beautiful"—Toussaint small man "Neber see him smile"—"Always seem cross" Call for generals" "Dey come, hold hat under arm," & he rose standing with his hat under his arm as if in Toussaint's pressence.

Toussaint stamp foot" using the gesture, "Had one favorite"—"Crabo"—"Dont stamp foot at him"—While relating these things he arose, gave the word of command in French—"En avant"!—"Porter armes"—"Presenter armes," saying he could go through every exercise now as well as when in St. Domingo—He said Toussaints soldiers were obliged to go to church, after church, they sung.—Then the old soldier sung most *perfectly* & spiritedly, Toussant's hymn,—the "Marsellaise"—One line was "*Vengo*.! Vengo"—"le pays, la liberte." At one time in Savannah, he was asked if he knew Toussaint's song?—Fearing the effect of its acknowledgement he

Photograph of Norice Wilkinson, who had fought with Toussaint L'Ouverture's army in Haiti. The picture was enclosed in a letter to Phillips from
Mrs. A. F. Pillsbury. See letter 47.

replied, "I forgot." The party insisted offering him five dollars to sing it. Tempted by the reward, he began, sang one half of a verse & said "I forgot." as he knew too well, how much the Southern hated its spirit of Freedom.

Norice is a noble soul & Slavery could not crush his manhood. He is very poor, cultivates cotton at .40 cents per. task. & lives with his son, now 58 years old, who was born two years after Norice was brought to Charleston.

I send an ambrotype, that, if desired, photographs may be taken from it.—You will pardon the length of this letter, as I thought the facts would interest one who has so highly honored the life of Toussaint L'Overture.[26]

Very respectfully,
MRS. A.F. PILLSBURY.

26. Phillips would have been fascinated by this account of one of Toussaint's soldiers, but he does not appear to have used it in his lecture, which was prepared before 1861.

2. Personal Philanthropy

BEFORE returning from Europe, the youthful Wendell Phillips promised his mother that he would "bear worthily the philanthropic" family name. Although it was not what his mother had in mind, Phillips's career can be seen as a long, consistent, and largely successful attempt to keep this promise. The Negro was his first but not his only client, and eventually Phillips became associated with scores of organizations supporting causes as diverse as temperance, prison and currency reform, and the rights of women, Irishmen, Indians, factory workers, and Chinese coolies.

In addition to his work with reform organizations, Wendell and Ann Phillips were heavily committed morally and financially to helping people on an individual basis. Although the door of their little Essex Street house may rarely have beckoned to friends and acquaintances for social occasions, it was always available to strangers in need. A former house servant, Mary Desmond, remembered a steady stream of visitors "constantly travelling up stairs to Dear Mrs Philips sick room receiving her aid." The striking picture that Mary Desmond also draws of the half-shaved Phillips rushing out of the house and down the street to obtain money for some unknown petitioner conveys the highly personal flavor of this kind of philanthropy.

Some of the people who came for help were poor and obscure, turning to Phillips as a benefactor of last resort. A surprising number, however, were simply middle class people down on their luck, some of them with far-fetched stories, who sought help from the wealthy Wendell Phillips as naturally as their counterparts today would go to the bank. A school teacher, living alone with an infirm mother, wrote, "A small fraction of your kingly income would buy me a home. True I have no claim on you, but will you not give me a small part when God has given you so much?" [1] A minister in Pocasset needed fifty dollars in a hurry and was willing to put up

1. Bell Russell to Wendell Phillips, July 19, 1866.

his library of some 200 choice volumes as security.[2] A man wrote for assistance with his plans for a sanitary bakery, a woman for help to establish a poultry farm.[3] A young soldier in 1861 wanted funds for a revolver, while a bankrupt bookseller-turned-performer needed money to buy an Indian headdress for his Hiawatha recitation.[4] The Blagden Papers do not reveal whether Phillips subsidized the purchase of the revolver or the headdress, but they do show the astonishing variety of requests made upon him, requests which he always tried to answer personally.

Legal training as well as money helped Phillips to play his philanthropic role. He spent much of his time as an executor of trust accounts, and his reputation as a successful legal and financial adviser was so well known that abolitionist friends frequently asked him for help. Writing to ask advice "and save lawyer's fees," Abbey Foster said that she and her husband often noticed "how eventually all of us abolitionists, consider you as belonging not to our cause only, but to our selves. It is your special business not only to attend all the conventions and meetings, to devise the ways and means for carrying forward our movement, to edit our papers etc., but also to help us individually." [5]

More often than not helping people individually cost money, and it was fortunate for Phillips that he had inherited money along with his philanthropic name. His wife's estate alone was enough to make him financially independent, and his share of his father's property added to that made Phillips, in Edmund Quincy's words, "very well off." In addition, there were lecture fees which would bring him as much as $3,000 for a single month's work. Phillips may or may not

<hr>

2. Rev. Richard Devens to Wendell Phillips, August 26, 1856.

3. John W. Sullivan to Wendell Phillips, January 17, 1872; Harriet F. Curtis to Wendell Phillips, August 1859.

4. Charles Smiley to Wendell Phillips, April 23, 1861; R. Spalding to Wendell Phillips, July 10, 1857.

5. Abbey Foster to Wendell Phillips, July 28, 1866. Marion C. Reed found almost 250 land transactions by Phillips in the Suffolk County Registry of Deeds. In about 90 percent of these he was acting as Executor or Trustee. The typescript list of these transactions is on file in the Boston Public Library.

have been one of the 1500 wealthiest men in Massachusetts as listed in a book of 1851, but it is clear that he had more to give away than most of his colleagues. When he died in 1884, he left only a modest estate of about $8,000.[6]

6. Irving H. Bartlett, *Wendell Phillips: Brahmin Radical* (Boston, 1961), p. 31. The $3,000 estimate is taken from a journal and account book which Phillips kept for 1867. The only precise figures available on his income are for 1864 when, according to records in the National Archives, Phillips paid $514.75 in federal taxes on a reported income of $12,353. This may not sound like much today, but in the middle of the nineteenth century when laborers made about a dollar a day and William Lloyd Garrison was struggling to get by on a salary of $1,200, it was a princely sum. For the valuation of Phillips's estate at his death, see Suffolk County Probate Records, 569:187.

48. From MARY DESMOND [CHALMERS]

WATSONVILLE SANTA CRUZ CO CAL

JULY THE 25TH 1876

To WENDELL PHILIPS ESQ

Sir I suppose you will hardly remember the writer of this letter but the impression that you and dear Mrs Philips have made on me more than twenty years ago while residing in your house will never be forgotten by me and I know it is recorded in Heaven your many acts of Charity to the poor and espessally to my Country People the world knows how your noble heart have been rewarded when you raised the slave to manhood yes you for I believe you elo- quence your unselfish noble purpose were watched by God and after years of trial to you for I think you were instrumental in the hands of God to raise the slave to manhood this is a late hour to congradulate you but I have often thought of doing so and as often said to myself it would be to presumtuous in me but a little incedent or the reading the letter of a boston correspondent to one of our daly papers which reads Wendell Philips out done himself in behalf of the old south he is grey his cheeks hallow he is getting old etc his many noble sayings I read every day in the papers but how little the world or newspapers know of the daily nay hourly acts of charity that is performed at his residence on Essex st in Boston where the poor are constantly travelling up stairs to Dear Mrs Philips sick room receiving her aid and comforting them how many annecdotes I can tell of you and Dear Good Mrs Philips which I observed and which I know the Angels in heaven have recorded ah I have seen philanthrophy but I tell some here with truth that the only real charity I have met with was in your house to every peopele of every nation in conversation last evening I said now gentlemen if a poor person came to the door to ask for alms and you were in the act of shaving one side of your face shaved and the other prepared to shave and you had to go out in a fashonble street to get that alms asked for would not you tell them wait untill you cleaned your face and you would be a good man an to do so yes but Wendell Philips would not wait to finish that part of his tilat but went out to the next store brought in a fave dollars and handed it to the beggar how many acts like this I have observed in you and dear Mrs. Philips sometimes I think I aught not have left her Mr Philips with what tears of gratitude I have read your lecture on O Connel your lecture flinging back his lies to that english historian Fraude by some accident or other I occasnally get some of your writings now Mr Philips I am going to ask you for a favor that is for your & Mrs Philips picture I have one child the issue of our marriage a boy thirteen years of age he is healthy intelligent we intend and can afford to give him a good education and if he grows to be a man I would like to show your picture to him and tell him to try and learn to follow your example so far as in his power to help the needy and oppressed as the great & good Wendel Philips have done for when he will appear before the judgment seat of Christ he will be told as much as you have done to my poor you have done to me enter the joys prepared for you (as the reward of your good work) for eternity hoping to hear from you soon

respectfully yours
MARY DESMOND

P.S. I heard a few years ago that Mrs Philips health was restored and that Phoebe was married and had a large family how glad I would be to see Dear Mrs Philips I was hoping that I could go east this summer but I am disappointed

Direct to Mrs Mary Desmond Chalmers
Watsonville Santa Cruz Co Cal

49. From THOMAS CASHMAN

STATE REFORM SCHOOL
WESTBORO MASS JULY 22/57

DEAR FRIEND
I take this opertunity to write you to inform you that I am well and hope you are the same. I was sorry that I could not see you when I

went to Boston I went to your office in Cornhill and the man there told me you went out in the country. When you see my father tell him that I would like if he would get me a place in Boston to work. I would like to work at his trade better than any other tell my brother to be a good boy and take good care of himself and I would like to know the reason he dont send the books and papers he promised me. And last but not least to my sisters tell then I am in good health and I hope they are good girles. I am here over two years and I would like verry mutch to get out. I dont know of anything more to say this time but Good bye

> yours truly,
> THOMAS CASHMAN

PS tell my father to give my respects to Mr. Prouty and I would like to know if he got the letter I wrote to him tell my father I wish he would writ once a month please answer this letter as soon as you can.

> T. CASHMAN

50. From THOMAS CASHMAN

> STATE REFORM SCHOOL
> WESTBORO
> JAN. 16, 1856

MY DEAR FRIEND.

I know take my pen in hand to let you know that I am well and hope to find you the same as this leave me at present. I would like to have you tell my father that I would like to have him come up and see me and fetch me up some things such as a handkerchiefs and some postage stamps to pay my letters with. And some money. I would like to have you tell my brother to come up and see me. I would like to know if he is at work now. I am doing well in my studies and in my work and in my writing. I send my love to you and all my father's family. Please to tell me if Mrs. Author and her sons are getting along and I hope that they are at work I send my love to my Aunts and my realations. I would like to have you send me up a pair of skates. and a pair of mittens. I would like to have you tell my brother to be a good boy and keep from all bad company. I would like to have you send me up some good books and some papers.

DEAR FATHER.

I would like to have you tell William Beard's father to send him up some things tell his sister to Come up and see him. He is well

> From Your affectionate friend
> THOMAS CASHMAN

51. From THOMAS CASHMAN

> STATE REFORM SCHOOL
> WESTBORO MASS
> AUGUST 13 1856

DEAR FRIEND

Having a few leasur moments i thought that i would ocupy them in writing these few lines to you to let you know that i am well and in good health and hope that you are the same. i do not know why my Father does not write to me I havent had a letter from him these 10 months and i do not no what keeps him from writeing to me if i could see him i would be contented. i am geting along verry well in my studies. i want to know if you have seen any of my friends yet. I am not at all sorry that I came here and I hope when I come out of here I will be altogether different than what I was when I came here for here I have every chance to improve and make my myself a better boy and I hope also I never will persue the course that I have persued I will now close my letter by hopeing this will find you in good health.

> From your Affectionate Friend
> THOMAS CASHMAN

52. From MRS. MARY BLAKE

ROXBURY   APRIL 20 1864

DEAR SIR

I beg you to excuse the liberty I have taken in addressing you as I do know you except by reputation but I could not think of any thing besides which appeared as wise to me; but I will state my case. I am a widow 50 years of age my husband was killed in the battl at Winchester Va about 2 years ago and I have no children of my own living; but have adopted a little girls 9 years of age. I hold in my own possession about 14 thousand dollars worth of personal property and about 3 thousand worth of real estate. We have always hired a house but I wish to own one of my own to live in, I have looked at several which are for sale and find but one that I like, and that owned by a woman and that is a nice house with 3½ acres of land attached scituated on 3 streets there is more land tan I wish but some time it might sell to the right kind of purchesers for house lots. I can have it for fifty one hundred dollars it is 11 miles from boston near the depo. The hous cannot be bought without the whole land. It is considered a fair price for the property the land yealds nothing but a crop of hay as there is but little fruit on the place. The hous is 14 years old has rented for $350 rents now for $200 without the land. The property is taxed at the rate of $13 on a thousand I cannot sell a part of the land to any one at present who would make the neighborhood pleasant. I depend entirely on the income of my property for a maintenance but my habits & tastes are not extravigant. My mind is in a sad dilemma to know whether to take the said place at $5100, or look farther for a lower priced place. Fifty one hundred dollars is a large sum to invest without endeavering to obtain the best of advice.

Now my dear Sir I have laid my case and circumstances before you and humbly beg your advice for my brain is not capable of knowing what would be judicious. I might have aded I have no one depending on me for suport except the little girl of whome I spoke

& also that there is no stable on the place nor do I intend to use one for any purpose.

I feel that i owe you many appologies for thus intruding myself on your time & notice but I counted very largely on your generosity. If you answer this please address Mrs. Mary Blake soon as convenient   Box 2648   Boston Post Office

Yours Respectfully

53. From G. H. COFFEY

Private

WILLIAMSPORT PA   MARCH 30 '70

MY DEAR MR. PHILLIPS,

You may be surprised to have me write you about myself—

I came here out of health—and remained hired, *not installed, boarding not housekeeping,* as I looked upon it as an experiment, as you know. The town, as all agree, will not grow much more for years. There are only a few Conglists here—all Presbyterians in my Chapel and they have built a new *Presby Ch* and wish their own. This decided me not to remain—As this fact was known it made some uneasiness, and a slander case made some feeling, and all decide me not to remain here at least, much longer. I have been sick and fear a large church as my old enemy, *indigestion* is upon me and will attack me severely under the demands of a large Church.

Yet I know my only success must be in a *large* field.

I have been had, on these accounts, and because I have gone through an *agony* of *doubt* on some *Church Dogmas* and do not like the way churches work, to think of seeking, for a time or altogether, some other employment. I confess when I am sick I fear *poverty* and think sorely of my children. I know it is rather late to begin any other business in life—I am 34—yet I am better fitted for some kinds of business than for the *managing* work of the ministry.

It occured to me that you might possibly open a door for me in some church field; or more probably in some secular work. I would

like newspaper life if I could support my family from the start and
have promise of success by energy and perserverance.

I am aware that I have no *claims* upon you and that my acquaintance is only one of life-long admiration, that was never before
connected with a selfish thought in relation to you.

I am ready to go any place and do any *honorable* work.

I should hope to have opportunity to make my education useful
wherever I went.

Hoping that you may be able to open a door

I am your Friend,
G. H. Coffey

54. From WENDELL PHILLIPS MARDEN

MONT VERNON   SEPT. 28/66

Mr. Wendell Phillips
Dear Sir.

I have heard several times that you helped poor boys. I would
like to give you an account of my past life and the reason of my
writing to you as I do.

I was born in this place. (Mont Vernon. New Hamp Hillsboro
County) Have lived here ever since I was named Wendell Phillips
Marden. I suppose for no other reason than that you are a great
man. I am now sixteen years old. I have been to school more and
less since I was eight years. I have not got a very good education
because I have not had many advantages. I would like to go to school
some more but dont know whether I can or not. I have been told
by many to write to you. They say you have helped a great many
boys. I *need* help and knowing you were so well off and seeing I
am your namesake perhaps I could get help from you.

Yours Respectfully.
Wendell P. Marden
Mont Vernon
N.H.

55. From DANIEL WOOD

GREAT FALLS JULY 13TH 61

Friend Philips for the last year or since the murder of John Brown
I have had my mind exercised much of the time in search of the
best method of liberating the slave and I wrote G. L. Sterns who
was Friendly to the John Brown movement that I believed I could
make a machine (Bird) that I could fly out South over their planta-
tions drop down call the boys to jump in and we would be out of
their reach before they could harm us for $500 I can make one that
could be worked by hand to carry two Persons and a modelle could
be made for $50 or less I received no answer but shortly after
Thadius Hyatt gave notice in the papers that he would give $1000
for the best flying machine We continued our experimenting and
last winter succeeded in producing a machine that would raise itself
from the floor and go ahead   at this time Mr N. C. Bean who is the
Mechanic wrote to the Cientiffic American what he what he had
done and making enquiry what the sise of the machine must be
to get the reward but received no answer I have been opposed to
taking the reward and would not under any circumstances other
than to use in experimenting upon the machine and motive power
which I design to use Electricity at pleasure taking it from the
Earth at pleasure or as we need making a self operating machine
the machine I think can be made for less than one hundred Dollars
but whether we can harness Electricity or not or the expence is
what we want to know will you mention this to some of the Heroes
of Harpers Ferry noteriety and write me the result   we have spent
every Dollar we can raise unless we can make a raise some way it
looks as though the whole thing would go down   you will ask why
not call on your Friends I will answer I have but few and they
are mostly poor   I have some that are in good circumstances but
they think me crazy and make many th[ink so?]   Gad if they should
require me to give a reccommendation of my character I can give it
and get nearly every person in town & vicinity who is acquainted

with me to sign it that I am Crazy as John Brown was that I was
first in the Temperance Cause and first in Abolitionism, Come
outerism & Spiritualism   you can ask Stephen S. Foster or Parker
Pillsbury and my apology for writing you is I read every thing I
see in the papers of your writing and I think you are as crazy as I
am   it has been generally believed by the people that the Air would
be navigated but when I tell them I can do it they turn aside and
say you are crazy what a pleasureable mode of conveyance how
convenient for John Brown to transport his Cannadians to Haty.
and their Cotton back   no danger of Privateers   will you send me
the Address of Thadius Hyatt I have been with him in sympathy
but have forgotten his wherabouts

Yours in truth love & Wisdom

DANIEL WOOD

3. The Politicians, The Press and the People

" I CONGRATULATE you heartily on Wendell's attack," Henry Adams wrote to his brother Charles Francis Adams in 1869. "Besides being a perfect gentleman he is a good thermometer. I confess always to a desire to do to him what we used to do to our dogs that misbehaved in the house—'rub his nose in it'." [1] Adams could afford to be condescending to Phillips, but politicians, especially those who opposed slavery, tended to treat Phillips with a kind of puzzled respect. On the one hand, as Charles Sumner pointed out, they found it hard to understand how Phillips could take such an active interest in their own behavior when he refused to vote himself. On the other hand, they suspected that he had genuine political influence, and like Henry Wilson and Salmon Chase, they sought to gain his approval.

For his own part Phillips saw nothing inconsistent in what he did. As a moral person he refused to take an oath or to vote for anyone required to take an oath to support a government that upheld slavery. As an abolitionist he sought to shape public opinion for moral ends. Believing with Tocqueville that majority opinion controlled American institutions and politics, he especially sought the ear of influential lawyers, ministers, editors, and merchants who helped to direct the course of public opinion at the local level. [2] He must have been gratified, therefore, to learn in 1856 that an Illinois lawyer by the name of Herndon had become almost a disciple and was doing some agitating of his own to get Phillips's speeches printed in book form. Herndon was Abraham Lincoln's law partner. Born in the South and brought up to hate abolitionists, he had been radicalized by the political developments in the 1850's and the eloquence of antislavery advocates like Phillips. Lincoln would not have shared his partner's enthusiasm, but the two Springfield lawyers would almost certainly have discussed and probably argued

1. Henry Adams to Charles Francis Adams, July 22, 1869, *Letters of Henry Adams, 1858–1891*, ed. W. C. Ford (Boston, 1930), p. 162.

2. Irving H. Bartlett, "The Persistence of Wendell Phillips," in *The Antislavery Vanguard*, ed. Martin Duberman (Princeton, 1965), pp. 102–123.

together over the merit of Phillips's work.

Eventually Phillips would denounce Lincoln along with Chase, Wilson, Sumner, and almost every other prominent Republican. Politicians were not to be trusted. Given a choice, they would always sacrifice principle to interest and compromise on moral issues. What Phillips saw happening as the federal government took control of the South during and after the war, and the horror stories of Reconstruction related at first hand by his abolitionist friend A. G. Browne, must have infuriated but could hardly have surprised him. Left to its own devices the American political system invariably became corrupt. What happened to poor Browne was a perfect example of what would always happen when the moralist tried to work from inside the system. The proper role of the agitator was to remain outside and force the public to come to grips with the moral implications of their political behavior.

When Phillips began his career, it was difficult for abolitionists to find an audience, as the letter of 1839 from Ann Phillips's friend Octavia explains. One of the reasons that he later perfected what some people called "the eloquence of abuse" is that attacks on famous leaders made news. One of the following letters shows that editors sometimes tried to muzzle Phillips, but by the time of the war his speeches were widely read and publishers were competing for the exclusive right to put his invective in print. Knowing that an explosive outburst of the famous Phillips rhetoric could sell tens of thousands of papers, an enterprising editor sometimes planted the seed himself, as Theodore Tilton did when he told him that the President was confessing to doubts about having issued the Emancipation Proclamation.

Although there was a time during and just after the war when Phillips's radicalism seemed to flow with the mainstream of American opinion and he had easy access to the most powerful people in Washington, he spent most of his career as a dissenter, sometimes a very lonely one. Like most dissenters, he never lacked for enemies. Some of his hate mail, like the comment on the impeachment petition below, is cryptically obscene. Some, like the letter which condemns the "fanatical schemes of you and your myrmidons" clearly reveals its middle class origins. These letters must have amused Phillips. It was not possible to intimidate him, and he loved to turn the table on his enemies, as he apparently did in the case of the angry slaveholder who sent him a lock of hair from "the head of that *Thief* & *Murderer* John Brown."

Surrounded as he was by strong-minded reformers as doctrinaire in their own way as himself, it was inevitable that Phillips should have been criticized by his colleagues. The bantering reproach of Elizabeth Cady Stanton is written in a good humor that did not always characterize the differences of opinion which flared up between him and the feminists. As his letter to Tilton indicates, Phillips tried to accept criticism from friends in a constructive spirit. This would certainly have been the way in which he read George Smalley's letter protesting his infatuation with Frémont. Phillips would listen to critical friends but he did not often change his mind.

An unreconstructed Calvinist who frequently reminded his audiences that he did not expect to find perfection in this world, Phillips still believed that if exposed to it often and long enough the people would see the light. The last set of letters in this section must have reinforced his confidence in the moral strength of rank and file Americans who looked to him as a beacon—Albert Browne, who told him about the conspiracy between greedy Yankees and malevolent slaveholders in South Carolina; the abolitionist teacher Sallie Holley; Private Reuter, who had made heroic sacrifices to enlist in the army and only wanted to be put in a place where he could do some good; the Virginia seamstress who had used her own money to buy spellers for the freedmen; or the man who in 1857 was courageous enough to mail a letter in Noxubee County, Mississippi asking for copies of the *Liberator*. Phillips was proud to be known as a leader and spokesman for such people, and it was his belief in them as well as his faith in the will of God that compelled him to say in the long run liberty would know "nothing but victories."

56. From CHARLES SUMNER

COURT ST   FEB. 4TH 1845

MY DEAR PHILLIPS,

I have read your pamphlet with the best attention that I could command, & regret that, agreeing with you in so much that concerns our relations to slavery, I must differ so decidedly from your conclusions with regard to voting, & otherwise acting under the Constitution of the United States.

I know of no Constitution or form of Government, in the world, from the ancient rule of China to the most newly-fashioned republic of our hemisphere, which does not sanction what I consider injustice & wrong. All of these Governments, for instance, sanction war, which is a sin as hateful & mischievous as that of slavery, productive, like the latter, of immoralities of the worst character, subverting the happiness of thousands, dissolving families, dooming to death women & children, & poisoning the soul with bad passions.

But because Governments lend their sanction to what I consider unjust, shall I cease to be a citizen? Shall I not rather, so far as in me lies, according to the humble measure of my ability, by the various modes in which I may exercise any influence among my fellow-men, by speech, by the pen, by *my vote*, endeavor to make an alteration in the Constitution, to expurgate the offensive passages? I think that you would *speak* in favor of an alteration of the Constitution, why not *act* in favor of it? Take your place among citizens, & use all the weapons of a citizen in this just warfare.

You already support the Constitution of the U.S. by continuing to live under its jurisdiction. You receive its protection, & owe it a corresponding allegiance. In simply refusing to vote and to hold office you proceed only half-way under your own theory. You should withdraw entirely from the jurisdiction; you should sever the great *iron cable* of allegiance, & not content yourself with cutting & snipping the humbler cords, by which some of your relations to the Constitution are regulated.

But what new home will you seek? Where, in the uttermost parts of the sea, shall you find a spot which is not desecrated by the bad passions of men, embodied in acts & forms of Government?

Our lives are cast under a Constitution, which, with all its imperfections, secures a a larger proportion of happiness to a larger proportion of men, than any other Government. Let us, then, continue to live under it; but, living under it, to strive in all ways for its purification. I am mindful of what our master Lord Coke says: "Blessed be the *amending hand*!"

Do you not feel animated by the results of the recent Convention? The people of New England will be lifted up to the new platform of Anti-Slavery, & all must join in the reprobation of Slavery.

I listened to Garrison with an interest, hardly ever excited by any other speaker. His position before that audience, as well as his words, spoke eloquently for him. I voted against his motion; but was most sincerely glad that he made it, & that he had so good an occasion to explain his views.

I abhor the bravado, & threats of the South. I hope we shall not imitate them in launching these *bruta fulmina*; but when the occasion occurs, let us *act*. If Texas be admitted, let us *then* consider, whether we can properly remain in the Union. It may be that this conclusion against Garrison's motion is to be referred to my native hue of *ir*resolution, which leads me to postpone action on important matters.

But in earnest opposition to slavery, I may almost assume the complacency of a veteran, while I survey the new-born zeal by which we are surrounded.

To you & your friends belong the honor & the consolation springing from the great spread of Anti-Slavery.

When shall I see you to converse on these things?

Pardon my freedoms & believe me, dear Phillips,[3]

with great regard,

Sincerely Yours,

CHARLES SUMNER

3. Sumner is criticizing Phillips's pamphlet, *Can Abolitionists Vote or Take Office Under the United States Constitution* (New York, 1845). Phillips's reply to this letter is discussed in Bartlett, *Wendell Phillips: Brahmin Radical* (Boston, 1961), p. 122.

57. From WILLIAM H. HERNDON

SPRINGFIELD, ILLS. SEPTR. 28, 1856

MR. PHILIPS

DEAR SIR

About two years since I wrote you a short letter, and you were kind enough to answer the questions asked. I now give you my thanks for the favors then confered. Though not acquainted with you and differing with you in politics, yet I know your kindness will overlook these differences and leap to the man, who is like yourself struggling for the advancement and development of the whole race of man.

You may want to know how things are moveing here in Illinois; and I propose to State how things look and how the fire-spirit feels. The heat & power come down to us from the North—Chicago and infloods us with warmth & intelligence. The waves of this light advance further daily—flashing into Egypt. Had we a few months longer to go on I think we would Carry this State for Fremont. Were the Republicans and the Americans to join, we could easily, now—at this moment, carry the State for Fremont. You may not hope as I feel & hope; yet the facts are as above stated. There is a chance for Fremont as it is, but either of the above alternatives would make it absolute. Two years since I never dreamed of this world-rush for reform; and if we shall advance as fast for the next two years as we have for the last two,—then there will be a grand earth-wide revolution. I mean the mind would be prepared to sow the charities, the hopes, the dignities and duties of man. This is the first thing: the teachings and developments are easily done. This progress—this advancement and development are the Causes why I say that Fremont stands a chance to be Elected. Two years since almost any man would have been burned for advocating the Republican plat-form in Illinois and most assuredly so if charged with abolitionism—Clap-trap & c. The world moves and Philips may see the day when he can say—the world does move—does it not?

Men, consciously, out here feel that the chains are broken: this is *now* but a sentiment; but will soon grow and expand into an idea which will work with a flame-like power in the future. The idea will before long work itself into a logical form; soon to be *booked* by philosopher & patriot and sent abroad to the schollars—the children—the future great men of the world. Men feel—cannot logically explain—the verge wave of the Good—the Beautiful & the True. Now more than in all the ages before. The world does move—it heaves as with a central fire-force.

My immediate object in writing this letter is this:—Are you not going to Collect, *soon*, your speeches and have them published in bound vols for the young which are to come after you? When will you do it? I in common with thousands of others ask you to do so: —pray do so.

Yours truly
W. H. HERNDON[4]

Private

I refer you to Theo Parker or Senator Sumner for personal character if more is wanted.

---

4. In his book on Lincoln, Herndon claimed to have been in correspondence with Phillips and other abolitionists in the early 1850's and to have read and discussed their speeches with Lincoln. William H. Herndon and J. W. Weik, *Abraham Lincoln: The True Story of a Great Life* (New York, 1901), II, 32. To the best of my knowledge the Blagden Papers yield the first documentary evidence of the Herndon-Phillips correspondence. The assistance of Professor David H. Donald in reading Herndon's hand is acknowledged with gratitude.

58. From WILLIAM H. HERNDON

SPRINGFIELD, ILLS. MARCH 9, 1857

Mr. Philips

  Dear Sir

Is any person writing a history of the Anti-Slavery progress?—
or has any person written such a book? if so, will you please tell
me *who* or *what*—Such a book is very much needed just now.
The whole subject is old to you, and more familiar than an "old
shoe" or a good, long-tried friend: it is part and portion of yourself:
it is you and friends. People in the future will thank God and you
for it. Your day is not yet—it is coming: the grey firey streaks have
commenced flashing and needling in the eastern horizon, soon to
flood the world with light. When this glowing light shall come;
so bright that the "Consensual" twitch of the eye shall close to
prevent the "excess of light"—then your day will be—not before.
Bear up, my Friend, and hug this Consolation. A few years since
I hated—say 1853—the very name of Anti-Slavery: never hated
men in my life; loved the race. I was born in and reared partly at
the South; hence my hate to agitation. But thank the "Stars" or
better still, thank God, that this obstructive malice has gone off,
and I am now prepared *to see*. I never loved slavery, yet I had deep
seated prejudices. O—what a change has come over me! Were you
to ask the question—"Herndon where are you going to Stop" I could
not answer to save my life. This depends upon the movements of
the South. I do candidly believe that this whole slavery question
ends and begins here—Universal freedom for all the race, or universal
despotism for *white and black*. *This* is the question, and the solution
is *here*—Peace or—War. The South have it in their own hands, and
can have peace or war. "God save the Queen"— God and man will
save freedom or die in the ditch. What say you to all this. I do not
want to see war; nor do I want our Union dissolved. My nature
cries peace at every pore—yet my reason says, that peace may be
purchased at too dear a price—that Life—Liberty, & the pursuit of
happiness may be ingloriously sacrificed under the piping, whining

cry of "*peace*"; when there is a subtle and cunning power waging war silently beneath this surface—peace; attempting to chain my body and crush my soul. Peace I want.

We have just this moment heard from the Sup^m Court of the U States: it has decided the "Dred Scott" Case; their decision is unfavorable to freedom. They decide that Slavery is almost national —slaves may be taken anywhere and kept—& c. This I had always supposed would be the case. *What are we to do?* It will soon be decided that Slaves may be taken and held in Boston and reared —yes and "*got*," beneath the shade of Bunkerhill monument. *How do you like it?* Whips and Chains around Bunkerhill—Eh? *What think you?* I once thought that the boast of Toombs, was simply a boast—an out-gush of gin; but I am rather distressed to think he was not "*a-dreaming*": he is a "cute" fellow—knows ahead of time: quite a gift, this. I try to be merry, yet there swells and rises up this question, within me—*What shall we do?* I have no answer to give and bid it down, and soon there comes this question—*What shall we do?* This is honestly and literally true.

Kansas is in trouble again and it was whispered into my ears a day or so ago—that the free people would let the Elections—Conventions & c. go by default; and so soon as Kansas was a State, that the People would *reform*, or if you will *Revolutionize*. I do not see much hope in any way. I have my doubts as to Kansas being a free state. The Slave States will make it just what they want. If it is to their advantage to make it free, it will be free;—otherwise it will be a slave state. All the free men in the Universe cannot make that Territory a free state, if the Slave drivers want it Slave, Except in one way—Rebellion—War. There is no use to lie to you—do no good. They have got the cards packed and can turn "*jack*" when and for whom they please. Free-States men are fooled if they think that numbers will do any good—in peace. Justice—Liberty—Good Lord people, hush. "Long live the Republic"!

Will you please have the kindness to answer my first queries, and the others if you will. I hope you will. Give my best

respects to Mr. Parker—send this to him, if you want to—when I
say private I do not mean to include him. — Private —

W. H. Herndon

59. From WILLIAM H. HERNDON

SPRINGFIELD, ILLS. MAY 12, 1857

Mr. Philips
   Dear Sir

   "That is a curious chap out west, writing to me"—says Mr.
Philips; and to which that chap says—"Cannot help it". I want
to ask you a question—Is that resolve of yours a just one, or an
unjust one? The resolve is about this—"I try to make my friends
write to me and yet not to answer them." I say is this just?—is it
fair? Do you love to put a man in hot irons and see him crisp? I
hope not:—then alter your cruel resolve and write. Since I wrote
to you I have been in Court pretty much all the time, and have not
much news to state, yet I must say a word to you by way of
encouragement. Since the *"Decision"* in the *"Dred Scott Case"*
many and many a man has changed from the nigger-driving gang—
has changed his way, and is now and will forever be a free man,
doing God's service of aiding and energizing human liberty, and
assisting man to get his rights. Our ideas of human rights and human
duties are becoming more and more expansive—more and more
liberal. People are brave enough to look the names of Theo. Parker
and Wendl Philips in the face; and no howl from the nigger driving
gang can much terrify our people. Thank God, *that* series of terrors
is gone. The people have crawled up the hill and can now look
down and over the subjacent plains; and see and gather at a glance
all the ideas and principles that constitute our foundation elements.
They see the main currents—the surface currents—the transverse
ones, sweeping north & south, and thus seeing all and feeling all,
there are no terrors in naked truth. Their ideas of human rights and
human duties are a *Becoming*—they are being embraced by thou-

sands whom I never supposed would do so. In our prairie State there are no commercial ties—no hunker families—no crystalized State of society that we cannot burst through or overthrow with a push or a whiff, if we see proper so to do. Our people are honest and all they want is *light—light—time*—time. Light & Time are great forces, aiding the onward sweep of truth: they are entities of great value, gemming the deep immensities of progress. Our Slave getting friends are looking "sorter" humble and condescending just now. —Hypocrisy is their leading trait—past—present—and future—must be so from the very nature of their calling. Truth would choke them—light would blind them.

You remember, I wrote to you sometime since a glowing description of Spring—I wish I had not done so—as we have been paid for it sence. The whole affair from that day to this has been a firie-frost dance, sarabanding and whirling up and down giddily, to see if it cannot provoke a quarrel and have a fight out of our People. Things—in the vegetation line, look sad. I am now in my office writing this letter, with a good hickory fire in the stove and several good jolly fellows keeping it warm. Lincoln—the joker—the funny man—is cracking his jokes:—he beats Hale to death *in that line*. By the by—do you know Lincoln? as we say west he is a "hoss" I am the runt of the firm and no "hoss," yet I suppose will pass among the crowd as a Liberty lover—a fool and a Reformer. This is a happy position—is it not? In fact our Spring is "Sot back" several weeks and things that shot up bravely are arrested in their march and development. They look sad crisped and, as it were, scorched. If Spring do not come quickly and send us a thrill I do not know what the fields and forests are to do. How is our friend Parker? Is he getting better? Is he very sick? or is he only prostrated by over mental exertion? *No wonder*—he has so much power—does him so much good to strike and crush a hoary error—*that he is exhausted*. He is a man—yes a double man—a double star with dual light and power. I hope he will soon recover and be well. I hope he is now forging his hottest—heaviest—grandest, bolt to hit slavery with. I want to see the accursed — d——d thing Killed, blasted, scorched and sent "*Hellwards*" for I am not safe while a human chain rattles & clanks upon a human Shin—No man is—No man can be. War to the knife—war to the hilt is its motto.

By the by, are you doing anything—what is it? You said you made me your confessor and now shrive yourself—What are you doing? How did Emmerson do in filling Parkers place a Sunday or so since? Emmerson is a pretty great man. In his way he is a transcendent genius. I hardly know as great a man. He is a greater man than Carlyle. He has not as much power, but more genius, he has. What say you? Write or I will get roaring mad.

Your friend

W. H. HERNDON

60. From WILLIAM H. HERNDON

SPRINGFIELD, ILLS. NOV. 26TH, 1860

MR. PHILIPS—

DEAR SIR:

It has been quite two years since I have written to you. At one time I said I would never write to you again. The reason was this:—You did not treat me well—did not even come to see me, whilst in Boston. But let all this pass, and if possible be forgotten. What I want to say to you is this: Another presidential Canvass will soon be upon us, and to assist the world you must publish your speeches: they are absolutely needed; they will be educative of the Spirit of 1864. If you can do no better let them be published which you have delivered since 1850. Let those be an unauthorized edition, if you so will, but let them come in some shape—how questionable soever. Others may teach the moral side of the question—some may teach the politico-economical side; and some one side and some an other; but ONE of your sides is equally beneficial—namely a soul hate of Slavery, decked in the eloquence of an armed vengeance, speaking in tones that make the tyrants quail. There are some few men—a good many men in the west who do and can understand you or any other man. Some are lawyers—Editors—speakers, & c. & c. and all these want your *live* speeches—must have them. What say you to this polite and natural request? We should like to have all your Speeches, but if we cannot get all we will take what we can get. This is moderate, is it not?

I have read your late Speech on the Election: it is eloquent, but not without a sea of hope rolling in it. My students read it with pleasure, all ablaze. So it runs.

My beau ideal of man—my model of our race is gone—Poor Parker.

Please answer this, stating what you think of doing. You may consider your letter *private.*[5]

Yours Truly,
W. H. Herndon

5. Herndon visited Boston in the spring of 1858 where he was cordially received by Garrison but brusquely treated by Parker and apparently ignored by Phillips. He refers here to Phillips's speech of November 7, 1860, which appears in *Speeches, Lectures and Letters*, First Series (Boston, 1863), pp. 294-319. Theodore Parker died on May 10, 1860.

61. From WILLIAM H. HERNDON

SPRINGFIELD, ILLS. DEC. 28TH, 1860

Mr Phillips
Dear Sir:

Your short letter is this moment received. You need not fear concession, nor secession. Neither will take place during your life time. To be mild but firm is not concession, nor do bluster—threats, & whisky make secession. You do not give the Republicans credit for anything. You forget that a young vital courageous civilization has burst up behind "Old Whiggery," commanding it— "Onwards & upwards": Republicanism must obey or perish.

Lincoln is "Jackson redivius" and though you may not believe it, I say to you, that Mr. Lincoln has a superior will—good Common sense, and moral, as well as physical Courage. He will in my opinion, judging from his nature, make a grave yard of the South, if rebellion or treason lift its head: he will execute the laws, as against Treason & Rebellion. If I had your private Ear close to my lips I could tell you much that bears on the present crisis.

Yours Truly

W. H. HERNDON

62. From WILLIAM H. HERNDON

SPRINGFIELD, ILLS. FEB. 1ST, 1861

MR PHILLIPS—

  DEAR SIR:

   Some few days ago I rec'd your late Speech. It was truly—it *is* truly an excellent & eloquent Effort. How different in tone—pluck & ring from Seward's late oration. I do not agree with you in your disunion views   Still I see that disunion is Freedom to the slave. Given therefore—the sequences follow from the premises. God speed the day of universal liberty—the freedom for all mankind —the Divine right of every man to govern himself for himself by himself. Your speech is a grand summing up of the world's highest experiences—a kind of philosophic *resuma* of what Phillips has often said in fragments before.

   I really sympathize with you in your troubles in Boston. What is to become of Boston? Is she drunk & crazy? Go on and stand up for the Liberty of speech right in Boston; & if necessary summon some of our western rifle men to assist you. You are not speaking alone for your own benefit—nor for the advantage of this age: but for the benefit of all men during all the ages. Be firm. Your day will come soon. I have just read the proceeding of the Boston mob & how shameful! Our merchants here are angry—mad —indignant; and they swear by all the gods that they will mark

those timid, cowardly, & truckling pro-slavery merchants of Boston.
I hope they will Spot them & keep them *Spotted*.

Our western men are still true as steel and are opposed to all
compromises of every nature. I told you once, if not oftener that
the great wide west would never flinch—never cower—never
back down. I told you at the same time that the East would, and
lo up pops Adams—up shoots Mr Seward! How shameful—how
deeply humiliating. I have just counted on my slate the number of
those men who help *here* to create courage—who make backbone—
who give vigor and fire to the crowd; & I find they stand Southern
men—say four brave Southerners to one brave Yankee. It is strange.
How do you account for it? The Southern men here are the most
genuine & truest anti-slavery men; and Oh! how they curse a
cowardly Yankee. Excuse me & don't get mad. The truth is the
truth, and I cannot do otherwise than speak the truth, as I see it—
know it.

Lincoln is still true—as firm in his convictions of Justice—Right
—Liberty as the rocks of Gibraltar. He has been approached here
for Compromise—Crittenden's border state one—Douglas', & c. & c.;
but he says—"Away—off—begone!" In substance he says—"If the
nation wants to back down let it—not I." I will, I hope, see you eye
to eye, and then I'll tell you to whom this nation is somewhat indebted for some of Lincoln's courage—for some brave words spoken
by Lincoln—& for some of his brave acts—This sentence—the last
few words are private *now*. So keep them housed till the right time
comes.

What in the d——l do the Representatives of Mass mean by sending delegates to Virginia to babble and twaddle over a subject that
God has said millions years ago shall exist—boil & bubble till Freedom or slavery is overthrown. Do not these men know that the
South will get the advantage by cunning, by fraud or by gold. Do
you expect to be dealt honestly & fairly with in a land of thieves. I
do not say that the south are thieves—yet the figure will do to
explain an idea. I am glad Sumner is true. Our Governor kicked

the resolutions—the Virginia ones and all applications to attend such conventions out of doors. He is a brave "Kentuck boy." [6]

Excuse me.

Yours Truly,
W. H. HERNDON

6. In January 1861, Phillips continued to advocate disunion before large, hostile crowds and was regularly threatened by Boston mobs. The Virginia "resolutions" refer to the 1861 Virginia call for a Peace Convention.

63. From WILLIAM H. HERNDON

SPRINGFIELD, ILLS. JULY 8TH, 1865

WENDELL PHILLIPS

DEAR SIR:

I thank you for your kind letter & speech made in Tremont Temple. The letter which you sent back to me was mailed to you by mistake. I thank you for it too. The reason why I wrote to you was—I can't get one man in a thousand in Boston to answer a note, asking some simple questions—postage enclosed. Hence I addressed you. Garrison will *never* answer my note. I once said to my friend Theo in a letter that Mr. Garrison was not a *great* man in the true sense of the word great—ie that he had no great generalizing mind—great in the sense that Newton was great. I suppose he got mad. I once said that Garrison was an obstinate man and I suppose he got huffed at that &c. You say in your note that I did not like your speeches. This is a great mistake. I like none so well— none are so classical—none so eloquent—none so sharp—none ring so like gold and now why should I not like them. I may have said that you did not exactly *hit* Lincoln's character. I saw & read your Speech on his death: it was eloquent—yours & Emmerson's are the very best made on Lincoln. I honestly say this much.[7]

Your Friend
W. H. HERNDON

7. On April 23, 1865, Phillips delivered a muted eulogy for Lincoln, claiming that his assassination was Providential because "The nation needed a sterner hand for the work God gives it to do." *Speeches, Lectures and Letters*, Second Series (Boston, 1891), pp. 446–454.

64. From WILLIAM H. HERNDON

Court Room Desk No 2
SPRINGFIELD, ILLS. JULY 24TH 1865

MR. PHILLIPS
MY DEAR SIR:

Your kind letter is this moment received, and for which I am much obliged. If there was anything in my letter scolding the men of Boston I take it back. They are & have been my teachers & masters: are the teachers & masters of America, and soon to operate on a world wide scale, if they have not done so for the last 50 years. Thank God for Boston brains! The New England men are not perfect beings, but with their imperfections they are the conserving fire that keeps faith from freezing. I *do* wish that you were all a little more spontaneous—generous—sociable & jovial. *We* of the west are spontaneous—generous—sociable & jovial. *We* leap forward to anticipate all wants. *You* ask what it will pay. However take you all in all, God bless you. You are the Educators of the world & the teachers of mankind. *Make 'em hum*. I remain still a strong progressive—on-going upstanding abolitionist.

Your Friend,
W. H. HERNDON

65. From HENRY WILSON

NATICK, JUNE 6TH, 1857

WENDELL PHILLIPS ESQ.

DEAR SIR,

On my way home from a trip to Kansas I read in the Anti Slavery Standard your speech before the Anti Slavery Society at its late anniversary in New York. I was much surprised to find in your speech this expression:—"If Henry Wilson thinks that Slavery is to be abolished by abusing us on the floor of the Senate, God increase ten-fold his power of abuse, and let him pour it on our devoted heads"! I assure you I read this sentence with surprise and pain. Never in the Senate or out of it by word or pen have I uttered an abusive word of the Anti Slavery Society. If I have done so I am utterly unconscious of it, and I would be under great obligation to you if you would refer me to any reported words of mine in which I have abused you or your friends. If any such words have been anywhere written or printed I am sure they have been manufactured for the purpose of misrepresentation. I have differed from you and your friends—not I trust in love of freedom and hatred of Slavery or in zeal for the cause of the poor bondsmen of my country—but in regard to views of the constitution & modes of action; but everywhere before your friends and in face of your enimies I have spoken of you with entire respect and with sincere regard. In the Senate and before the people I have been called upon to point out the differences between us but I have done so by always giving you credit for great talents, lofty character and self-sacrificing devotion to the cause of the Slave. I have done this too where it would have better served the cause of the friends with whom I act to have denounced you and your friends. Your positions, words and acts are put before the people in some portions of the country and we are held responsible for them by the people who are ignorant of the anti Slavery movement. When called upon to show your position and to define ours I have spoken, as I know my heart dictated with entire fairness and justice.

I have been rather severely criticized by your friends during the past few months. I have borne it all although I have sometimes felt that I was rather hardly delt with. That some of your blows have caused pain I am free to admit. While I can look foes in the face and hurl defiance at them I have little of that feeling that can receive unmoved the censures of friends. Of fair criticism I do not complain, I hope to profit by it, but words have been uttered by some of your friends that seemed to me to be unjust and intended to wound my feelings. But I have made up my mind and taken my position. I shall not be unjust even to those who have been unjust to me. At all times and in all places I shall when duty requires it explain the differences between you and our friends but I shall indulge in no misrepresentations, denunciations or reproaches. If I have blows to give they shall be given to the oppressors of the bondsmen of my country—not to men I know to be the friends of the Slave, although I may not agree in their modes of action, and may feel their blows—blows that I may think ought rather to be aimed at the head of the oppressor, not mine. I shall do this because it is in accordance with the dictates of my heart and the convictions of my judgement, and in the confidence that I can better serve the cause of Liberty and I may add in the hope—though it may be a vain one—that when my race is over the friends of the Slave may acknowledge that I at least endeavored to serve the cause of the oppressed.

Yours truly,

H. WILSON[8]

8. Henry Wilson (1812–1875) had come into the Republican Party by way of the Free Soilers and Know-Nothings and had been a Senator from Massachusetts since 1855.

66. From HENRY WILSON

NATICK, JUNE 28, 1857

WENDELL PHILLIPS ESQ.

DEAR SIR,

Your note came duly to hand and I write now to say that I should be glad to meet you some day and talk over these matters. If you can do so I will at your convenience arrange a meeting.

I do not think we disagree quite so much as we may seem to—at any rate I should like to see you and to talk over some points. I wish fully to declare to you that I have never intended to say a word in or out of Congress that you or your friends could regard as disrespectful. If you are at Framingham on the 4th I may see you.

Yours truly,

H. WILSON

67. From SALMON P. CHASE

WASHINGTON, DEC. 26, 1862.

My dear Sir,

I never saw you; but I must obey the impulse which bids me thank you for your most eloquent article on Daniel Webster, which I have just read in the Liberator. Your censures are just: but I cannot help wishing that they had been relieved by a portraiture of the better qualities of his heart. He was, in earlier manhood, my father's friend. In my own commencing public life he showed some personal kindness to me. While, therefore I acquiesce in the justice of your stern judgment of his great apostacy, I acquiesce mournfully and wish for some drops of melting charity mingled with the flashes of just indignation.

How earnestly—how more than earnestly do I wish that you could act with us! Oh, if we could but have your voice to cheer us on in our battle with the giant wrong—your voice in the public meeting—your voice in the halls of legislation. Will the time never come when the opponents of slavery will see eye to eye—and work shoulder to shoulder?

Very sincerely yours
S.P. Chase[9]

W. Phillips, Esq.

9. Salmon P. Chase (1808–1873), a former Governor of Ohio and a founder of the Republican Party, was Lincoln's Secretary of the Treasury from 1861 to 1864, when he was named Chief Justice of the Supreme Court.

68. From SALMON P. CHASE

Private

WASHINGTON, FEB 7, 1865.

My dear Sir,

I have often regretted that talents so rare as yours were not devoted to more practical uses than that of the rostrum. I have wished for you at the bar, in legislative councils, in administrations,

& wherever else the hard work of reform was to be done; and have been, sometimes, not a little provoked by what seemed ungenerous & was unjust criticism upon those who were doing that work—most provoked, of course, when these criticisms were directed against me!

But a few days ago I read your speech in New York—your grand plea for universal suffrage and was forced to doubt whether, after all, you had not chosen your sphere of usefulness most wisely. I felt when reading your words as I did when I first read Milton's "Speech for the Liberty of Unlicensed Printing," which the "world will not willingly let die." My heart said Amen to each glowing sentence, and bid me write you my earnest thanks for what you so nobly did.

I have had some trouble in bringing myself to do so; fearing misconception of my motives. But somehow I feel as if I must & so I write. Pray accept my thanks as those of one who feels most profoundly the absolute necessity of the action you recommend.

Since reconstruction was first thought of I have never doubted that a constitutional guaranty of universal suffrage or at least of suffrage for all loyal blacks who might be of sufficient education or had been in the national military service ought to be made an indispensable condition of the readmission of any rebel state to participation in the National Government. My own conviction is that universal is better & more practicable than any kind of limited suffrage, though I would not insist on the former, if it endangered the securing of the latter.

You will necessarily infer that the nominal state organizations of Louisiana & Arkansas, which exclude the mass of the loyal people from suffrage because of their complexions are exceedingly unsatisfactory to me. I have not ceased to remonstrate with our friends against their recognition as properly reconstituted states. To write or talk in this sense to somebody & do all I could, every day since this question became imminent, has seemed to me a duty.

It was with peculiar pleasure, therefore, that I read your brave defence of equal rights, guaranteed by equal laws, enacted under universal suffrage. It is most gratifying to hear the steady & rapid progress of opinion in the same direction. A few days ago I was in Baltimore, surrounded by some of the most able & influential young men in Maryland and was delighted by their general concurence in my views. There is a manifest change going on in Congress, greatly helped by the Constitutional amendment.

You may be of good courage therefore. Not many months will pass, I believe, before all yokes will be broken from all necks and universal suffrage will be recognized in the Constitution of every restored State as the only sure & perpetual safeguard against a new Slavery.

> Yours very truly
> S P Chase

Wendell Phillips Esq.

69. From SALMON P. CHASE

WASHINGTON, MAY 1, 1866

Dear Sir,

I cannot attend the Annual Meeting of the American Antislavery Society, on the 8th, except by sincere wishes for the complete accomplishment of its purpose to achieve the deliverance by our country from the spirit as well as the fact of Slavery.

Among the most urgent duties of the hour I count that of pressing upon the intelligence and the conscience of our countrymen the expediency as well as the obligation of unqualified recognition of the Manhood of Man.

The nation has liberated four millions of the people from Slavery, and has made them citizens of the Republic.

That all Freemen are entitled to suffrage, on equal terms, is an axiom of Free Government. Neither color nor race can be allowed, without injustice and damage, as grounds of exception.

If, in the first movement toward national reconstruction, this truth had been distinctly recognized by an invitation to the whole loyal people of every state in rebellion to take part in the work of State reorganization, can it now be doubted that the practical relations of every State with the Union would have been already reestablished, and with the happiest consequences?

Nothing is more profitable than Justice. Does not suffrage promote security, content, self respect, betterment of condition? With suffrage will there not be more and more productive labor than without? Will not suffrage ensure order, education, respect for law, activity in business, and substantial progress?

I have heard the difference between the production of the lately insurgent States, with universal suffrage, and the production of the same states, without it, estimated at one hundred millions of dollars a year. At this rate, the injustice of the denial of suffrage will cost those states—will cost the nation—five hundred millions of dollars in five years; enough to pay nearly one fifth of the national debt.

Is it too much to expect that sensible and patriotic men, in those states, will, before long, see their true interest in their plain duty, and join hands with those who seek, not their injury or their humiliation, but their welfare and their honor, in equal rights for all?

However these things may be, this, at least, seems clear. The men who so long contended for justice to the enslaved, & now contend for justice to the emancipated, will not, cannot, must not cease their efforts till justice prevails.

Yours truly
S.P. CHASE

Wendell Phillips, Esq.

70. From WILLIAM A. RICHARDSON

TREASURY DEPARTMENT
SEPT. 11TH, 1873

DEAR SIR:

I have the honor to acknowledge the receipt of your note of the

11th inst., enclosing a letter addressed to President Grant which you desire to have put into his own hands. I have today forwarded your letter to the President, and it will be in his hands tomorrow.

Very respectfully Yours,
WM. A. RICHARDSON[10]

Wendell Phillips, Esq.
Boston, Mass.

10. William A. Richardson (1821–1896), Massachusetts Republican, was Secretary of the Treasury from 1873 to 1874.

71. From ALBERT G. BROWNE

BEAUFORT, FEB. 19, 1864

DEAR PHILLIPS

The bearer Mr. James Damon a good anti-slavery man will hand you a ring which I took from the brick pillar in the basement of the house of Bishop Barnwell. It was about 6½ to 7 feet from the floor evidently used to "*trice*" the poor negro up by the arms previous to flogging.

I promised to send you a set of stocks used for the same purpose, but by some misunderstanding they were sent to Syracuse for an anti-slavery Fair—I have just returned from Florida, we have met with no opposition, shall bring her into the Union as a Free State within 60 days.

I go again tomorrow to remain there an indefinite period. I *now* consider myself a citizen of Florida and shall perhaps go into the convention—I am confident that our arrangements are such as to make all things sure.

Yours truly,
ALBERT G. BROWNE[11]

11. Albert G. Browne (1835–1891), Massachusetts abolitionist and lawyer, was a Special Agent of the Treasury Department in South Carolina, Georgia, and Florida.

72. From ALBERT G. BROWNE

TREASURY DEPARTMENT
FOURTH SPECIAL AGENCY
BEAUFORT, S.C.   OCTR. 28, 1864

My Dear Phillips,

I could never 'till the present moment heartily and cordially ask you to come and visit me, altho I would have been very glad to have seen you here. Heretofore my accomodations have been scant—now I have ample "range and scope"—I am having fitted up the "J.J. Smith" house, where South Side Adams lived—alternating between the house in town and the Smith plantation. I now give you a most cordial invitation to come here this winter *with your wife*. I believe it would benefit her health—I have a beautiful Reserve Cutter Steam Yacht at my command, with saddle-horses and carriages which shall all be yours. I visit Florida as often as once a month, having just returned from St. Augustine—a day or two since I was at the fleet and Morris Island—and had the satisfaction to witness the shelling of a blockage vessel. She was completely knocked to pieces—having got on shore while running in. 'Tis wonderful with what accuracy, having got the range, they throw these shells—I saw two 300# Shell strike the hull, out of four—the first fell short, the second went over, both in range—the third and fourth struck the hull. While at Ft. Grey—now Putnam—showers of *rifle* bullets were thrown in from Sumpter. one man standing near the spot where I had stood was killed, being obliged to be exposed while standing in the embrasure, loading the gun. The range was near 1500 yards! I took good care to keep under cover. I sincerely wish you could come here to look at the *"freedmen"*! as they really are *not*! I am full of indignation when I think of their treatment. I have written to the Governor to withdraw his agents and wash his hands clear of the iniquity. The state Agent may be honest enough, I don't know him, but he is weak as water. We pay to our *recruits* on enlistment $325—out of a great many who have been examined, Col. Hallowell tells me he can find but *one* who has received over $25. What has become of the balance? I intend to search this thing to the bottom. It would appear that we (our State) are obliged to turn over her recruits to the United States officer, Col. Littlefield, who *says* he is the confidential friend of Pres. Lincoln, having read law in his office. Littlefield it would seem, intended to make "a big thing of it," gobbling not *only the recruit but his money*. I have been in consultation with General Saxton, who, altho a weak man in some things, is essentially a *just man* Provost Marshal General Col. Hall, as noble a man as breathes —Cols. Hallowell and Hartwell;—*and Littlefield*'s *flint will be picked*. Col. Hartwell is in Massachusetts, on a furlough. I want you to see him and get from him the particulars. I wrote to the Governor that I *had not* mentioned the subject to any one out of my immediate family, and I therefore do not wish you to use my name—as it may mix me up (in ways I will find it out here) in a disagreeable business. Genl Saxton instituted a commission to look into the subject, of which Col. Van Wycke and Hallowell were members. They both assure me they think Littlefield is a rogue. So soon as Littlefield *found what was going* on, he proposed to deposit some $30,000 in the hands of our Paymaster, and offered to place $9000 in the hands of Mr Judd, Saxton's agent for the freedmen—which he declined unless he could hand him the *names* and the *authority* of the men (soldiers) for whom he wished to deposite. Just so at the Savings Bank here, he offered to deposit $6 to 7000. It was declined for the same reasons as stated by Mr Judd. I know this Littlefield to be what Gen Wm Birney called him, a "boasting humbug." I *think* he is a rogue. He went North by the last steamer to forestall opinion, but he should have no quarter from our friends. He will, I doubt not, try to manipulate Wilson. I do not think however that either Wilson or the Governor can be influenced by the fellow. I cannot tolerate such scamps, and when he spoke to me on the steamer I told him never to address me again, as I did not *recognize him as a gentleman*, and would hold none but official intercourse with him. He is also a lying mean mischiefmaker—or would be *if any dependence could be placed in his word*—and he *says* he has influence with Pres. Lincoln. I do not credit his assertion—but if he, or such as he has, God help us I say. I have written nothing about this rascally business to my son, as I do not wish to have him mixed up with me in it. But I am determined to follow it up and make this fellow disgorge his ill gotten money. I have no doubt *if* he has the influence of which he boasts I shall not be in good odour at Washington—I am content when such dogs bark at me.[12]

> With sentiments of respect
> I am yours truly
> ALBERT G. BROWNE

12. Nehemiah Adams, a Boston minister, had visited a plantation near Beaufort and written a favorable account of slavery entitled *A South-Side View of Slavery: or Three Months in The South in 1854* (Boston, 1854). In Massachusetts Browne had helped raise a black regiment, the Fifty-fourth Massachusetts Infantry, originally led by Colonel Robert Gould Shaw. After Shaw was killed, Colonel M. S. L. Littlefield was temporarily assigned command of the Fifty-fourth. General Rufus Saxton was the commanding officer in charge of the Reconstruction effort at Port Royal.

73. From ALBERT G. BROWNE

> TREASURY DEPARTMENT
> FIFTH SPECIAL AGENCY
> HILTON HEAD JULY 16TH 1865

DEAR PHILLIPS,

I am detained here on my way to Florida, by the breaking down of one steamer, which will be ready tomorrow, when I shall proceed to Jacksonville, from thence to Macon Geo. via Tallahasse Fla. Thence returning to Savannah in about three or four weeks, I shall wind up the business of my office, resign, and return North. I was in Massachusetts for two or three days two weeks since; going up with a quantity of gold and silver coin and bullion, which I placed in the SubTreasury at N. York, which was captured by Wilson's forces, and which belonged to the Rebel government. All private property (with the exception of that belonging to Beauregard and Pillow) with the assets of the Georgia Central Rail Road I gave up. I felt it to be only just and right to do so. I will not war upon individuals, or corporations, such as the Georgia Central, whose stock is owned principally in Holland and at the North. Besides, had I taken their specie, said to amount to $243,000, they could not have gone to work to repair their road, and without this facility of communication great distress must ensue. Without meeting many genuine Union men, I do find that this whole people are sick and tired of the war; they believe they have been duped by politicians, and feel bitter towards them, and acquiesce in the abolition of slavery. When in Boston I hoped to have seen you, and called at your house. I had many things to say that cannot be put on paper. Before I left here the last of June, which I did quickly with my treasure (I believe the fact has not yet been published), I felt much uneasiness about the treatment the negro was receiving at Savannah and Charleston: There had been collisions between them—them and the white soldiers—and the negro had to go to the wall. He could receive no justice at the hands of the military. True, some of the Officers would not be sparing of their platitudes in speaking of negroes rights, but most of this talk was for "bunkum" and to serve their purposes to get Brevets—some of them have effected their object. The command of Gen. Grover (a Maine man), a part of Sheridan's corps, which succeeded Sherman's in Savannah, were utterly regardless of the negro, and Grover of the regular army, was a regular toady to the prominent Rebels, a pig-headed martinet with no sympathy for the negro. Hatch at Charleston is a "hard boy," a "regular" cavalry officer—a libertine, and whiskey drinking coarse fellow. Gurney (Brevet Genl) Col of the 127th N.Y. *then* commanding the Post, is a weak man, and *trimmer*. His men frequently insulted negroes, and were a brutal lot. But they were saints in comparison to the rake hellish Zouaves, who with the 107 and 47 Pensylvania regiments succeeded them at Charleston. Murders, rapes, robberies were of daily and nightly occurrence. The negro is placed between the upper and neither millstone—and is ground to powder. There troops are in collision with the white rebel rowdies, men and boys, and always protect and defend them in their frequent collisions with the poor blacks. In my experience here of two years, I have never known of a quarrel between white and black *where the negro was the aggressor*. For the past two weeks at Charleston there has been a reign of terror. These infernal brutes, the Zouaves, with their coadjutors, the low white rebels, have systematically raided upon the negro. They frequently waylaid the negro, with his fruits and vegetables coming to market and after beating him, and perhaps ravishing his wife or sister who may have been in his company, stealing his entire load. Thefts innumerable have been committed in the open market in broad day from the negro market men and women by these demons. On Saturday the 8th inst. a theft was committed in the market upon a negro, he resenting it, and trying to retain his property—at a signal a body of Zouaves rushed in and drove every colored market man and woman out. The white mob rushed in and they with the Zouaves stole every article in the market. Some of the negroes in attempting to defend themselves were most brutally beaten—some of them have since died. The 54th Mass. Regt., or rather a part of them under a Seargent, hearing of the work, armed themselves, and proceeding to the spot a regular fight took place between them and the 50 hellhounds, in which the detachment of the 54th was discomfited—and a number killed and wounded on both sides. The particulars are studiously repressed by Gen Hatch who is down upon the 54th and the negro in general. He had some 40 or 50 negroes arrested and *without examination* thrust into prison. Gilbert Pilsbury told me he saw the 47th Penyy white soldiers thrust the negroes into the cells with clubbed muskets,—on his protesting he was grossly insulted. A Seargent of the 54th was brought in and a *drunken* Capt. of the Pensyl. Regt. would examine no papers he offered to show showing his right to be out nor listen to his defense. "We mean to hang all you damned niggers" said he.

Pillsbury said he saw a white boy throw a razor into the street, and then pick it up, and hand it to a policeman, telling him that "a negro dropped it." There has been a night of terror in Charleston. Dr. Ramsey told me that a short time since, two respectable, well behaved colored girls, in open *day*, *were* passing in a *public street*— two Zouaves, one of these brutes said to the other "let me show you the new moon" and seized one of the girls around the waist, threw her over his arm, with her head down and her feet in the air, thus exposing her person. Does not such conduct exceed anything the rebels ever charged to "Butler the beast?"

I say unless different treatment is meted out to these poor people they will rebel against so much injustice and every true man will say Amen. I will do more, I will give them "aid and comfort" I will fight in their ranks—to right their wrongs.

Let me be just toward Genl Gillmore. He is as fair and just as such a cold selfish nature as is his can be. He has been in Charleston removed the Zouaves with their officers to Morris Island, and taken away their colors. But cold calculating selfishness should not be here. We want fair, just, sympathising natures, men of noble views and purpose, and friendly Christian principles. Unless we have such here we shall have to fight our battles over again, and I say God speed the right. In such a combat God can have no sympathy with the oppressor. There are a host of these new Brevet Brig and Major Genl who have been toadying for promotions, and *talking* "justice to the negro," but who are now acting like the devil, and who have no more love for the negro than the devil has got for holy water. I loathe, I despise all such. Brevet Brig Gen Burnett, the successor to the command of Higginson's Regt is one of these trimmers. He is in command of Charleston post. Some people distrust the Chief of Staff of Genl Gillmore, Brev Brig Genl Woodford. I confess there are some things I have *heard* which I do not like, but unless I *know* them to be true, I cannot give him up, for he has done some good things, and I sent in for his Brevet. If I find out he is false, to the devil with him I say—some of our friends find fault with Genl Hartwell. I believe they are unjust towards him. I think him perhaps a little politic, but generally fair minded, and just and true. Hallowell and Beecher are right up to the mark. I wish Beecher was a bigger man, and better soldier, but he is a *brave* soldier, and a true and fearless friend of the colored race. He, nor his good, pure, little wife, will hold no social intercourse with Genl *Hatch and his woman.* Therefore, and because too of Beechers out and out anti slavery doctrine Hatch is persecuting Beecher and has sent him out of Charleston with his regiment His H'Quarters being at Branchville a low unhealthy bay—and his regiment is along the line of the RailRoad. Beecher used to teach in the colored schools with his good little wife, and preach to the colored people on Sundays at Zion Church. A petition from hundreds of these people was presented to Genl Hatch to keep Beecher in the City but he would not yield to it. *In my judgment not a white soldier should be allowed in the Slave states.* Black regiments only should be here and officered by men who are in sympathy with their commands and not by demagogues. Neither should civil government be allowed but such men as William Burney and Geo Gordon should be military governors. I have written you a long but hasty letter but I deemed it only my duty to cry aloud and spew out.[13]

Truly yours,
ALBERT G. BROWNE

13. The fighting between Northern white and black soldiers which Browne reports here is discussed in Joel Williamson, *After Slavery: The Negro in South Carolina During Reconstruction, 1861–1877* (Chapel Hill, 1965), pp. 240–274.

74. From ALBERT G. BROWNE

TREASURY DEPARTMENT
FIFTH SPECIAL AGENCY
HILTON HEAD, SEPT. 17. 1865

DEAR PHILLIPS

I have been wandering to and fro and up and down the States

of South Carolina, Georgia, and Florida, and have probably seen more of the working of the new *system* of labor if system it may be called, when there is endless confusion, and absurd contradiction, and when in most cases the poor freedman is worse off, so far as food and clothing goes, than in a state of bondage when, in fact, he is made to do more work for less pay—and is subject to the most cruel treatment. "He's nobodys dog now." and everybody has a right to kick him. Tell about loyalty, there is no loyal sentiment in the South, *not a bit of it*. I think in South Carolina, as their elevation was higher, so was their fall heavier and apparently there is more *seeming* submission or acquiescence in the new order of things. They are in a sort of stupor—so abject as to say they are willing to submit to anything, but it is from the lips only, not from the heart. Withdraw the military and see how defiant they would become. In Georgia they are openly defiant, or doggedly determined to place any stumbling block in the way. Their treatment of the negro is infamous. He is cruelly whipped and frequently shot down, and the perpetrator often goes off with impunity. I am following up a case where a poor boy had a double barreled gun discharged at him, *and I counted fifty seven* bird shot in his left side, there were many on the back of his head, and on the left side of his face. The infernal drunken brute then rode plumb over the poor boy. I have caused the arrest of this demon, his name is Duncan Sinclair, a *whiskey jug* and parolled rebel soldier. At the preliminary examination some of his friends tried to *bribe* the negro boy to confess that he *stole* the pistol which Sinclair took from him, but *without effect*. Sinclair is to be tried by court martial at Darien in a week or two. If my business permits I intend to be at the trial to see fair play, for I find many of our officers have no back bone, indeed, many are inimical to the negro. Such is the case here in the 21st Reg. U.S.C.T. Lt. Jacob of Co. D has been in the habit of kicking, striking with his fist, and sword, those under his command. *I was* arrested by this *drunken rascal* a few days since for calling him a disgrace to his profession, and a cowardly poltron. I saw him strike a colored boy, a harmless inoffensive individual, and civilian, a terrible blow in the face for merely speaking to him, and contradicting a white rowdy who was misrepresenting the truth. I was in the 3d story looking out of the window. In ten minutes after I was marching up to the Provost Marshal officer in charge of some of my colored friends member of Co. D 21st U.S.C.T. from whom I received an account of this reprobates rascality. I did not remain long in duress, but long enough to gather facts by which I hope to pick this Lt. Jacobs flint, and have him dismissed. I tell you my friend the poor negroes redemption is not yet complete— neither will it be 'till those are appointed to rule over them whose hearts and minds are in accord. Bad as the military Govnmt—yet it is *better than civil rule* for which these people are no more fit than wild indians.

Yours truly

ALBERT G. BROWNE

I think Florida has a better Gov and Genl Commanding   Marvin & Foster, than South Carolina or Georgia, and is far advanced of either. But here cruelty—whippings, shootings prevail. I have in my trunk a cowhide which the Marshal took from a Mrs. Holden The wife of *a Senator in the rebel Congress*, who was whipping a negro girl with it—*last month*. This I intend to give to you. I am tired of this mode of life, shall close up my Agency & come home— within a few weeks. There is no encouragement held out to do one's duty. I think as a general rule the Treasury Agents have taken care of themselves and the imputation is upon all. Unless I am paid my commissions I shall come home as poor a man as went away.

75. From ALBERT G. BROWNE

SAVANNAH, APRIL 20 1866

DEAR PHILLIPS,

Writing to the Secretary of Treasury to day, I said, after informing him of certain transactions, *"I am chagrined, but not surprised.*

I am not surprised at anything happening here, going to show fatuity of mind, or direliction of duty."

Will it be believed that an officer upon whom I charge theft, bribery, corruption of the basest kind, and having the most irrefragable proof to convict him;—and also that a firm (rebels) in this city have been acting as his agents in selling the stolen cotton—having *now* in their hands, which I made them acknowledge under oath, Fifty-five hundred and forty 01/100 Dolls. to the Credit of this officer, being the balance of three several consignments of Cotton—will it be believed I say, that this officer is mustered out of service, and of course the charges cannot now be sustained against him? There must be corruption somewhere of the most gross and shameless character. I am thoroughly disgusted with all I see and know of the doings at Washington. I am convinced that I am not in favor there. I deal and talk too plainly to suit them. This is only one of the many, many infamous transactions which have been going on to shield villany. Will it be believed too that this officer has always been on duty, but a poor young man a soldier of his regiment who *was a witness* was imprisoned four months and two days! So soon as I knew the facts I immediately took measures for his release and could only effect it by becoming his bondsman for $1000. He was an entire stranger to me. You may say it was imprudent for me so to do—granted. But I hate oppression, come from whom, or fall on whom it may. This young man was a white man, a member of the 12th Maine Vol. I am to day relieved from the bond by reason of the discharge of the complaint on Major Hastings. The Col. Kimball of the same regiment was equally guilty. Albert was anxious to bring on the trial at the same time with Lamar's *but Genl Brannan would not consent to it*. It was a great mistake or something worse!

I wrote to Alley to day saying to him I wanted Lt. Col. Bogert and Lt. Felix Brannagan Adjt of the 103d U.S.C.T. to be summoned before the reconstruction Committee. This regiment (the best I ever saw) is mustered out. The regulars who have taken their places

are raiding here and at Macon & c.—with a vengeance, being
English rogues, German demons, Irish reprobates, and New York
roughs. robberies and assaults are committed by them every night,
perhaps it is wrong in me to feel so, but feeling so, I must say, *I am
glad of it*. These people will now have an opportunity of judging of
the relative merits of Colored and white troops. Col. Bogert told
me that two negroes were arrested in Central Georgia for some
alleged offense, and were tried together, a white man came up and
shot one, *then ripped his bowels open, and twisted them with the
screw on the end of his ramrod and pulled them out!!!* In Wayne
County an intelligent negro by the name of Avery who knew how
to read and write had communicated some facts to a paper published
in Memphis, Tenn. a few days after the fact was known Avery
was found drowned in a well, with a bag of stones tied to his neck!
I believe I told you of a man by the name of Roberts assaulting one
of his colored children the yellow boy defended himself, slightly
wounding his white father—The next morning the poor young man
was found hanging to a tree. Roberts the father with some of his
white neighbors doubtless did the deed. Roberts tried to kill another
yellow son (he has six) and cut him severely. This young man I
saw, as well as the father—and advised him if attacked again to
kill his father. I told all the negroes standing by the same thing, if
attacked by white men to be sure to kill them. This I did in the
presence of twenty white men. Roberts is now at liberty, released
in and through the peace proclamation of Johnson. I learn that by
order of Genl Brannan a number of the 103 U.S.C.T. are to be
sent back, after being mustered *out, to Macon, to be tried by Civil
law for some alleged offences*. one for bayoneting a boy by name of
Bell, who going along in the streets of Macon deliberately stabbed the
colored guard with a jackknife; I might instance hundreds of such
atrocitys. I advised the colored soldiers to retain their guns. Col.
Bogert tried to dissuade them from doing so, as he knew they would
be assaulted, their guns taken from them, and they perhaps killed—
about one fifth kept their guns, paying $6 for each. I may be wrong,

but my advice always is *keep your guns,* and kill if you are assaulted—I think if this was the usual result, there would be a certain defference paid to them— to their prowess at least, and we should hear less of these barbarous murders and assaults.

Truly yours,

ALBERT G. BROWNE

I have fully made up my mind not to remain here after the 10th May., but my business cannot be brought to a close at that time. But I will finish in Boston—

ii) *The Press*

76. From JAMES M. W. YERRINTON

MONDAY, A.M.

DEAR MR. PHILLIPS:

I am mortified and enraged at the conduct of the *Bee* in not print-ing your speech after having solicited it. Last night, when I went in to read the proof, I found that it had not been put in type, and learned that some very powerful influences had been brought to bear to prevent, not only its publication, but all mention of it, by the Boston papers, and that the *Tribune* had been telegraphed to, to observe the same silence. You see that you are considered of con-siderable moment, in these times. I propose to get hold of the Ms. as soon as possible, and have it issued at once in pamphlet form. I think it not well to wait the slow issue of the *Liberator*. There are other types in Boston than those used on the daily press, and the people shall read what they so gladly heard.

Of course, I cannot consent to accept any thing from you under these circumstances, and so enclose the amount you so kindly handed me.

Truly, yours,
J.M.W.Y.[14]

14. James Manning Winchell Yerrinton (1825–1893) was the official stenog-rapher and reporter for the Massachusetts Antislavery Society.

77. From THEODORE TILTON

NEW YORK, 1859

MY DEAR MR. PHILLIPS,

Will you write for *The Independent* a letter giving your views of John Brown, with whatever else you might wish to say on the present aspect of slavery?

I wish that *The Independent* might speak a great voice at this crisis, and I want you to utter it. Write over your own name, and

to as great length as you choose. If you wish to say, the lesson of
John Brown is *Disunion*—SAY IT.

I will give you the first page of the paper, with large type & will
advertise your letter in every city in the North; will print as many
thousand extra copies as may be needed; and will pay you for it
whatever you ask.

> *Will you strike the blow?*
> Yours in haste
> THEO. TILTON[15]

15. Theodore Tilton (1835–1907) was the editor of the *Independent*, an influential radical journal throughout the Civil War and Reconstruction years.

78. From THEODORE TILTON

OFFICE OF *"The Independent"*

MY DEAR FRIEND,

I have just received a note from Mr. Bowen, proprietor of the
Independent, which I enclose to you. He is a large-minded man, and
so near a radical abolitionist that there is but a hair's breadth between him and the American Anti-Slavery. You will see that he
wishes you to write for the Independent.

Now, my dear friend, if you knew how long I had been trying
to *mellow the soil* of this newspaper, you would rejoice that now
the time had come when there is an actual *asking for the best seed*
to sow in it. Think of it! Lowell and Whittier! Mrs. Stowe and
Mrs. Child! Cheever & yourself!

The columns are offered freely to you—not by the editors, but
by the proprietor. The proprietor has power over the editors,
and is supreme dictator. The door, therefore, is opened wide to you,
without bar.

If I could make any appeal that would induce you to accept
this opportunity, I would make it. Lord is my witness, that it is
not the profit of the paper but the good of the cause that makes
me solicitous that you should not throw away *a golden chance*.

You will have the ear of 30,000 subscribers, 6,000 of whom are clergymen. If you begin with the elements of anti-slavery, and make a wise use of occasions for applying principles, you might soon move *half a million of readers* to put on armor for a crusade against Slavery.

My heart leaps at the idea of seeing you in the Independent!

The proprietor has a delicacy, and so have I, in proposing terms of payment. Will you not say, "Yes," and propose your own?

I am, yours with much love,
THEODORE TILTON

79. From THEODORE TILTON

[NOV. 6, 1862]
BROOKLYN, THURSDAY

MY DEAR MR. PHILLIPS,

I have just heard some bad news from the President. He has spoken to at least six persons, lamenting the issue of his Proclamation, and calling it the great mistake of his life.

That looks ominous!

There begin, already, to be clamors by Democrats for a revocation of the Edict. This is the first echo from Tuesday's election. Otherwise, that election, in itself, was almost as much a victory, in one sense, as a defeat, in another. It gave the Administration a fit rebuke:—a rebuke which, failing to come from its friends, came at last, more fatally, from its enemies. This much is salutary in the election.

But even this, I fear, in view of what I hear from the President, will do the Administration no good: for, acting under Seward's advice, the whole ruling element in the Cabinet will connive with the Democrats. Will not this necessitate a recall of the Proclamation? And will not that send us all straight to the Devil?

But, just at present, everything is in chaotic confusion.

I drop you this line only to mention the remark of the President —foolish, perhaps fatal.

Yours in a hurry,
THEODORE TILTON

80. From ELIZABETH CADY STANTON

Dear Friend,

I hold in my hand abundant evidence that you are still a subject for missionary effort. Here is a letter for "Susan Anthony to the care of *Mrs. H. B.* Stanton". Only think of it; one of the noblest champions of freedom, at this late day denying to woman her own name. Now my dear friend, did you pen that insult? or was it done by your private secretary?—a perfumed young man who never heard that women & negroes were beginning to repudiate the names of their masters?—& claiming a right to a life long name of their own.! Perhaps I do injustice to your chirography & this "Mrs." may be Mr. after all, but if you are guilty I shall feel it my duty to make a special effort to convince you of the heinousness & criminality of your offence. But how shall I present to you the new gospel of individual sovereignty.! Not by pen—your benighted condition would require folios of paper!—I cannot go to that part of the Lord's vineyard where you dwell, for I am anchored here, surrounded by numberless small craft, which I am struggling to tug *up* life's stream. May I hope that during the coming winter you will stay a few days in Central New York. Do accept all the Lyceum invitations you may get from this part of the state, that you may thereby place yourself in the way of being converted, to my idea of right & at the same time refresh us with your presence at many a breakfast & dinner also. You little know how sadly disappointed we all were, at not seeing you last winter, nor how many pair of blue eyes & rosy cheeks watched at the gate to herald your coming.

From what I have said Mrs Phillips must not infer that her Husband does not always do honor to the admirable home influence, which we all know he has, but in spite of the purest angelic influences, all Husbands & sons will occasionally let the old Adam stand

out. With much love & admiration for Mrs Phillips & yourself,
(in spite of your shortcomings)

> From sincerely your friend
> *E. Cady* STANTON

81. From LUCY STONE

79 E. 15TH ST.   N.Y.   OCT. 15

DEAR MR. PHILLIPS

We have engaged the Tabernacle for the 25th & 26th of Nov.
and will expect you on the evening of the 25th.

We are very grateful that in addition to all your anti slavery
labors, you get time for us too.

> Yours truly
> LUCY STONE

P.S. Dont ever add Blackwell to my name.[16]

16. After her marriage to Henry Brown Blackwell, the abolitionist and feminist
Lucy Stone (1818–1893) insisted on being called "Mrs. Lucy Stone."

82. From GEORGE W. SMALLEY

OFFICE OF THE TRIBUNE
NEW YORK,   MARCH 15, 1864

DEAR UNCLE,

Yrs. with check re'd, & we are much obliged. Phoebe about the
same today—mostly keeps her bed & gains slowly.

You ask why not publicly join the Fremonters. For two classes
of reasons—the first against Fremont generally—the second specially
against *your* appearing as his advocate.

I think you sacrifice your position, the moment you pronounce
decisively for any man as President. One strong hold you have on
the people is your absolute independence of politics, & being beyond suspicion of *personal* motives. If you speak as the partisan
of Fremont can you retain it? Losing it, do you gain, or can you

79 E. 15th St. N.y. Oct. 15

Dear Mr. Phillips

We have engaged the
Tabernacle for the 25th & 26th.
of Nov. and will expect you
on the evening of the 25th.

We are very grateful, that
in addition to all your anti-
slavery labors, you get time for
us too.

Yours truly
Lucy Stone

P.S. Don't ever add,
Blackwell, to my name.

Lucy Stone's letter protesting Phillips's use of "Mrs. Blackwell." See letter 81.

accomplish, anything to compensate for it? The weight which your opinions now have, the force of your criticism on Lincoln's policy, and on men—Banks for instance—can they be the same when you give people the chance to say they are made in the interest of a Presidential candidate?

This I speak of not as affecting you personally, which I know you would not listen to, but as affecting your influence on affairs, of which not one iota ought to be thrown away. I need not follow out the suggestion. You see how far it would carry me.

2. As you ask, let me say frankly I don't believe in Fremont for Pres. I do believe him able & personally as honest as most public men. I grant all you can say about his executive capacity &c. But he is the worst judge of men in America, and is surrounded by swindlers. Men enjoy his confidence & abuse it, which would make his Administration rotten to the bottom financially—sink it utterly in public esteem—to say nothing of what it would cost in money.

I am bound to say also I think him vain & selfish—his natural simplicity of character corrupted by the men who have long been his personal followers, devoted to making their own fortunes under pretence of advancing his.

The inevitable corollary is that he is a *weak* man, sure to be a tool in others' hands.

Further, I reluctantly believe that his morals are rotten. That he seduced a governess in his own family & that the exposure of it carried his wife to Beecher for advice are facts which I have only at second hand from Mr. B. himself. That he has been habitually a libertine I have heard asserted so often & sustained by so many seeming facts, that I don't know whether to believe it or not.

It is another reason against him—tho' of less moment—that he is said to be resolved to run against Lincoln—or perhaps any Baltimore nominee—anyhow; preferring to give the election to the Copperheads rather than not gratify his revenge. Don't say that I judge him harshly when I say that I think him capable of this. I know what scores he has to pay off—I know his Virginia quarrel with L.

& how shamefully he was treated—but I remember also that even at that moment he sank into bitterness against the Gov't & asked to be relieved not because Pope's appointment over his head would destroy his usefulness, but because it "largely reduced his rank and consideration in the service." That is not the language of a man of generous impulses & unselfish purpose.

Not believing for one moment in the honesty of the Democratic Anti Slavery policy—if it is to be—I regard the independent candidacy of Fremont as a stab at the Republic—draining the life blood of Freedom out of it. Weak as another Lincoln Administration would be, would a gov't which McClellan swayed—or rather which James Barlow & Wood & reinstated Rebels swayed—be better? Yet that is what Fremont would hand us over to, rather than see Lincoln reelected.

Finally I believe there is a better chance to unite against Lincoln —& to carry the Baltimore convention—with Butler or with some candidate not yet prominent, & I regard the F. movement as a diversion in favor of Lincoln.

But whether I am right or wrong about all this I should profoundly regret to see you at this moment taking any part in the wrangle about men. I believe—I know—you have better work to do & cannot be spared from it.

Faithfully yours,
GEORGE W. SMALLEY[17]

17. George Smalley (1833–1916) married Phoebe Garnaut, who was practically an adopted daughter to Wendell and Ann Phillips. Smalley worked for the New York *Tribune* before beginning a celebrated career as a foreign correspondent. Phillips regarded him as a kind of son-in-law. Like Smalley, many of Phillips's closest friends repudiated his support of Frémont in the 1864 campaign.

83. From THEODORE TILTON

JUNE 30, 1864

WENDELL PHILLIPS, ESQ.

MY DEAR FRIEND,

Am I not right in supposing that you will not take unkindly

the criticisms I have made upon your letter? Please tell me so and relieve my mind. I have been so utterly unhappy ever since your letter came, & my duty came with it, that this morning I am sick. If I have wounded you, God knows that I have wounded myself more. I am nothing to you, but you are everything to me. You never can know, for I have never had the boldness to tell, what a place you hold in my heart. If this controversy—which I never expected to fall to my lot—shall shadow or alienate our friendship, I shall account it one of the chief calamities of my life. But I am sure you cannot doubt my heart and motive. On reading my article this morning, it seems more harsh than it seemed yesterday while writing it. But I know you will speak a good word to relieve my anxiety. This is a foolish note, but you will pardon it.[18]

> Yours affectionately,
> THEODORE TILTON

18. Tilton had criticized Phillips's endorsement of John C. Frémont in the presidential election of 1864.

84. To THEODORE TILTON From WENDELL PHILLIPS

DEAR TILTON

Dont be troubled   your criticism has not hurt my feelings the least. The milk of my kindliness for you is as fresh & sweet as ever & the cream rises thick & even—witness some of it which I inclose as my reply for the next Independent.

It did amuse me to see in your charge of inconsistency, how little you read the speeches you think you admire so much. But I've always known & said nobody ever reads speeches. Only dont ever praise them hereafter. If you do I shall laugh in your face.

> Goodbye my
> W[19]

19. Draft in Phillips's hand.

85. From S. A. MAPES

JACKSONVILLE, ILLINOIS, JULY 30, 1868

MR PHILLIPS
  Boston
    DEAR SIR,
Some few years Since I was in Boston   and I was informed that
there was a parcel sent to you by a carrier boy, or by express and
on opening it you found it to be the carcass of a cat   the cat was
shot in Fowls upholster store and was supposed to have been sent by
Geo Fowl. You probably knew at the time from whence it came
if not it gratifies me to tell you

From a Friend
S A MAPES
Jacksonville, Ills.

86. From JOHN H. WHITE

WENDELL PHILLIPS

If you are willing to make a "nigger" of yourself you can do
it. (without much effort) no one but God! can make a white
man of a Negro. to attempt to make the affrican Slave, equal
with the educated white man is repugnant to common sense. none
but radicals and fools would dare propose such monstrous non-
sense, and you say the man that differs with you is a Davis syco-
phant. I differ with you. I despise you and any other man that
denounces his neighbor because he does not agree with him. did
God almighty create you the sole arbiter in this matter or any
matter that you should judge and you should denounce   should
decide who are lovers of liberty and who are sycophants. how
dare you to presume to dictate to intelligent citizens and men
that are and who ever have been Loyal. Yes I say you who are
and ever have been a traitor and resist and would rebel, if you
had the power against any administration or any law that did not
please you. are you not a pretty subject to talk about traitors—

permit me to tell you that you are a contemptible, impertinent scoundrel & ought to be yoked with Jef Davis—are only fit for such Company. You are an ass. you are unbe

I am getting vexed
JOHN H. WHITE

87. From O. B. TUGMUTTON

ELBERTON APRIL 18TH 1851

Sir   I See from your remarks in a meeting Held in Boston on the 4th ult. that you are determined to oppose any man that will attempt to arrest a Slave in Boston & further advise your followers to follow any man that gets possession of his Slave to the Line of this State   I wish you would follow them to Savanah and I am sure that would Show you a Sight that you never has Seen   you have got more paupers now in your free States than you feed. attend to them & let the Slave alone and you would be much Better off. I am for one for having Laws passed in these States to have any northern man tared and feathered and that done by a Slave as Soon as he put his foot upon Slave Soil. I have a Slave   I generally Reed to him about Such Rows as you have in Boston and he has often Said to me if he had his way he would have the whole of you hung by the neck   you may think by your Rows that you are gaining the good will of the Slave in the Southern States but you are mistaken   our Slave have the Benefit of the Gospel well fed and clothed and that is more than you can Say of your State   our Slave are better acquainted with the Scripture than a majority of you whites you contend that Slavery is contrary to Scripture   I will tell you what is the matter   the Devil has always had a people and he has Selected the northern States to carry out his design   you are working for the Devil and knot for god   all I will Say for this time you had better Stay on your own Side of the fince— you Ministers of the gospel pretends to be doing the will of god when they are telling

An example of the abusive attacks to which Phillips was subjected. See letters 85–88.

the people knot to respects the Laws of the Land and Constitution
if that is knot carry out the will of Devil I do knot know what is
for all Christians desire peace   when you here from me again you
will here Something more serious than this

I want to here from you and If you Refuse to answer this I
Know you ar a Scoundrel

Yrs Respectfully
O. B. Tugmutton

To
Wendel Phillips
& Rev Thos Parker

88. From AN ANONYMOUS SLAVEHOLDER

NORFOLK 19 DEC/59

Sir

A short time since I sent you a lock of hair cut from the head of
that THEIF & MURDERER John Brown (I assure you it was his hair)
I notice in the New York Herald of 16 Inst your speech in which
you refer to that hair, saying it came from one who sympathized
with the old scoundrel   I have always look'd upon you as a KNAVE
but not as a fool & how you could have constru'd my motives in
sending you the hair as you did I know not unless it was to serve
your Knavish plans—I sent you the hair because I thought one
Scoundrel would like to have a rememberance of a Brother scoundrel—(pardon repetition)—

On the 20– of last Sept you & I met near the Tremont House. I have
an account to settle with you so look out for

A Slave Holder

Wendall Philips
        Boston
            Mass

89. From "ALL UP"

[DEC. 8, 1860]

Sir.

The writer of this warns you against taking part in the Meeting to take place at Tremont Temple on *Sunday the 16th inst.* An organised party of "Conservatives" will be present on the occasion to escort you and Mr. Ned patch to Boston Common where you will be treated to a "dress of tar & feathers." If you question the prediction of the writer, you have only to test it by your presence on the 16th. That day will witness the "Second Christening of American Liberty!" and the death blow of "niggerdom," and the fanatical schemes of you and your myrmidons.

Beware of the 16th!

"ALL UP."

90. To ANN PHILLIPS From OCTAVIA G[ARDNER]

BOLTON, MAY 7TH, 1839

MY DEAR ANN

I thank you for your kind letter, and my first leisure morning shall be devoted in replying to it and on your own principle, "duty first, pleasure afterwards." I will proceed to *business*. In the first place, I will give you a statistical account of Abolitionism as it exists in Bolton, its rise, progress & prospects. And dear Ann, how I wish with my whole heart & soul. it could be more satisfactory to you, as to me—more in accordance with the principle of Right & with our own feelings & sentiments.

Until within two years, the subject of Abolitionism was not agitated, or perhaps named, at all, about us, or if named, but with sneers, by those who scarce knew its meaning. The first lecture was given here by Misses Grimke, at the instigation of a quaker of this town, Mr Fry, who is now gone & is reaping his reward for his "zeal in well doing." I was surprised at the general attendance of the people on the occasion of their Lecture for I knew there was prejudice among them in relation to the subject. It gave satisfaction & about twelve came forward & acknowledged themselves interested, sincerely, in the Anti Slavery Cause. I thought this a good beginning & a foundation & opening for a regular Society, & proposed it to them at the time, but they thought it inexpedient, & declined, urging as a reason, that the subject had not been generally discussed & public opinion was in opposition, & a society could not be supported satisfactorily to them. Misses Grimke lectured in many of the adjacent towns & those interested in them followed them & seemed much gratified. A Mr. *Stratten*, particularly, a man of discernment & intelligence exerted himself much to create in his friends a taste for their principles & sentiments, & succeeded in a degree. I've often begged of him to establish a Society; if it were but small at first, it would increase, like the 'Leaves' of old. Last autumn we had another lecture & a small society *was* formed, consisting of about twenty, men & women, & I hope the result will prove it expedient as successful, but my fears are as numerous as my hopes. Dr. *Thomson* & family, consisting of Mrs Thomson & Mother, (Mrs Marsh) & sister, & our neighbors, (you remember the *Withington Cottage* do you not?) are much interested in the cause & we often gather together to talk of those 'in bonds' & what is to do, & to be done. I laid the subject of your letter before them, & after deliberating, pondering & weighing we came to the conclusion that to try for a "table" would be useless, but we would among ourselves do "what we could" * & send a package if ever so small to some one who will have a table. The approbation of our own consciences will more than reward us. As for myself, dear Ann, from a child I've felt for the unhappy children of the South, & been impressed with the certainty of the moral, as well as physical evils of Slavery. At times it has seemed that I *would* concentrate all my energies to its extinction; that do what I might it would fall far short of what I would wish to do, & what it was my solemn duty to do. Every one has some influence, you know, & I feel that mine is not the most limited, that I have friends who would listen to me. But Ann, I am not *free myself to act*. My Parents both of them were ever opposed to the subject of Anti Slavery. My dear Sainted Mother, was educated in an old aristocratic family who owned slaves themselves & as "the twig is bent the tree is inclined" you know. She knew I was interested for the slave, but it grieved her, & in her last advice she said, "Octavia dear, I would that you could give up Abolitionism, it has often troubled me, all will yet be well, Your Father as well as I disapprove of your connecting yourself at all with it." "Children be obedient to your parents in the Lord"   "Honor thy Father & Mother that thy days may be long upon the land that the Lord thy God giveth thee." Now *could* I, *should* I disobey these commands have troubled me much. I feel *both* to be *duties*, & yet at war with each other. "I'm in a strait betwixt two" but still feel as tho' I MUST be *obedient* to

*which is just nothing at all

my *parents* who have done so much for my comfort & happiness. I've told you all, Dear Ann & prithee condemn me not, but be charitable, & tell me what you think, candidly.

I was, indeed, sorry not to see you while I was in Boston, I would have called to see you at any time, most happily, but I was told you were not well, & I fear'd you might think you *must* see me and I thought how really *disinterested* I [letter torn] *you know* that I *love* you dearly. I heard a fine Lecture, the "History of Inventions," from your husband, at the Odeon! I do not know when I've been more interested, & I heard others speak in its favor. I think the intelligence of George's marriage was communicated in a most abrupt manner, to you as to us. I'm glad you are pleased with *her*, she seems the very one for him. He has relinquished the habit of smoking, is not that *another* triumph! I think he merits the esteem & respect of every one. We are much attached to him. I thank you & *yours* for your kind congratulations, & wishes for my happiness. If *wishes*, could alone suffice for happiness, I'm sure, I should feel in a Heaven on earth already. For *of late*, especially, I've found friends where I've least expected them. I think I've a right to expect to be happy, & with reason, & Dr. Dupre is one who will make me so, if any one could. George & wife visited us last week, they send their love to you.

I am glad there is to be a "Fair" in Boston. I think much good will be the result & I sincerely wish I could take an active part. But I *must* be satisfied with knowing of its success.

My sisters desire their love to you, Mary thanks you for your message to her. She hopes to see you before you go to England, she says, but you say nothing of going? Shall we not see you in *these* parts again? O how much pleasure it would give us to see you, as blithesome & gay as the birds, as was your wont! & will it never be? Would you not like to sit beneath the shade of those spreading elms once more. I've not seen Mr Allen yet to deliver your message to him. Mr & Mrs Gilbert are well.

I had a delightful visit at Salem, at Mr Saltonstalls. Caroline said she would love to see you much, but she feared too ill. Charles Burston has gone to the West. Mary just came in and said, tell Ann I hope to see her this month. "Ossian" is coming to pass the summer in Harvard & will wed his thoughts to musick. There he will find time to think on "what I am or what I was," dont you remember *his song*? Now I must e'en say Farewell tho' reluctantly, for 'tis long since I've talked with you. Remember me kindly to your "better half" & believe affectionately &

> truly you friend,
> Octavia W.G.

I went to Norwood the day on which this was written & it was not sent as I intended. Mr. & Mrs. Green are well & seem *very* happy. I think she is a very amiable & pleasing woman, & he seems to be improving constantly. I could say more relative to abolitionism but have not room.

91. From MARVIN H. BOVEE

WHITEWATER, MD.
MARCH 15, 1865

MY DEAR FRI.

I have been watching your career for the past three years and am happy to know that I can endorse you as a man of *genuine consistency*, which in these days is a curiosity.

I have ever been a willing member of the Democratic Party, repudiating its errors and endorsing its principles when I believed them right. Land Reform, *Anti Hanging, free suffrage*, regardless of *color*, all received my earnest support when a member of the Senate, and on all occasions since.

I am thoroughly radical in my nature and love to disturb old theories when I believe them wrong.

I have been frequently abused for not casting my fortunes and influence with the Republican party, but I must say that it never had my sympathy in the least degree. Why? Because I saw that party sought only to limit the power of the South. In other words it was a mere question of political preponderance and not a question as to how it could benefit the slave, hence I preferred to remain where I was and where I had influence.

I am glad to see you still at work. You have your mission to perform and are doing it faithfully.

I am quietly resting on my oars waiting for the American conflict to cease that I may resume my labors on Penal Reform. An effort was recently made to restore the Gallows in this State but it has failed. I feel that it is necessary to hold what we got if nothing more is gained at present. It is useless to talk of saving life where we are killing by thousands. Cant elevate mankind when Government is debasing them.—

Do me the favor to send me some of your speeches if you have any in pamphlet form.

Believe me, dear friend,

Yours faithfully,
MARVIN H. BOVEE

Wendell Phillips Esq.

P.S.   I hope to take you by the hand again before the expiration of the year   M.H. Bovee

92. From MARY MOORE

WILLOW PARK, WESTBORO, MASS.

JAN. 8, 1867

WENDELL PHILLIPS ESQ.:

DEAR SIR,

I attended your Lecture, delivered in Westboro Jan. 2; when all, that was high and human within me, rose up and wanted to thank you for the words you said; for the great work you are doing; and for being *Wendell Phillips*. But as I could not then, I take this means of doing it.

I would beg pardon, but honest appreciation needs no pardon.

I thanked God for you, and for the blessed privilege of hearing you speak.

You would not wonder at my earnestness, if you knew, how for weary years, I have tried to do my humble duty, away in Central New York, with a heartsick longing for a more congenial atmosphere. When John Brown, brave old man! was captured and hung, I was crawling from room to room, with a sick baby in my arms, and fire in my brain. I knew no responsive soul, and might have gone mad, because no one would cry out, but for hearing your words through the New York Tribune. Thank you again. I never thought to look in your face, but I have, and God is good. May He bless you forever.

MARY MOORE

93. From GUSTAV REUTER

IN THE FIELD, CAMP OF DET. HEADQUARTERS 24TH A.C.

ARMY OF THE JAMES, BEFORE RICHMOND, VIRGINIA

MARCH, THE 6TH 1865

VERY DEAR AND HONORED SIR,

Will it please You, to pardon me, that I, a private in the army, do now respectfully address you.—I will try, to be short and not weary you with many words. I am a German, but, having been only three years resident in this dear dear Country, I am not a Citizen of it, as yet.—In Octbr last, I enlisted to fight for my adopted country, for the reestablishment of Order, of Obedience to its Laws, for the Perpetuation of a free republican form of Government, but, above All, for the Liberty of a Race, a People, brethren, for whom Christ died, as well, as for me; whom I pitied, when but a boy and reading in those young years the cruel story's of their Opression. Oftentimes have I opened my young heart, full of simpathy for the needy and lowly slave, to a pious mother, expressing the wish, that when I should become a man, that then I would go to America helping them a attain their

Photograph of Private Gustav Reuter, a German immigrant who joined the
Union Army to fight for the abolition of slavery. See letter 93.

Liberty. And now, dear Sir, the petition I bring to You, is this: Can and will You please, do something for me, that I may truly be usefull to the People, I love; to be permitted to fight side by side with them against their Opressors, that so a boys wish, grown into a burning Desire of manhood for Action, may be fully realised? Having been in business for myself five years in London, Engl. as a Confectioner, I have had Opportunity to learn more of slavery and its wrongs and also sitting for eight years under the faithfull ministry of Mr. C. H. Spurgeon, I have been unmoveable established in my princip for Liberty to all men.—Three years ago I came with my familie to New York, to make this land our home. Even than, I would have gladly gone to the war, but for my child and my wife, whose heart was then sorrowing for the late loss of both parents and whose only friend and stay, I was, and because, too, that the poor runaway was flogged back to his tyrant master by the soldiers of the Union. I opened a buisness as Confectioner in Jersey City and for near 3 years, God blessed my toil with Success. Trouble than came to my home. I was bereft of my two little boys, Gustav and John C. fremont, and next failed in buisness. My path of duty seemed plain and clear to me now. till now, two angel boys and an affectionate wife, her Tears had kept me back from it. I reason'd with her, whom I had sworn but 4 years ago to provide for and to protect, that, believing as we both do, the cause of the needy to be that of God, we must be ready to surrender anything, however dear, for it! that we ought to be practical Christians in our day, doers of the word as well as hearers of it, that I could not attend to Dr. Cheever's Church any longer, without being accused by my consciense. I told her, that the Children, whom God would please again to bless us with, would one day be proud, to call this country, that of their birth and should our boy in after years be ashamed of his father and shut his mouth, when others could say: "my father too assisted as a man in that great Struggle between good and Evil, he too helped, to break the chains of the millions, who stand now, disenthralled, free, as God made them before Him, lifting their hearts in Thanksgiving and praise." True to the impulse of a Christian wife, she too made the sacrifice with many tears. I became a soldier. My friends in Boston thought I was wrong; that the society in the ranks would either make me low or else, dwarf my mind in misery about my sad lot, that I had been too long accustom'd to comfort, to bear hardship or privation now, that I ought, should not go. I have proved to them, till now, what I then answer'd, that the princips for the which I lived, was willing to lay down, if need be, my life for, would and should uphold me, and Sir, never shall a sound of murmur or complaint from me reach them, though it is hard, to respect and treat as Superiors a swearing, gambling, drinking crowd of Officers.— But, very dear Sir, to you I come with Confidense, knowing you now some years personally as the advocate of the weak, the despised; in You, I know, I find the large hearted man, the patriot, that will simpathize with me. I came out here for to fight, but my regiment is not a fighting one, as it is called; it does orderly and provost duty now and than. All through this army, it is called the 4th Circus, is its laughing stock, because of the Officers in it, as Lieut. Col. Hutchins of Gen. Weigal's staff remarked to a friend of mine the other day. Three of our Companies are at the Dep. Headq. The remnant of 2 Comp's. (I with some 30 men) 2 Capt., 4 lieutenants, stay in this "old Camp" of ours, doing nothing whatever. Not an hours drill is given, no tactics studied by noncomm. Officers or men, though formally the Order from the war department in Washington, to this very effect, has been read out to us by an Officer some weeks ago. These 6 Officers have some 16 men to attend to their various wants, three to cook for them, of whom, sorry though I be, am one, since January the first. Yes Sir, Volunteers raised for war by the people of that old Commonwealth Massachusetts are detailed, as Officers drudges, out here, at a cost to them of 1000 dollars each. Most men have got their horses too, but some not, though the Officers have not uncommonly two or three, which all, but one, belong to them,

thei are made by some fair ? way by them out here and eat out
of the government crip. If no money is left, to gamble with, these
horses change hands and so called owners for no company mark
or letter is burnt into them. I was allowed till late my horse and
Equipments, which I loved, to clean and attend to, but now even
that privilege they have stripped me of. I had to turn it all in by
order of my Captain Mr. Thomas; not even the sabre is left me,
a soldier, in an Enemy's Country without Arms. I remonstrated,
but was reminded if I heard my Order. I could say much here,
but forbear. Having gone into the service of my Country, I love
it, for my principle is pure, and so I learn'd easy, nothing seems
hard to me. but I must do a soldiers duty be usefull to my people.
The waiting, hoping blacks, whose Freedom is not yet secured,
their solitary cause wich allways lays nearest my heart and posess
my whole soul; if I think over it, bends my spirit down to sadness.
I love my adopted country fervently and no American can love it
better. I long and strive to love it more, because even in this, a
Mass. Regmt. how great the number, who glory in their shame,
of not caring for it at all, and yet, here am I, worse than useless
to the people and the Government, who are and have been paying
so freely for my supposed Service; useless to my color'd brother,
the weary bondsman, whom I have come to help deliver, with
whom I would fain wish, to share the hardships of a soldier, and
to whom I long, to speak the word of good will and Cheer to.
When, during the watches of the night I have contemplated, that
the ground, on which I stood, was not long since moistened by the
sweat, the unpaid for sweat of the one, whilst the other, getting
riches by that man's toil, wielded the cruel lash on the victims back,
that here is the place where only shortly since the Sigh of the Needy
ascended to heaven, whilst Cruelty and Crime for a time held sway,
oh, than I feel, that this thought alone, which swells my heart with
righteous anger, will be all the martial Music my soul shall need,
to stir it to deeds of valor and making me victorious, when meeting
the wicked foe. I came, dear Sir, to the Old Commonwealth because

I would not be accredited to a Copperhead State or City, am now in one of its Vol. Regmts, but, believe me, Sir, and (without reason or truth speaks no Soldier of a Comrade's shame) I have looked in Vain for one whole hearted man among them. All around me I see none others, but a slave hating, unconcerned Crowd, men, that boast of want of patriotism, that would hail with utmost glee any kind of patched up peace, even were it dishonorable and unjust.

Must I stay the whole precious 3 years among these men, remain inefficient & idle, whilst there is need for brave and fearless hearts still? Does not the country need my services? than, why not send me home, put me to work on my trade, if you please, and what more I can earn, than my soldiers pay, put it into the treasury for the common good. Is there no patriot or Statesman, influential & willing, to help the right, true hearted man in the right the usefull place? can I not be transferred to some color'd Regmt., sharing danger & honor alike with men, with whom my whole soul is and will be? These thoughts have forced themselves again and again upon my mind. I have thought of you, honor'd Sir, remembering your goods works on behalf of the needy, Your patriotism, Your readyness to assist the friendless but true ones. I hope, I believe You will kindly listen to this my Entreaty, regarding this my earnest plea, which is: to assist me by Your influence with other great and good men, like Gov. Andrew, so, that I might be transferred to a Cavalry Regmt. of color'd troops. I would go as a private if that could be done, but this not be allowed, I ask for the humblest post, I care not what, as long as I can be but with the people, I love, the Objects of my and my wife's prayers. If granted the privelege, to lead a handfull of these men against their former Opressors, I know, that I shall honor that trust so, as a noble cause and a great trust are worthy of. And should in His own time, He, who leads men and nations in the way, which in wisdom He laid out for them, appoint a soldiers grave, to be mine, I would want none other, than that of the immortal Col. Shaw, fighting beside his black Comrades in the thickest of the fight, laying down his charge in the midst of his good work, going before Him, who leads men and battles, to receive a "well done thou good & faithfull servant" from the great Master. I do not care, where the Spot, or if ever men shall know it, where a board may or may not mark as my last Restingplace, all I wish for, is, to rest among those, whom the World hated and despised. My two little Angel boys slumber in death in that same green little Hill in Jersey City, where the Africans of that place are allowed to burry their dead. I and my wife thought, we sink our young Seeds for Eternity there, for methinks when God shall call the dead, to rise, to our doubled Joy shall we again see them among those, once rejected on Earth.—May I ask now one more favor of you, dear Sir, and will it please You, to give to me, an answer to this, in Your own handwriting, for I would keep it as a token of honor from a good and noble man, but more especially, to bequieth it to my young Son, born on the 10th February last, and whom we called after you. Our fervent wish is, that he may live, but live to honor the name he bears; may he be ready and willing too, to assist the weak, lift up those, that are cast down & to cheer the heart of the needy and humble. May it please God, to spare his parents, to bring him up in the fear of the Lord, fearing None, but Him. But if I should not return, to see my boy and he grows up, to distinguish wrong from right, he will than read the words of mine, I sent home, on the news of his birth. With this my charge to him in after years, I would give or leave to him the letter, written by you. and perhaps these means may remind him of his duty to God & men, when time shall be with his father no more, that he may worthyly bear your honor'd name, Sir, and not treat, with coldness even, the people, for whom his own father gave up all, that is dear to life, seperating himself from dear and loved ones, to be helper of the helpless, and for whose liberty, good men have spent long and valuable lives, to bring about a healthy sentiment in favor of justice to all.—I have every comfort since January the first, that I can wish for, a good and warm bed and tent, to my self, where I do cooking now for 2 Officers. I may sit up late, none interferes, though lights in all tents have to be blown out by 9 o clock. My Officers think well of & treat me kindly, but they dislike a color'd men, and the three dark friends of mine, who were formerly employed, to do my work, are since the old year discharged. As for chance for promotion here, I think I have a better one, than any other men in my Company, but willingly I give up all these things, if, by so doing, I can be but of service to my people and be with my friends, who are still the despised here.—please pardon this lengthy letter, dear Sir, and this intruding so much on Your valueable time. Being a stranger to You, I thought best, to enclose my card. Mr. Augustus Meisel, Lithographer of Phonix building Boston, is a friend of mine and knows my motives better than any other man, Mr. Daniel Fobes of 8 Brattle street Boston, also knows me, having done buisness with him for the last 3 years, in confectionary. And now, dearest Sir, may it please the God of a kind providence, to spare for many years to come, Your valuable life, for still to be able to benefit your friends the despised and to see the ripe fruit of Your toil and labour; liberty to All on the American continent. With great Esteem for You, I shall ever be, honor'd Sir,

> Your obedient Servant, GUSTAV J.L. REUTER
> private, Comp. K, 4th Mass. Cav. Vols.

94. From SARAH A. MANIS

ESTILLVILLE SCOTT CO VA
AUG 25TH 1866

MR PHILIPS:—

DEAR SIR—

Please forgive me for interrupting you. My subject is one of interest to the poor freedman of the south of this town.

I have done every thing in my power to better their condition—to instruct them in the rudiments of learning. You must know that we are very poor out South and unable to do a great deal.—hence I appeal to you for what aid you can give—

I have out of my scanty earnings as seamstress, bought one hundred and eight Websters Spellers for the poor freedman, at a cost of twenty dollars, they seem anxious to learn and to improve their condition. Now the people of Mass are *Rich* and can do a great deal of good—indeed I know they do a great amount of good.

Will you make me up a little money to pay me for teaching the freedman this fall and winter? If I was able I would teach them for nothing, but I must make at least my board and clothing. Almost any little boy and girl in Boston will give you ten or twenty cents for the purpose which will not injure them but do a lasting good to the poor *colored*.

I will refer you to the post master and to our minister—also to the Clerk of the courts, at our Town for the honesty of my motives and intentions, and should you give any thing, it will all be appropriated to the benefit of the poor colored people here.

Hoping that my appeal will not be altogether in vain—I will close for the present by impressing a desire to here from you soon.

Very respectfully
Your Obt Servt,
Address   Miss Sarah A. Manis
Estillville
Scott Co
Va

P.S. Any referince you desire you can have—the very best.

S. A. Manis

95. To WILLIAM LLOYD GARRISON
From ROBERT CRAIG

NOXUBEE CO
BROOKSVILLE POST OFFICE   MISSISSIPPI
APRIL 18/57

W. Loyd Garrison Esq
   Dear sir———
   Living in a remote section of Country and a Slave one at that

and there Being but few friends of us in an enemies Country we wish you to send some good Liberal Documents   I wish you to send me a few Copyes from time to time of your Liberator and I will send you the money shortly

and you will Obli your friend

& Co

ROBERT CRAIG

96. From SALLIE HOLLEY

LOTTSBURGH VA.

APRIL 20TH 1873

MY DEAR MR PHILLIPS

It is a wonderful comfort to us to have *you* care to hear of what fills our eyes and hearts in Virginia. And if a letter of mine amuses you for a moment—I would not miss writing it for a great deal. It is a small but only return I can make for all your very delightful interest and sympathy. Yesterday we celebrated Lexington & Baltimore—with the Flag flying free over our schoolhouse. Joseph Armstrong, one of our colored men—planted the pole (which we keep for safety on our own grounds, except holidays) and run up the beautiful stars & stripes. Novella Middleton caught sight of it a mile off—You can scarcely imagine what a rare, pretty sight *The Flag* is in this region—And our scholars sang over the score of patriotic songs they have learned to the edification of the mail carrier—and all our souls. No where do we realize their significance as in this semi-loyal land. Julia Clark, Pyramus Johnson, Novella Middleton, Rachel Gordon and Georgeanna Payne Emma Hooper & Lizzie Burgess—all recited passages from Mr. Phillips speeches about the Equal Rights of woman and of Black men—with a clear distinct idea and correct enunciation that seems to me *miraculous*—when I recal what an incoherent, unintelligible mess their sounds and speech was four years ago. Of course, Paul Revere's Ride was spoken.

FREEDOM TO SLAVES!

Whereas, the President of the United States did, on the first day of the present month, issue his *Proclamation* declaring "that *all persons held as Slaves in certain designated States, and parts of States, are, and henceforward shall be free*," and that the Executive Government of the United States, including the Military and Naval authorities thereof, would recognize and maintain the freedom of said persons. *And Whereas*, the county of *Frederick* is included in the territory designated by the Proclamation of the President, in which the *Slaves should become free*, I therefore hereby notify the citizens of the city of Winchester, and of said County, of said Proclamation, and of my intention to maintain and enforce the same.

I expect all citizens to yield a ready compliance with the Proclamation of the Chief Executive, and I admonish all persons disposed to resist its peaceful enforcement, that upon manifesting such disposition by acts, they will be regarded as rebels in arms against the lawful authority of the Federal Government and dealt with accordingly.

All persons liberated by said Proclamation are admonished to abstain from all violence, and immediately betake themselves to useful occupations.

The officers of this command are admonished and ordered to act in accordance with said proclamation and to yield their ready co-operation in its enforcement.

R. H. Milroy,
Brig. Gen'l Commanding.

Winchester
Jan. 5th, 1863.

A poster announcing the Emancipation Proclamation to the inhabitants of Winchester, Virginia, and surrounding Frederick County, on which an anonymous abolitionist has written a triumphant comment.

Florence Bailey recited "The Black Regiment" very nicely—
Mary Ann Johnson & Charlotte Washington spoke an admirable
Dialogue on "Mischief of Bad Air" which made us all laugh—Then
"*The Wonderful Machine*" (The Hand) was spoken by Henry
Washington and Jimmie Blackwell. All the children were unex-
ampled in their neat, clean attire— I could not help praising them
upon their pleasing appearance—I kept a nice lot of girls dresses,
from the boxes sent down to us—and coaxed a score of hands to
bring grass sods for our garden borders—or weed our strawberry
beds—and all manner of little employments so I could bestow these
dresses—and the result was they "all came out in a bloom" as good
John Carter said "to keep company with the fruit trees"—I wish
you could have had a look at them! Little four-year-old Wendell
Phillips Parker wore a little navy blue sailor suit that was given me
last Dec. and was immensely proud and happy in such unusual
dress—a whole nest of little ones—an Infant class sat on the platform's edge—one tiny mite we address as "little Miss Newton" (to
her great satisfaction)—mother—Letitia Leland altogether a pic-
turesque looking and agreeable mannered group of children that
we are beginning to look upon as the Hope of the Future. They
performed a little part quite dramatically. "Good Night said the
Plow to the weary old horse" &c. No child ever thinks of *not* taking
a part but all do it as naturally as to eat a ripe peach. These little
ones in a row sat each with a pretty colored picture like a chromo
in their hand—after I began "distributing the presents," which is a
most enjoyable feature of these holiday occasions. Mrs. Theo Brown
of Worcester had sent down a quantity of old parasols which carried
joy to many a breast—and some painted trap balls made the boys'
eyes glisten—pocket handkerchiefs—ribbon bows—fans—aprons &c.
Honest old Albert Smith received new warm flannel for a shirt.
Poor old man—he walked six miles to be here with his little grand-
daughters Julia & Gethsemane Smith—at the close of exercises he
made a pathetic speech expressing his sense of the "monstrous good
thing this learning was"—Everybody who had children must feel

"mighty proud to see them get up and make speeches about things they never thought on or heard of before"—out of his aged bent form so long crushed by Slavery's power came a cheerful voice and a tender joy beamed in his face for the blessing he too was sharing with his grandchildren in the school.

Thornton Chapman & his bride got down with their oxen and cart (brot grass sods and I gave her a bedquilt)   They said they "worked right through Easter Holiday so as to take this 19th of April at the School—He spoke nicely too—Told how much he learned hearing Frederick Douglass here last Nov. "wouldn't have missed it for fifty dollars"—So our little happy festival has come and gone again—Every anniversary like this marks to our senses the progress we have made—It gathers our much scattered fold into view in one scene, which is inspiration to continued effort   We never waver for a moment, of the wisdom and value of our work here—Nothing can destroy what has been done. The past is secure—We are only anxious to save the future with the best advantage possible—from the malignant group of these rebels—

One lovely morning last week Miss Putnam and I walked four miles up to see Mary Ann Digger in her new home—"A pretty snug house isn't it for a poor man?" Thornton Chapman asked us—as we saw with pleasure—his three glass windows (four little panes in each) —*brick* chimney, good plank floor—doors with locks & hinges—a pair of stairs and upper chamber—&c.—As we walked out of their just-burned clearing—where they would soon plant corn—he remarked "ground as rich as cream!" My grass sods have yielded one bright golden bunch of dandelions—six in a cluster—a rarity in this country—the children don't even know the name.

Miss Putnam has a nice class in Botany "How plants grow"—by Prof. Gray—The best passage in Mr Stearns' Book is where he tells us how Mr Phillips strengthened, refreshed and exalted his disconsolate soul—and I am very glad to have read it.

Our strawberry beds are in promising bloom. We have nearly conquered the viper's Bugloss—an ugly weed our people call "Blue

thistle" that almost wholly possessed "Our Farm of Two Acres" —
when we began.

truly and affectionately from Miss Putnam and myself
SALLIE HOLLEY[20]

20. Sallie Holley (1818–1893), an Oberlin graduate, feminist, and antislavery
lecturer, and her friend Caroline Putnam carried on a freedmen's school for more
than twenty years after the War. Phillips must have been struck by the contrast
between her description of Reconstruction and the demonic image of the post-war
South communicated by Albert G. Browne.

4. Phillips and Garrison

DURING the 1840's and 50's Phillips and William Lloyd Garrison collaborated powerfully in a common cause. Letters from Garrison during the period reflect the satisfaction both men took in their relationship and Garrison's almost painful awareness of his wealthy friend's many acts of personal generosity.

When civil war came, Phillips's reputation soared. Commanding vast audiences denied to other abolitionists, he seemed to embody the principles that Garrison had first enunciated. Although Garrison was still the nominal head of the movement, and the one man who more than any other held it together, he almost seemed to be standing in his friend's shadow. His letters to Phillips in 1861, for example, can be read as an expression of Garrison's unconscious resentment at not being at the center of the stage himself. He was forced to content himself with directing the action from outside.

Ironically enough, the war, which did so much to unify antislavery sentiment in the North, finally drove Phillips and Garrison apart. Although disagreeing with Garrison on some matters, Phillips had always been willing to bow to his friend's moral judgment. However, he could not agree with his judgment of Abraham Lincoln. Garrison believed that Lincoln was leading the nation on an essentially just course thus making a separate antislavery movement obsolete. Phillips condemned the President as a weak leader and sought to have abolitionists agitate for the rights of the freedman as determinedly as they had for the rights of the slave. At the annual meeting of the American Antislavery Society in 1865, Garrison proposed dissolution. Phillips successfully opposed the motion and was elected president of the society in Garrison's place. Many loyal Garrisonians followed their leader into a retirement replete with public honors and recognition, while the radical remnant under Phillips struggled to make a reluctant people confront the moral implications of reconstruction.[1]

1. Irving H. Bartlett, *Wendell Phillips: Brahmin Radical* (Boston, 1961), pp. 276–293.

The break with Garrison came over a matter of principle. Neither man had ever been able to compromise on such matters and each tended now to treat the other as they had once spurned a common enemy. As usual, Phillips could justify himself, but as Lydia Maria Child discovered in 1868 he felt hurt and lonely.

Garrison did not die until 1879. By then the two old comrades had been brought together many times at the graves of other abolitionists. A kind of reconciliation was inevitable and when it came time to say the final words for Garrison, Phillips chose to forget that there had ever been differences between them. "For myself," he said, "no words can adequately tell the measureless debt I owe him, the moral and intellectual life he opened to me. I feel like the old Greek who, taught himself by Socrates, called his own scholars 'the disciples of Socrates'." [2]

97. From WILLIAM LLOYD GARRISON

BOSTON, SEPT. 12, 1842.

MY DEAR PHILLIPS:

Am I never to have an opportunity to see your face again? I believe two, perhaps three months have elapsed since we met. It is not your fault, it is not mine; but so it happens. There is one consolation that I have left me. If I cannot see *you*, I can and do see your little namesake every day; and a more charming boy, (though he is my mine,) I challenge the world to produce. O, such eyes! such a head! such a complexion! such every thing! May he prove to be even a better man than he is a handsome child, and not disgrace the fair name that he bears.

I have a piece of intelligence to communicate. On Friday last, my dear Helen, for the fourth time, presented me with a fine boy, fairly weighing 10 lbs. and in all respects "a marvellous proper" child. So, you see, "Garrisonism" is steadily on the increase, in spite

2. Wendell Phillips, *Speeches, Lectures and Letters*, Second Series (Boston, 1891), p. 466.

of all opposition. Thus far, every thing has gone most favorably, both for the mother and babe. What should the name of the new comer be? I have several beloved friends, whose names I should be proud to incorporate with my own; and it is difficult for me to choose one name from among the number. True, "a rose by any other name would smell as sweet"; but it is not best to call a rose a pumpkin, you know.

Now, for business—my principal object in writing to you. You have seen doubtless, in the last Liberator, a notice of a grand Anti-Slavery Pic Nic, to be holden at Princeton on Friday next. Circumstances will conspire to render it exceedingly inconvenient for me to attend it; and I promised our brother J. T. Everett, (at his urgent request,) that I would do my best to secure your presence on that occasion. Perhaps you are aware that you are quite a favorite in all that region, and they would prefer you to any other person. Do go, if you can. Give them a trumpet-blast, and let the winds carry it all over the land. If you should decline, they will probably not be able to get any one else, of the right sort. All your expenses will be promptly liquidated, and many thanks given to you besides. Let me hear from you by return of mail, if practicable, It will be necessary to leave Boston on Thursday.

I wish to see not only your face but that of your afflicted, estimable wife. How is her health, at present? Where do you intend to live during the ensuing winter? When are you coming to the city? Desiring to be remembered in terms of sympathy and friendship to Mrs. Phillips, I remain,

Your faithful friend,
Wm. LLOYD GARRISON.

98. From WILLIAM LLOYD GARRISON

BOSTON, AUGUST 5, 1845

MY DEAR WENDELL:

I see nothing of you—I hear and get nothing from you—but presume all is well with you, at least as usual. On what day do you start for Philadelphia? I shall probably leave on Friday morning, via the Long Island route—stop over night in New York, and on Saturday morning take the cars for P. Can you go at that time? Or, for the sake of your company, I will not leave till Friday afternoon, and so will go through to N.Y. during the night. The meeting, you will remember, takes place on Monday forenoon. I see by the last Penn. Freeman, that they have advertised me to speak twice on religious subjects during Sunday, and in the evening, a lecture is expected from you on the subject of slavery. It is possible that you might reach Philadelphia in season on Sunday to fulfil that appointment, if you should not leave Boston till Saturday afternoon—as I believe there is a train that leaves N.Y. for Philad. on Sunday morning (at least, there was last year at this time) at 9 o'clock; but there would be some risk about this, and I therefore hope you will go on with me. My company is worth something, you know! Should you fail, for any reason whatever, to arrive at the State meeting in season, our Penn. friends would feel as if an avalanche had been precipitated upon them, and each particular hair of my head would stand on end. The conflict is to be a severe one, and we must not on any account be away from it. Let me hear from you immediately.

My warmest regards to your beloved Anne, who is, I hope, improving in health by her sojourn in the country.

> Yours, faithfully,
> Wm. LLOYD GARRISON

99. From WILLIAM LLOYD and HELEN GARRISON

BOSTON, JAN. 3, 1846

DEAR WENDELL AND ANN T. G. PHILLIPS:

According to human device and calculation, it is the commencement of another new year—the season of good wishes, friendly congratulations, loving gifts. To allow it to pass by, without invoking upon you both, whatever of felicity or health kind Heaven can bestow, would be to put a gag into our mouths, and a seal upon our hearts. Words are cheap, it is true; but only when they are the progeny of flattery and formality. They possess a rich, inherent value, when they breathe of true affection and deep sincerity; though they should rarely be multitudinous.

Among a somewhat extended circle of choice friends, you are very dear to us. Your friendship we prize at a high rate; your kindness, as unweariedly manifested to us from year to year, we gratefully appreciate. Neither in the one nor the other case is it in our power to return you a suitable equivalent, though we are unreservedly yours to serve and cherish. More you will not desire; less we cannot proffer. Be assured of our lively and perpetual remembrance of all your virtues and kind deeds, though we say so little to you about them. In your eyes, they are modestly estimated; in our own, we are sure that they are not exaggerated. But this is a subject too sacred for personal address, and we will not press it. May this be the brightest and happiest year that you have spent together, happy as you have been hitherto.

Is the exclamation, "I wish you a happy new year," on the part of every body to every body, at this season, a mere form of words? Sometimes it is, doubtless; but generally otherwise. Is it not a prophecy of the arrival of a period when "men shall sit under their own vines, and there should be none to molest or make afraid"; when it shall be every body's business to make every body happy, not for one day annually, but during the whole cycle of life? O, if mankind could only see and realize what it is that lies in the way of their happiness—to what extent and in how many ways they are the artificers of their own misery—and how they are rendering it impracticable, by their follies or errors, for their good wishes to be consummated—how soon we should have Eden come again! Let Heaven be exonerated from all blame. The source of all the discord, confusion, suffering on earth, is beneath the skies. It is not to be traced to any arbitrary fiat of the Creator, who causes his sun to shine as genially on the unjust as on the just. Our race, to be truly happy, must be positively good. Alas! if human goodness be the measure of human happiness, no marvel that misery so widely abounds. The earnest wish for each other's happiness, expressed on each new year's day, is the evidence of general liability to disappointment and sorrows else it would not be uttered.

Dear Mrs. Phillips, we often think of you, confined almost exclusively to your chamber by permanent ill health—cut off from all the advantages and enjoyments of active life—deprived of all participation in the gatherings of those whose philanthropic object is so dear to your heart—unable, except rarely, to enjoy the society even of your most attached friends; and, while we deeply sympathize with you in being necessitated to suffer bereavements like these, and in the bodily pains and infirmities which you are called to experience, we admire and wonder at the patience, fortitude, resignation, cheerfulness, and elasticity of spirit, which mark your character, and enable you to keep up a lively interest in the reforms of the age. "Is there no balm in Gilead," that will prove a panacea in your case? O that your health might be entirely and speedily restored! Pardon us for saying that you must be resolved on a cure! True, it is safer and better to try nothing, than to try every thing that may be recommended; but you must not be wholly devoid of faith, nor regard your case as a hopeless one.

Beloved friends, the year is before us, for good or for evil. We know not, of course, what may be its vicissitudes and mutations. It is doubtless well that we are thus ignorant. To be prepared for the future, it is for us rightly to improve the present. There is no lack of work to be done in the vineyard of humanity, and should be no cessation of effort, until we are called away to a higher and nobler sphere. The friendship which now binds us together as with "hooks of steel"—shall it not survive the life of these frail bodies, and be as immortal as our spirits? Trusting and praying that it may, and renewing our best wishes for your temporal and eternal welfare, we remain,

> Yours, unitedly,
> WM. LLOYD GARRISON,
> HELEN ELISA GARRISON.

100. From WILLIAM LLOYD GARRISON

BOSTON, JUNE 30, 1846.

DEAR PHILLIPS:

Thanks for your *private* note, and your *public* communication. Success to the cause of Woman's Rights, the world over! "There's a good time coming" for the whole human race, yet. In this faith, I mean to live, and hope to die.

Isn't it surprising that Douglass should have allowed himself to be seduced by the London Committee, for their benefit, after all that he has known of the conduct of that Committee toward the American A. S. Society? I fear (with you) that G. T. advised to this step—and without due reflection. Strange that *he* should be willing to give that Committee any countenance. But how few men can stand perfectly erect, where all is sunshine, and prosperity!

I am, at this moment, almost "solitary and alone." Helen and the three youngest children are in Providence, where they went on Friday, and from whence they will not return till Thursday. I went to Providence on Saturday, lectured on non-resistance and the Mexican war to a full audience on Sunday evening, and returned yesterday forenoon. I will give Helen your message on her return. Are you not almost afraid to trust me on the other side of the Atlantic?

I enclose a private note, just received from Pillsbury, in Ohio. You will see what he says about the liberty Stephen is taking with your name, and those of others, to give credit to his idle and impracticable scheme of rallying the no-union voters at the polls.

Certainly, he does not mean to deceive any body; but just as certainly, he is deceiving them, in making such statements. If you think best, will you give me an article on the subject, without any particular reference to P's letter?[3]

You fill me with horror, in saying that you shall not be at the Dedham celebration on the 4th! Whether you can speak or not, you *must* be there—or you will grieve the hearts of a great multitude, and throw a shade of disappointment over all the proceedings. What excuse can you offer for not being present? You are at leisure —Ann's health, I trust, is better, at least not worse—you can come and go back on the same day—the occasion has been magnified from a local to a State celebration—and your absence cannot be tolerated! I beg you, on my bended knees, to attend, in the name of thousands. Your absence would be next in enormity to the volunteer support of C. U. Clay in the Mexican war! Come, and bring Henry Wilson along with you for a companion, and God's blessing be with you both!

Of course, I must see you before I leave for England. I still have some misgivings about the mission, but trust it will turn out well for the cause of humanity.

Give my most affectionate regards to Ann. She does not know how much I esteem her, nor how much I yearn for her speedy and entire recovery. Tell her that I know she will so far abandon the non-resistance principle as to *drive* you to the Pic-Nic, if necessary. Seriously, do not fail to come.

Lovingly yours,
WM. LLOYD GARRISON.

3. Stephen S. Foster (1809–1881) was one of the more radical abolitionists who with his wife Abigail Kelley Foster (1810–1887) frequently balked at Garrison's leadership. Garrison's concern here with the behavior of Foster and Frederick Douglass is characteristic of his attempt to play the role of "chief arbiter of a religious community, the American Anti-Slavery Society, the keeper of its traditions, the creator of spiritual consensus among its members." James Brewer Stewart, "Garrison Again, And Again, And Again, and Again," *Reviews in American History*, 4 (December, 1976), 542.

101. To ANN PHILLIPS

From WILLIAM LLOYD GARRISON

THURSDAY AFTERNOON,
APRIL 20, 1848

DEAR FRIEND:

The dew-drop is exhaled—the bud withered and fallen to the earth. We have the form of our dear babe still left to us—very beautiful even in death;—but her emancipated spirit is in that other and better world, which it is a part of our religious faith to believe a gracious Creator has prepared for his children, at the close of their earthly sojourn. "Of such is the kingdom of God." How beautiful the illustration of Jesus!

Little did I imagine, when I wrote you that hasty note on Tuesday afternoon, that our darling Lizzie was so soon to be taken from us. True, I knew she was feeble, emaciated, and very ill; but her fever seemed to have turned somewhat favorably—the doctor thought she was gradually improving, and his visits were less frequent—and when I went to my office yesterday morning, she gave promise, from the better repose of the previous night, of having an unusually comfortable day. During the afternoon, however, she became wild and restless, and her symptoms grew alarming. At dusk, the doctor came, and pronounced her case extremely critical. He left a prescription, saying that if it did not operate, she must die. He spoke truly: the medicine had no effect, and at half past 12 this morning, the edict was fulfilled in her case—"Dust to dust, and the spirit to God who gave it." Her exit was so gentle, that no one in the room knew when she drew her last breath. "Night dews fall not more gently to the ground, Nor weary, worn-out winds expire so soft."

To-morrow afternoon, at 3 o'clock, is the time we have assigned for the funeral. We hope dear Wendell will be able to be with us, (we are sure you will both be in spirit,) and perhaps he may feel like saying a few words on the occasion—many are not needed. No strange event has happened unto us, distinct from the history of human mortality; there is nothing dark or mysterious in it, but it is natural, and inevitable to us all. Tenderly do we feel our bereavement, but there is no dark cloud upon our spirits.

Accept from dear Helen and myself our renewed assurances of great personal esteem and affection.

WM. LLOYD GARRISON.

102. To ANN PHILLIPS From HELEN E. GARRISON

BOSTON   JULY 18, 1848.

MY DEAR ANN.

I feel as if I could not refrain from sending a line to you, as I am denied the privilege of going to Essex St. to see you face to face, which would indeed be refreshing to look upon this moment. I feel lonely and forlorn without my darling, for who is there that can supply his place. Not one I miss his cheerful countenance, his pleasant voice which was always music to my soul. It was a severe trial to me to think of parting with him for so long a period, and for a time I could not think of it with the least composure. But when I saw the struggle was equally as great on his own part and that nothing but a sense of duty that he would be doing a greater work elsewhere than here, would compel him to leave home, I felt resolved to be resigned let the consequences be what they might, and I have thus far been wonderfully supported with a degree of calmness I thought I never possessed. Still to look forward to three months; it seems an eternity without him, but with him how like lightning speed it would pass away. As the time drew near for his departure the thought of leaving us weighed heavily upon him, but we comforted ourselves with the reflection that a reunion would be sweet indeed; so bitter was the pang of separation. Blessed with a fond and loving husband yourself, dear Ann, I know you will sympathise with me as few others can in my hours of sadness, for already do I keenly feel his absence now I know he cannot return to me. How did we long for a quiet retreat for a few hours to be by ourselves without intruders, that we might have time for thought and reflection. But from the fourth of July we never had an hour without interruption. A great many strangers happened here to pass the afternoon, and others came to stay that we had no particular interest in. We had three at a time staying here, they seemed to think because Lloyd was going to England he could see his friends from far and near. They came from every quarter to say farewell. Kindly meant I know, but provoking at such a time when we covet the hours we had to spend apart so near the time of separation. But I must leave this subject for I did not think of talking so much about ourselves, when I commenced this letter, but I beg you will excuse it at this particular time when I feel so much.

I was rejoiced to see Wendell at Dedham for next to seeing my own husband, there is none I look upon with so much pleasure as yours. He said you were still feeble which news I regretted to learn. I hope you will be prevailed upon to try the water cure in the Autumn, though I shall not be willing to part with you just as I can make you some friendly calls, which I look forward to with delight. Still if you can only enjoy your health once more, it will seem like a new creation to you, so long have you been shut out from its beauties. I cannot feel too grateful that Wendell is spared you, always so watchful, and kind, and never weary in making those around him happy. I received a letter from sister Sarah, who is in New York under Dr. Doolittle's care. He draws out cancers with a plaster, and he has taken out hundreds, but never knew one to return. He had applied two plasters when she wrote, she wore them ten minutes then had a soothing one applied. She writes in her usual spirits, evidently feeling encouraged, and hoping she should derive great benefit from them, and seemed to feel she should be cured. Her hope is very large, and she always looks upon the bright side of everything. I fear dear I have wearied your patience with my long epistle, if so, forgive me this once, and I will promise not to do the like again. I have expressed my feelings to you, because I know you are kind and sympathetic, and I have no one to whom I feel so near as yourself in the vicinity of Boston, and to whom I can open my heart without reserve.

I have been in quite a desponding state, and have written just as I felt, and what came in my head first, so I shall oblige you to commit it to the flames as soon as read, and let no eye but your own see the contents. Give my love to Wendell, and accept a large share for yourself. When you feel able to send a line you may be assured I shall delight to have it.

Your loving friend,
HELEN E. GARRISON.[4]

4. Helen Benson Garrison (1811–1876). There are several letters from Garrison's wife to Ann Phillips, suggesting a hitherto unsuspected intimacy between the two women.

103. To ANN PHILLIPS

From WILLIAM LLOYD GARRISON

65, SUFFOLK STREET, APRIL 27, 1849

MY DEAR FRIEND:

When, the other day, Wendell put into my hands five dollars, in your name, to be expended in that amount of omnibus tickets in my behalf, in consequence of the enlarged distance between my present residence and 21 Cornhill, and especially of my indisposition since the demise of my beloved boy, I was most deeply affected by your kindness, but had been indebted to it so largely, and so many times, that I really felt as if I ought not to take the gift. But Wendell persisted in my acceptance of it, as a matter of real pleasure to you, which would be turned into pain by my declining it; and so a consideration was presented, which I could not resist. The money shall be faithfully appropriated as you desire, though I promise you it shall not abridge that amount of bodily exercise in walking which a due regard to health requires. The liberty of transportation which it will purchase for me will save me many a weary step, and often prove of very great convenience.

I am almost afraid to offer thanks. You and dear Wendell have done so much for me and mine, that I feel as unable to express my obligations, as I know you both are averse to any special mention of them. Your united gifts at the last Bazaar were various, valuable, and most serviceable. What have we to offer you in return? Nothing but the assurances of our heartfelt gratitude; nothing but the confession of our deep indebtedness; nothing but the conviction of our unworthiness.

But it is your confidence and esteem, your sympathy and love, which we prize "above all price." Such friends are rarely to be found on earth—so disinterested and kind, so faithful and devoted. We feel that our spirits are blended with yours, not merely for time, but for eternity.

How I long for your restoration to health! My heart saddens within me, whenever I think of your long imprisonment as an invalid. Yet I am filled with wonder and admiration at the patience, fortitude and resignation manifested by you; at the buoyancy of your spirits; at the vital and untiring interest which you take in the reformatory movements of the age; and especially at the vigilance and zeal which you manifest in the noblest and most trying struggle of our day, for the complete emancipation of our enslaved country-men. There are few permanent invalids who feel or can be induced to believe that they have aught to do, except to deplore their situation, and to be wholly engrossed by it.

As for Wendell, he has long been an object of my unfeigned admiration, of my deepest love. I know not whether I most esteem the goodness of his heart, the brilliancy and strength of his intellect, or the moral heroism of his spirit. But I am writing to you, and not to another, and must suppress what more it would delight me to add.

Dear, loving, noble Charley! Ever since his removal, my heart has been heavy, and relief comes slowly. Our household seems to be almost voiceless, now.

Pray excuse what I have written, and accept the gratitude of dear Helen, and

Yours, truly,

WM. LLOYD GARRISON.

A.T.G.Phillips.

104. From WILLIAM LLOYD GARRISON

BOSTON, JAN. 3, 1851.

MY DEAR PHILLIPS:

There is no one to whom I can more freely unbosom myself, in any emergency, than yourself; and I therefore confidingly submit my present situation to your friendly consideration.

On the first of this month, I find that I am owing, for absolutely necessary family expenditures, above what I have a farthing to pay with, something over two hundred dollars.—This deficit, it is just to state, is not all to be put down to the past year, but a portion of it belongs to the year previous,—as the expenses of each quarter, during that entire period, has gradually entrenched upon the receipts of the next. Various circumstances, however, during the last three months,—sickness and protracted medical attendance, incidental expenses arising from the visit of our beloved G. T., to the purchase of a large parlor stove, &c. &c.,—have served to make the sum total of indebtedness greater than it would have been ordinarily.

I need not protest to you, my dear Phillips, that I have not thoughtlessly or needlessly got thus straitened. If my conscience is lively in any direction, it is in regard to the use of money, especially while I am occupying a somewhat dependant position. I am neither a spendthrift nor improvident, but careful, considerate, scrupulous, and ever anxious to keep "square with the world." But, in spite of my best endeavors in this respect, (seconded uniformly by dear Helen, whose dread of being in debt is intense, and to whose prudence in regard to personal expenditures and household affairs,

I most gratefully testify,) I find myself, pecuniarily, at the beginning of this year, just as I have stated above. My family, you know, is large, and as they grow in years the children unavoidably augment the burden of support. My connection with the anti-slavery cause is such as to increase my family expenses,—i.e., to exhibit any thing like hospitality; though I endeavor to keep the number entertained at my table as much reduced as I can with civility. Still, my liabilities on this score are constant, and in the aggregate onerous. My own personal expenditures are very limited; for the indulgence of my taste, fancy, and gratification, nothing. "Bread and butter," rent and fuel, and necessary clothing for the family, absorb my income. But details like these are not needed by you to remove doubt or inspire confidence, and I will not multiply them.

It is true that, in addition to my usual stipend, I have received something for my lecturing services; but, with this incidental aid, I am still embarrassed.

Before the past year terminated,—foreseeing how I was coming out,—my mind was greatly exercised as to how Providence might open a way of deliverance. My deep indebtedness to you and dear Anne, and to my kind friends Philbrick, Jackson and Hovey, on various occasions, made me "sick at heart" to think of increasing it by any statement of my real situation that might lead to further assistance; especially when you have so many calls upon your liberality in the anti-slavery cause in particular, and in the cause of suffering humanity in general.

Fortunately, there is no need of taxing any of you to the amount of a shilling, to afford me the relief I need. For the first time in its eventful history, the receipts of the Liberator last year exceeded its expenditures, leaving a surplus of nearly five hundred dollars. Could I have two hundred of this sum, I could get along for the present, though fifty more would just enable me to commence the year, owing no man any thing but love. I leave the matter to the decision of the Financial Committee of the Liberator, if you will be so kind as to lay my case before them. Perhaps you can do this to-morrow forenoon, after the meeting of the Massachusetts Board.

Perhaps you may say, "The income of the Liberator, above its expenses, is your own, to be used according to your necessities." I know it is. I know that the Financial Committee make no claim to any of the Liberator earnings. At the same time, I desire to act with their approbation, and under their guidance; and I trust they will not infer that, if what I need is granted, it may induce less economy during the present year. Not so. My effort will still be, assiduously, to keep to the lowest point, and I have a direct personal interest in a steady enlargement of the income of the paper, through its subscription list, as I love my wife and children.

One thing further. I have long wished it might be among the pecuniary possibilities of the Liberator to admit of a donation being made to our worthy and faithful friend Wallcut. As I heard him say, a few days since, to Mr. May,—the fact was extorted from him in reference to the meeting at Milford and Hopedale, which he said he strongly desired to attend, but had not the means,—that he was "under water to the amount of fifty dollars," it would be very gratifying to me if the Financial Committee should feel willing to make him a donation to that amount from the surplus income of the last year, if he has not yet found relief. He is an extremely diffident, as well as highly conscientious man, and never wishes to trouble any one with his difficulties. But his salary is small, so as to keep him continually cramped. I have said nothing to him, or to any one else, on the subject, and leave the suggestion to be acted upon as may be deemed expedient.

This letter is for your and Anne's perusal. Perhaps it had better be destroyed, after its perusal. If, however, you should prefer to lay it before the Committee, do so.

I remain, your debtor beyond all cancelling,
WM. LLOYD GARRISON.[5]

Wendell Phillips.

5. A draft of this letter in another form appears in *The Letters of William Lloyd Garrison,* ed. Louis Ruchames (Cambridge, 1975), IV, 45–47.

105. From WILLIAM LLOYD GARRISON

BOSTON, JULY 2, 1858.

DEAR PHILLIPS:

Enclosed, I send you a letter to your address, received from Mrs. Chapman, (which she authorised me to read,) respecting an official expression of sentiment at Framingham, on Monday next, with reference to the friends and opponents of the Anti-Slavery cause in the old world—the attitude of the British Government on the right of visitation as pertaining to the foreign slave trade—&c., &c. If you can prepare anything for that occasion, to be adopted by the meeting, or refer to this matter in your speech, I think it would prove very acceptable.

I also enclose a letter from W. H. Herndon of Illinois, (the third one I have received from him on the same subject,) urging the publication, in separate volumes, of a selection of your speeches. I second the motion with all my heart; and if you will get the speeches ready, this summer, and allow me to issue proposals, so that subscribers may be obtained in advance, I will do so forthwith. I think two volumes, of the ordinary size, (say 400 pages, each,) *as the first instalment*, would be best—selling them at a dollar a volume. Of course, a portion of the edition might be printed on finer paper, and bound handsomely, at an enhanced price; but for the public at large, I would not exceed *dollar* volumes.

I beseech you, for many considerations, to attend to this matter, and consent to the desired publication.

Give my *warmest* remembrances to your beloved wife; for I write in a melting mood, sincerely hoping that you have it cooler in your country retreat. Also, give my regards to my favorite Phebe. In all which, dear Helen joins, of course.

Yours, admiringly,

WM. LLOYD GARRISON.

Wendell Phillips.

106. To ANN PHILLIPS

From WENDELL PHILLIPS GARRISON

BOSTON, JULY 21ST 1858.

My dear Mrs. Phillips:

If there ever was a person who could lay claim to double parentage, I think it must be allowed that I am he; for my feelings towards yourself and Mr. Phillips can be best likened to those entertained by a son for father and mother. At the remembrance of your motherly kindness, especially, my heart is filled with overflowing gratitude and thankfulness, though I regret that the state of your health has not permitted me more frequently to visit you, and to become as thoroughly acquainted with your face as I am with your goodness of heart. Not that I have forgotten your features—they are indelibly fixed in my memory, and rise clearly up before me, whenever I think of you.

I know how much I am indebted to you for my present advantages, and I feel the poverty of words when I attempt to thank you. I can only give you the same assurances that I have given Mr. Phillips,—that I will keep untarnished his fair name, and will endeavor to satisfy you both that I have not abused the confidence reposed in me, nor the liberality which has placed me where I am.

I feel doubly fortified in the fact that I shall always have Mr. Phillips' experience to guide me, and your constant sympathy to support me. One year of the course of four is over; I feel strong to encounter the other three. I have been very happy the past year, and I hope have made a creditable progress; but as learning is nothing without health, and health nothing without morality, I shall especially cultivate the last two, and the third will "follow as the night the day". Would that I could impart strength to you by acquiring it for myself!

Give my affectionate regards to Phoebe, and accept for yourself, my good mother (if you will allow me to call you so), the love and gratitude of

WENDELL P. GARRISON.[6]

6. Wendell Phillips Garrison (1840–1907). The Phillipses paid their namesake's expenses at Harvard.

107. From WILLIAM LLOYD GARRISON

14 DIX PLACE.
SUNDAY MORNING, JAN. 20. [1861]

DEAR PHILLIPS:

I am sorry that I cannot hear you to-day, but I shall hear *of* you, and *from* you, by the members of my family, and hope to read your testimonies in the morning papers.

It is impossible to tell whether you will have to run the same gauntlet that you encountered before at the hands of the Bell-Everett ruffians; but the venom is not lacking on their part, and perhaps they will attempt your annoyance. Trying as your position is, it is enviable and sublime in the highest degree; and may all the brave spirits of the past, with the strong arm of Omnipotence, be with you to inspire your lips and protect you from all harm! It is thus only can an enthralled world be redeemed.

I have a suggestion to make, and please give it your consideration.

It is particularly desirable to avoid, if possible the street concourse (whether of friends or foes, or both combined) that attended you home before; for the anxiety of your friends, should you retire immediately from the hall, and go home on foot, will induce them to gather around you in a throng, and thus there will be an appearance of a mob to the public eye. To avoid all this, my suggestion is, that, at the close of your lecture, you retire (with half a dozen friends,) to the ante-room *behind the organ,* and there wait, say, till a quarter past 8 o'clock, (by that time the crowd will have been dispersed,) at which time let a hack be driven up to the door nearest Bromfield street, and drive you home.

At any rate, I would ride home, and not walk. But I hope you will think well of my proposition.

You should go early this morning, retiring into the anteroom, to which I have referred.

God bless and protect you![7]

> Ever truly yours,
> WM. LLOYD GARRISON.

Wendell Phillips.

7. At this time Phillips was threatened by mobs every time he appeared at the Boston Music Hall to lecture on disunion. "The Bell-Everett ruffians" were the supporters of the Constitutional Union Party that sought compromise with the secessionists.

108. From WILLIAM LLOYD GARRISON

14 DIX PLACE, SUNDAY NOON.

[1861]

DEAR PHILLIPS:

I congratulate you upon the admirable manner in which you met the great and solemn issue of the times this forenoon: it was discriminating, exact, right to the point, and loyal to the cause of the slave, which made it possible for you to stand encircled by the drapery of stars and stripes without compromising your abolitionism. The impression produced was manifestly deep and powerful. Just as you were about to close, the lines of Burns came in to my mind, and I was wishing they might occur to you, *en rapport*, to repeat as your climax:

> "Who would be a traitor knave?
> Who would fill a coward's grave?
> Who so base as be a slave?
>   Let him turn, and flee!
> Lay the proud *usurpers* low!
> Tyrants fall in every foe!
> *Liberty's in every blow!*
>   Let us do or die?"

The recital of these lines would, I believe, have brought the whole audience to their feet, and "made the welkin ring." Excuse my officiousness in suggesting that you append them in the printed report of your speech—taking both an orator's and a poet's license—as tens of thousands are to read your speech besides the thousands who listened to it. You will know how to preface them by a few words, that the conflict is not with "the people," but with *traitors* and *usurpers*, who dare not submit what they have done even to a Southern popular vote, through the ballot-box. Of course, give no heed to my suggestion, unless you like it; but I feel certain an electric effect will accompany the reading of the lines thus affixed.

The scriptural selection you read, I can testify, made a marvellous impression upon the audience, flushing the cheeks of some, and drawing tears from the eyes of others. I hope the Atlas will print it entire.

And now, not to bother you again, I remain,

Still more admiringly yours,

WM. LLOYD GARRISON.

Wendell Phillips.

109. From WILLIAM LLOYD GARRISON

14 DIX PLACE, JAN. 30.
[1861]

MY DEAR DISOBEDIENT:

I must confess, you made a very compact, terse and creditable argument in support of the Personal Liberty Bill, yesterday, before the Legislative Committee at the State House; which, of course, you would not have done, if you had given heed to my advice! All my counsels in your case go to the winds; so that, henceforth, I must change my tactics, in order to have any chance of success. I must advise you strongly to do every thing I hear you are inclined to do, especially in these perilous times; and, then, perhaps—shall I say, in all probability—you will change your mind in the direction I really think for the best! Like the boy who excused himself for being late at school, on the plea that he slipped back two feet for every one that he took forward. "And how did you get here at last?" said the schoolmaster. "O," said the boy, "I just turned round, and *tried to go the other way*!" That is a secret worth knowing, and I will try to make use of it in the way of giving advice!

Wife was much gratified in having an interview with Ann this afternoon. It is a long time since I had that privilege; but I shall "hope on," and, if necessary, "hope ever." However, I am growing less youthful every day; and before my personal charms are utterly gone, a special interview must be provided for! Then old age may do its worst.

Unless he has mended greatly since he left this mundane sphere, Daniel Webster must be delighted to see or hear that, yesterday and to-day, the Anti-Slavery Convention in Syracuse has been mobbed by a body of organized rowdies, after the manner of Boston and "Wightmanville." This looks as if the ruffianism of the North had its wire-pullers in Charleston and Washington. I doubt whether we shall escape civil war, after all. Prepare for the most astounding movements, during the present month, that have yet been made by the Southern conspirators! The Capital will be seized—Lincoln pushed from his stool—a Provisional Government instituted in derogation of the present one—then Northern resistance—then a jubilee for all the "roughs," "short-boys," "subterraneans," "shoulder-hitters," &c., &c. And then—"we shall see." "Wait a little longer."

This is not discouraging—is it? "Through much tribulation we enter," &c.

Yours, unalterably, whatever may come.

WM. LLOYD GARRISON.

Wendell Phillips.

110. From WILLIAM LLOYD GARRISON

SUNDAY MORNING, APRIL 21. [1861]

DEAR PHILLIPS:

I dare say you have already selected a portion of Scripture to read at the Music Hall to-day; but I have ventured to *condense* the 50th and 51st chapters of Jeremiah, and herewith send you the most striking and pertinent passages, to be read from the manuscript, if you think proper. You can lay it upon the opened Bible. It seems to me marvellously adapted to the state of our country, North and South, in the present warlike attitude of things. Babylon, in which were the traffickers "in slaves and the souls of men," represents the South. The war against her is retributively "the work of the Lord God." Then the reference to the oppression of the children of Israel, and the assurance that their Redeemer is strong, and that he will thoroughly plead their cause, "that he may give rest to the Land," (how beautiful the figure!) is very touching. Israel and Judah typify the North; and a recognition of their guilt, also, is made, with discrimination and hope:—"For Israel hath not been forsaken, nor Judah of his God; *though their land was filled with sin against the Holy One of Israel*"—i.e., the sin of complicity. Then separation and disunion are clearly enjoined:—"Flee out of the midst of Babylon, deliver every man his soul, be not cut off in her iniquity," &c., is directly to the point. Then the statement, "We would have healed Babylon, but she is not healed," is significant of the desires and efforts of the abolitionists to put an end to the curse of slavery. Finally, the declaration, that the forces against Babylon shall come "*from the north country*," is geographically very literal. The whole description is wonderfully graphic, I think, and the reading of it cannot fail to make a thrilling impression upon the audience. Still, do not read it, if you prefer any other portion of Scripture; for there are many other passages to be found, singularly applicable to our anomalous condition as a nation, now.

I told Phebe, last evening, that I should also venture to send you a text to read at the commencement of your discourse. Here it is:—

Jeremiah, 34th chapter, 17th verse:—"Thus saith the Lord: Ye have not hearkened unto me, in proclaiming liberty, every one to his brother, and every man to his neighbor: behold, I proclaim a liberty for you, saith the Lord, *to the sword,* to the pestilence, and to the famine."

Marvellously striking this also! How it sums up, in a single sentence, the cause and the consequences of our national trouble! How it vindicates the abolitionists, who would have averted this shedding of blood by an early and peaceful abolition of slavery! And how it shows that *the cause must be removed* which has brought civil war to our doors! This is a point which we can enforce at the present time with great power and success. "No more compromises—down with slavery, at whatever cost!"

Pardon me, still further, in making a suggestion or two.

1. You will, of course, have a crowded house. The bulk of the audience will be there nearly an hour before the time. Therefore, be *in your seat* even before the usual time, so as to begin at least as soon as half past 10—or sooner, if the house is crowded. Do not let them keep you in the ante-room too long, on the plea that others may yet come—for after a house is crammed in advance, some consideration is due to those thus situated.

2. Speak throughout *as loud as you can* without straining your voice—remembering the intense desire there will be in every part of the house *to hear every word you utter*. In reading your hymns and the scripture, you usually drop your voice too low to be easily heard even by those tolerably near the platform. Let them be *emphatic*.

3. Proclaim that the issue must be in this war, either the abolition of slavery or the dissolution of the Union, or we of the North will be doubly damned in the sequel.

God be with you! Faithfully yours,

W.L.G.

P.S.   I send you an extract from a letter just received from Oliver Johnson, which please read before meeting, if you have time.

111. From WILLIAM LLOYD GARRISON

BOSTON, DEC. 20, 1861.

DEAR PHILLIPS:

Noon fills my parlors with friends who are joyous, exultant, and mightily strengthened and delighted by your morning discourse, and by the overwhelming demonstration of friendliness made on your return home. Your success gives me unbounded pleasure, of course. I only regret that you did not quietly ride home, as I suggested, and for the reason given; but I would not have had you alter your usual course, unless you felt it best to do so. I understand that Dr. Thayer was waiting with his sleigh in Bromfield Street, to convey you home; and that he drove round to Winter Street, hoping to take you up there.

I hear that your discourse is not to be published in the Atlas. I hope, therefore, you will assist Wendell in preparing it for the next Liberator. I hope to see you to-morrow at the Board meeting, should the weather warrant my leaving the house.

Love and congratulations to Ann and Phebe.

Yours, admiringly,
WM. LLOYD GARRISON.

Wendell Phillips.

112. From M. D. CONWAY

28 NOTTING HILL SQUARE W. LONDON ENG
APRIL 21, 1865

MY DEAR PHILLIPS,

I see with some anxiety the indications that the A. S. Societies are to be dissolved. That the conditions under which the friends of freedom are to act are materially altered, is unquestionable; and yet the probability remains that the poor we shall always have with us; and so long surely there will be need enough of united and organized effort. What was the Anti-Slavery Society? The national organization of the Spirit of Humanity with reference to the chief outrage on that spirit—Slavery. When the Spirit of *In*-humanity ceases the organized efforts of Humanity may cease also. But we know that the Old Serpent of Slavery has a great way of slipping from one skin into another; and wherever Slavery has a new skin Freedom should have a fresh Avatar, ready to bruise its head. Major Cartwright has lately proved to the English people this proposition: —that to be free is to be governed by laws to which we ourselves have assented; that all not having a right of suffrage are slaves, and that a vast majority of the people of Great Britain are slaves. The Major's logic is remorseless; and it proves that in America all women, and a vast majority of negroes are slaves. The Reformers of America ought to face this fact, and they ought not to suffer themselves to lay aside their armour until every woman and every negro has an equal right to vote with the white man. Now as to the Anti-Slavery organization, its power has been proved: its trophies are the enthronement of New England principles in every state of the South—trophies obtained by earnest agitation, and, on its part, by no carnal weapons, not even votes. To destroy this organization—to give up its meetings and lectures—to wipe out the A. S. Standard's list of subscribers, is to my mind, like smashing a good strong locomotive because the cars it used to draw have become worn out. Can it not now draw a new train as well as it did the old one? The good old cry of the reformer is—"Liberty, Equality, Fraternity". Having gained Liberty let us now enter into the work of Equality. My belief then is that it is the duty of the Anti-Slavery Society at its May Meeting to enter simply upon a higher phase of its existence. Let it form itself into an *Equality Society*. Let the A. S. Standard continue as the 'Standard of Equality'. Let it be declared in a constitution that the object of this anointed Son of Abolitionism [is] to expunge the words "*white*" and "*male*" from every State Constitution or Law in America. And as for those states (the Southern) which in the mercy of God are given to the Nation for reconstruction, let it be the aim of this transformed Society to resist to the uttermost the entrance of one of them into the Union until it shall come with a basis of the perfect freedom and equality of persons and sexes. This aim can be shown to be an eminently practical one. The present *élan* of Freedom in America will at once be followed by a Reaction as was the case in the War of Independence,—after which the noble Declaration cooled down to the Compromising Constitution. There will be a tremendous effort of the Democratic Reactionists to control the nation again; and the only security against their success will be the alliance of the radicals with their natural friends, the women & the negroes. Meanwhile as a question of principle is it not too bad that the *Liberator* should cease whilst cars "for colored people" are passing through Boston Streets under the windows of the Emancipation rooms, or the Standard is furled whilst nearly two million slaves remain whom the government might liberate but will not. The Equality Society would include the uncompleted work of abolition whilst stretching into the new epoch. I implore you to give your voice for this new society or something like it. If it shall be formed please put my name to it as a subscriber to the ultimate of my ability and say that I am ready to devote myself to its work

Yours most cordially

M. D. CONWAY[8]

8. Moncure D. Conway (1832–1907), American writer and reformer, served as minister to a liberal Unitarian church in London at this time. He refers to John Cartwright (1740–1824), British political reformer and advocate of universal suffrage.

113. To ANN PHILLIPS From WENDELL PHILLIPS

TUESDAY NIGHT [MAY 9, 1865]

DEAREST

I've tried to obey all my darlings direction in her letter which [GWS] brought me. It seems as if we should carry the vote 2 to 1— Lucretia H. Mott not here: their daughter too ill to allow their coming—Lots of Pennsylvanians here all on my side. E. M. Davis says "I wish I could see thy wife, perhaps there are some things I could tell her which we cannot well tell thee"

Dora Weston's face was the first one I saw in the meeting!
How right you were

Darling baby
good night

Wednesday
My cold all gone. Breakfast with Mrs. Stanton[9]

9. Phillips's hasty notes to his wife on May 9 and May 10 convey his sense of
satisfaction over Garrison's defeat on the resolution to dissolve the American Anti-
Slavery Society.

114. To ANN PHILLIPS From WENDELL PHILLIPS

[MAY 10, 1865]

DEAR ANN
        Wednesday abt 5 o'clock
The vote has been taken we carried it 118 *nays* to 48 yeas in the
question to dissolve. Then we nominated WLG for President &
loud, most unanimous applause followed—Mrs. Gibbons & Down-
ing begged him to serve. I had sent Tilton to him to intercede with
him to serve—But he declined. Purvis wd not serve & they chose
me—
Our officers are nominated & we are holding a good meeting. Our
business meetings have been held not in the vestry but in the church,
so large has been the attendance.

L
W–

115. From AARON M. POWELL

OFFICE OF THE NATIONAL ANTI-SLAVERY STANDARD
39 NASSAU STREET
NEW YORK MAY 7, 1868

Private
DEAR MR. PHILLIPS:
    I send with this a letter received yesterday from S.J. May,

which he desires printed in the Standard. It is my purpose to decline it—as I have also recently declined one from Beriah Green reviewing Mr. Garrison.

In Mr. May's case, as he refers to you personally, I would like you to read the letter and advise me before I write him. Please return it to me immediately with any suggestion.

I shall be decidedly averse to reopening the controversy in the paper for Mr. May, or for anybody, aside from yourself & I think it well that you do not answer Mr. G.

I have had two very long letters from Mr. G. intended only for my own perusal. The first assumed that as I made no comment upon his *Standard* letter I agreed with his view & expressed his pity that "*For the sake of employment*" I would allow myself to edit the *Standard* and be made thereby responsible for the great wrong and injustice done to him by you and Purvis. In his view you are now a very bad man and I am simply your tool. He has scrutinized every line in the paper with an astonishing watchfulness in reference to himself, displeased alike by what has been said of him and by its silence.

Not wishing to treat him with contempt I answered him so far as to disabuse his mind of the notion that I was in agreement with him & told him very plainly wherein I regard him as in error. In answer to this he sends another very long letter written in the vein of the one in the Standard. To his second I have not replied and do not intend to. It will, I suppose, practically end the relation of personal friendship which has hitherto existed between us. He intimates that without retraction, you too must be dropped from his list.

I think there are two ways to do—first to go on with our main business (for which only the paper is worth to me the labor and cost) and let Mr. G., May & c. severely alone,—which I think is much the best; the other is to take up the matters of the difference thoroughly, and push hard in the way of criticism & reproof. For such a fight in the paper I have no heart or inclination. Beriah Green thinks it a duty on the part of the Standard and is offended that I decline his article. So far I think the Standard has done no injustice to Mr. G.—having printed in full his very elaborate answer to the only directly critical reference it has made to him. I should not have deemed it right to have denied his answer. He has no claim now which I feel bound to admit. Mr. May can simply withdraw his cooperation if he can no longer continue it. His protest I do not deem it necessary to print.

I shall be glad to know if in this view you concur.

Please return the letter and private note by next mail.

yours

A M. P[10]

10. Aaron M. Powell (1832–1899) was editor of the *National Anti-Slavery Standard* which continued as the official publication of the American Anti-Slavery Society after Garrison withdrew from the organization and stopped publication of the *Liberator*. Phillips and Garrison had come into conflict as trustees of a bequest left by Francis Jackson for antislavery purposes. After Garrison successfully prevented use of the money for the *Standard*, Phillips used the columns of the paper to criticize him. In a long reply published in the *Standard* March 14, 1868, Garrison argued that the paper had become Phillips's "personal mouthpiece" and accused his former colleague of "great self inflation" and "a pitiable hallucination of mind." Samuel J. May (1797–1871), Beriah Green (1795–1875), and Robert Purvis (1810–1898) had all been founders of the American Anti-Slavery Society. During the dispute with Garrison, Green and Purvis sided with Phillips.

116. From H. I. BOWDITCH

DEAR SIR,

You are respectfully requested to meet Ex-Governor ANDREW and a few other gentlemen, at No. 113, Boylston Street, (Dr. BOWDITCH'S,) on Wednesday Evening next, March 28th, at 8 o'clock, to consider the propriety of a National Testimonial to WM. LLOYD GARRISON, and to take any action in regard to the same which may be thought advisable.

BOSTON, March 22, 1866.

DEAR WENDELL

Can't you be with us? It distresses me to think that there can be anything to separate two such true friends as I deem you two to be   You will pardon the delay in Sending this note. My house is the place of meeting but I have not sent out but a very few notes. because I did not attend the preliminary meetings.

  Love to Anne
    & believe me ever
        Faithfully your friend
        H I Bowditch[11]

11. Along with the formal invitation, Henry Bowditch sent his personal plea for a reconciliation between Phillips and Garrison.

117. From CHARLOTTE L. FORTEN

BOSTON OCT. 2, 1867

My dear friend,

I did not know that you had returned to town until I saw you at Mr Emerson's lecture last night, & envied the fortunate people who could get to shake hands with you, & welcome you home again.

I want to thank you for the kind letter you wrote me in the summer. I think you were very good to send it. I cannot tell you how much it added to the pleasure of my vacation.

I wanted also to say to you that I think the Court decided most unfairly to the "Standard" in regard to the Jackson Fund. And I deeply regret that one of whom we do not like to think with anything but reverence & esteem, should with so much unfairness have influenced the decision of the Court. Dear as the cause of the Freedmen is to me, I would not have it receive one cent to which it is not justly entitled; however great its need—and its need is great.— I deeply feel the need & importance of such a valuable paper as the Standard. But however opinions may differ in regard to its worth, I do not see how anyone can fail to understand that the decision of the Court was unjust. I know my opinion is not of much importance, but I cannot bear to have you suppose, —as I thought it *possible* you might—that I could feel differently about this matter. How many times I have wished that I had money, myself, that I might give to the A.S. Society the share to which it is justly entitled.—

I hope you are feeling benefitted by your summer sojourn among the hills of Sterling. Although I see you so rarely, it is yet one of the greatest pleasures that these golden October days bring me,—the thought that you are in Boston again.

Please give my kind regards to Mrs. Phillips, if she will accept them, & believe me, dear & noble friend,

Ever yrs. most gratefully

CHARLOTTE L. FORTEN[12]

12. Charlotte Forten (1837–1914), Negro teacher and author, refers to Phillips's losing battle with Garrison over the Jackson bequest.

118. From LYDIA MARIA CHILD

WAYLAND, MARCH 16TH, 1868.

DEAR MR. PHILLIPS,

Your letter from Cleveland filled me with emotion. Why, you precious man, it never occurred to me that the expression of our sympathy could be of consequence to you. I have always been accustomed to think of you as a pillar of strength, against which the waves of a stormy ocean might beat in vain; and I have so long been in the habit of considering myself an obsolete old woman, that I never once dreamed of your caring so much for such a letter as I wrote. No tongue can tell how glad I am to have been of any service, and how proud I am that you care for it. Truly, I might have *known* that neither you, nor any other human being, (however strong by nature, and however sustained by a righteous purpose) can always work cheerfully without sympathy and encouragement from others. One of the greatest trials in the pathway of reformers is the necessity of estranging so many who would otherwise be friends, or else of being untrue to our own convictions of duty. I have myself frequently fainted, almost to gasping, for want of sympathy; but it never occurred to me that poor, weak little me .

could do anything to sustain *you*. Now that I know you think so, how sorry I am that I did not sooner put my weak shoulder to your big wheel!

The debt of gratitude I owe you, for public reasons and personal reasons, cannot be estimated. What a pile is heaped up, you can imagine, when I say that all you have done for *Freedom* is the same as if you had done it for *me*. I have never attempted to tell you how much I loved and honored you, because, in the first place, one does not like to seem a flatterer, and, in the second place, I was possessed by the idea that you did not care much for me, and that such professions might be valueless, if not distasteful. How often I think of you when your fresh, strong young soul first entered the Anti Slavery ranks, cheering us onward with your clear, ringing voice! But more still do I honor you for so steadfastly standing by the remnant of our great army, helping them to pursue the enemy, who is ever ready to turn and re-take all he has lost. Never was there a greater fallacy than the theory that our work is done. Where is the politician (always excepting Charles Sumner) who does not need to be continually pushed up to his duty by the point of the moral bayonet? There are, indeed a few, beside Sumner, who I think would not desert their post as sentinels on the watch-tower of Freedom, even if the old Anti Slavery trumpet should become silent. The old veteran Thaddeus Stevens would not, Geo. W. Julian would not. But even those faithful and dauntless few, strong as they are, I imagine may feel somewhat stronger for hearing the old trumpet tones resounding from afar.

You say The Standard is now floated on as far as June, without debt. When I see you, I want you to tell me what you intend to do *then*. I expect to be in Boston the last of March, or the first of April, when I shall call to see you, and ask for $100.

Ever cordially, gratefully, and affectionately your friend,

L. M. Child.

Our letter in The Standard seems to have nettled Mr. Garrison. I don't know why it should, for no allusion was made to him.